MAZZINI

MAZZINI

From Rupert S. Holland, *Builders of United Italy* (New York: Henry Holt and Co., 1908).

M A Z Z I N I

A Life for the Religion of Politics

ROLAND SARTI

Westport, Connecticut
London

Library of Congress Cataloging-in-Publication Data

Sarti, Roland, 1937–
    Mazzini : a life for the religion of politics / Roland Sarti.
      p.   cm.
    Includes bibliographical references and index.
    ISBN 0–275–95080–8 (alk. paper)
    1. Mazzini, Giuseppe, 1805–1872. 2. Italy—Politics and
government—1815–1870. 3. Revolutionaries—Italy—Biography.
4. Statesmen—Italy—Biography. I. Title.
DG552.8.M3S34 1997
945′.08—dc21   96–37112

British Library Cataloguing in Publication Data is available.

Library of Congress Catalog Card Number: 96–37112
ISBN: 0–275–95080–8

First published in 1997

Praeger Publishers, 88 Post Road West, Westport, CT 06881
An imprint of Greenwood Publishing Group, Inc.

Printed in the United States of America

∞™

The paper used in this book complies with the
Permanent Paper Standard issued by the National
Information Standards Organization (Z39.48–1984).

10 9 8 7 6 5 4 3 2 1

To my wife, Rose,
who has lived with Mazzini as long as I have,
and suffered more.

Contents

Acknowledgments

My intellectual debts for this study are too diffuse to be acknowledged
adequately. They go in as many directions as Mazzini's own interests,
which touched on history, literature, philosophy, religion, social science,
and, of course, politics, and spanned many countries. In the nearly
fifteen years that I have worked on this study I have learned to
appreciate the efforts of generations of scholars who have devoted their
lives to the study of Mazzini. Even when I have not known them
personally, the intelligence and dedication of their efforts have been an
inspiration. I will mention only the late Emilia Morelli, for whom the
study of Mazzini was a lifelong passion. For many years secretary and
then president of the Istituto per la Storia del Risorgimento Italiano in
Rome, Emilia Morelli would have been uniquely qualified to tell the
story of Mazzini's life.

Anyone working on Mazzini must acknowledge the indispensable tool
of research that is the national edition of Mazzini's writings. More than
one hundred volumes have appeared since the Italian parliament first
authorized the project in 1904. The publication still goes on and will
continue as long as writings by Mazzini remain to be discovered. Among
the many scholars who have worked on this project, Mario Menghini
stands out as the editor and moving spirit of the ninety-four volumes
that make up the first series. It was casual reading through some
volumes of correspondence that aroused my curiosity and prompted me
to undertake this study.

Closer to home, several friends and colleagues have been extremely helpful. Like other American Italianists, I am indebted to Alan Reinermann of Boston College for his effective promotion of Italian history in his capacity as Secretary of the Society for Italian Historical Studies. The crowd from my department that meets regularly for lunch at the cafeteria of the Newman Center has listened patiently for years as I unburdened myself on the subject of Mazzini. Their comments have sparked ideas that I tested against the evidence. A special note of thanks goes to my colleague and friend Mary C. Wilson for her invaluable suggestions on the content and style of the first drafts of this manuscript. My discussion of Mazzini's approach to issues of labor owes much to the advice of Bruce G. Laurie, colleague, friend, and department chair. I would also like to thank the entire staff of the Interlibrary Loan Office at the W.E.B. Du Bois Library of the University of Massachusetts for their unfailing courtesy, efficiency, and helpfulness; without their help this research could not have been completed. Needless to say, no one but me is responsible for anything that critics may question about this study.

Since it takes a family to write a book, my final thanks go to my wife, Rose, to whom this book is dedicated. Her patience and understanding have made it possible for me to combine commitment to this project with my desire and need for family support.

Introduction

Giuseppe Mazzini's life is part of the history of the Risorgimento, the movement that led Italy to national independence and unity. Born in 1805 when the ideals of independence and unity were shared by few Italians, Mazzini took the lead in propagating the national idea and helped it to succeed. He lived long enough to see Rome become the national capital in 1870, an event that brought down the curtain on the Risorgimento and concluded Mazzini's political mission; he died eighteen months later, in March of 1872. His disappointment that Italy was unified as a monarchy rather than as the republic of his dreams does not change the objective reality that he was on history's winning side as a "prophet of nationalism." One reason for studying him is that winners demand attention. Another reason is that he won grudgingly, posing as a victim of his times. The victor/victim complex is a challenge to the biographer.

Biographers of Mazzini face many other questions. How does Mazzini the patriot relate to Mazzini the humanitarian, or the man of peace to the revolutionist, or the educator to the conspirator? The revolution envisaged by Mazzini respected no boundaries. Workers, women, peasants, serfs, and slaves were to be among its beneficiaries, but the Mazzinian revolution did not exclude the better-off people, whose grievances were of a different order. He was proud to be called a patriot, but refused the label of nationalist, because nationalism implied exclusive concern for the interests of one's nation. When he lost faith in Italy's ability to take the initiative, he looked elsewhere, to the Slavs of eastern

Europe and to the United States of America after the Civil War. A nation could not be the ultimate object of allegiance, because nationality was a link between the individual and humanity.

The cosmopolitanism that characterizes Mazzinian thought was not incompatible with those subtle and insidious forms of nationalism that claim national primacy in the name of some universal good. It was Italy's mission, he claimed, to show the way toward a better society. Mazzini was nationalist enough to resent French claims to primacy in revolution. The "initiative" belonged to Italy, he insisted, because France had exhausted its revolutionary mission in 1789 and Italy was poised to surpass it. To support that claim, he cited the precedents of ancient Rome, Italy's flourishing medieval communes, the splendors of the Renaissance, and the Roman Catholic tradition of universality. To the objection that Italy was too divided and weak to shoulder such an historic burden he replied that spiritual resources were more important than material ones. The power of the spirit over matter was his trump card. Mazzini's nationalist temptation was as real as his humanitarian vocation.

Mazzini was both a patriot and a revolutionist. To understand his view of revolution one must refer to his experiences abroad. The choice he made in 1830 to leave his homeland made him a political exile for the rest of his life. He discovered the Social Question in France and England, where he lived for almost forty years. In London he experienced deprivation, saw extremes of poverty and wealth, witnessed the rise of working-class radicalism, organized labor, and the Chartist movement, and rubbed shoulders with political exiles from other parts of Europe. The abolition of slavery and serfdom, the emancipation of women, the liberation of religious minorities, and political independence for all oppressed nationalities were international causes that attracted Mazzini in his London years.

Labor, socialism, and the strategies of revolution were never far from his mind, but he would not cater to class resentments. He saw revolution as an encompassing experience that affected people not only in the way they lived materially, but, more important, in their hearts and minds. To succeed, revolutions must invoke ideals shared by all and play down the clash of material interests; interests divide, ideals unite. His major objections to socialism were that it stressed interests rather than values, divided the forces of revolution, and discouraged initiative and innovation.

Mazzini was a republican, which meant several things in the nineteenth century. Republicans agreed that government was not the appanage of royal dynasties and titled nobility, but beyond that there was little consensus on goals. Nineteenth-century republicanism was an open road, not a fixed destination. Mazzini added the concept of democracy to the classical definition of the republic as *res publica*. He may have been the first to speak of government of the people, for the people, by the people. Other republicans were more moderate, settling for guarantees of individual freedom. These "liberals" often disagreed on the relative merits of political liberty and economic laissez-faire, not always connecting the two or preferring one to the other, and were also the most likely to abandon republicanism for a constitutional monarchy. Republicans who stressed the goal of economic equality were socialists and communists. Mazzini was neither liberal nor socialist. His republicanism is best described as democratic, which means that he claimed the political space between liberals on the right and egalitarians on the left. In his view, redress for social and economic inequities would come when the people acquired political power. Mazzini's concern for the welfare of workers put him in socialist territory, but he called his strategy "associationist" rather than socialist. Government should exert itself to keep the playing field level for everyone, promote popular education, and counteract the monopolistic tendencies of capitalism, but not to eliminate distinctions or erode private property.

Mazzini is hard to classify ideologically and politically. In his time he was a radical to conservatives, an extremist to moderates, and a moderate to extremists; people of common sense regarded him as an impractical dreamer. Coming to grips with his ideas was always difficult. He had followers in his lifetime, but they seldom came together as a group. It is misleading to speak of a Mazzinian movement or party, because Mazzinians were a varied lot who seldom stayed together for very long. That is one reason for his neglect. Another is that his impact beyond Europe was limited, probably because the Risorgimento had little resonance in world affairs. Until recently, there had not been a biography of Mazzini written in English in sixty years. Some recent studies of nationalism do not mention him at all, and his name seldom appears in studies of socialism. That is all to the detriment of historical accuracy, because Mazzini was a presence in his time.

How he became a figure to reckon with is the story of his life, a story full of ironies and paradoxes. He had intelligence, charm, humor, and generosity, but only the extremely devoted sustained long relationships with him. Followers dropped in and out of the movement for reasons that had to do with both his personality and his politics, which were often hard to disentangle. There was a dissonance between Mazzini's seductive outward manner and the authoritarian core of his personality. The first stood out in personal relations and in his capacity as publicist and educator, the second took over when he donned his hat as politician and conspirator. The publicist advocated democratic openness, while the conspirator practiced secrecy and intrigue. Mazzini often built bridges toward those with whom he disagreed, but he did not regard politics as the art of compromise. In his organizations he wanted homogeneity of views, and preferred the "few but good" to the many who were lukewarm. The problematic relationship between the conspirator and the democrat makes Mazzini a figure of the political penumbra.

When people questioned his creed Mazzini appealed to religion and the eternal verities. There is no doubt that his religious faith was sincere, but the biographer cannot overlook that it was also an instrument of political struggle. He recognized it himself when he called religion a necessary element of revolution, and faith in God the necessary underpinning of political conviction. A baptized Roman Catholic, he rejected both the theology of the Roman Catholic Church and its conservative politics. Christianity, he complained, spoke only to the need for personal salvation. He accepted the notion that religion is a private matter and defended religious freedom in principle, but he also believed that there could be no progress toward a just society without the stimulus of religious enthusiasm. Secularists welcomed the separation of church and state, while Mazzini deplored it as evidence of indifference to moral principles. It was a major disappointment for him that Italians showed no interest in religious reform. Insistence on the unity of religion and politics separates Mazzini from the political mainstream of his time and ours. He would have agreed with the criticism of religious fundamentalists that modern civilization shows a dangerous tendency to ignore moral concerns.

It is not the intent of this biography to present Mazzini as a precursor of our time. In these pages he is allowed to speak for himself as often as the evidence allows, and the judgments expressed, both positive and negative, are those of his contemporaries. His vision was always controversial, and this biography tries to convey the strong feelings that it and he aroused. In considering what he aimed for, one is struck by the disparity between the grandeur of his vision and the modest means at his disposal. But he was no mere dreamer or posturer. Mazzini matters not only because he lived his ideas like no other figure of his generation, but because he knew how to communicate by word and deed, because he captured the imagination of his contemporaries, and because he convinced them that one individual could make a difference. Although the story of his life is not of our time, the issues that it raises are timeless.

CHAPTER 1

Pippo: The Family Years (1805–1819)

Biographers often ignore or pay scant attention to the formative years of Mazzini's life, perhaps because they are the least documented and most obscure years. In Mazzini's case, obscurity is compounded by distortion. His public image, which was his strongest political asset, left little room for considerations of human frailty. In fact, his political reputation required that the image be stripped of most human qualities, leaving only the martyr and the prophet; the status of political icon that he attained after his death perpetuated this tendency. Those who knew him best made a concerted effort, amounting to a conspiracy of silence, to hide or gloss over incidents and traits that might damage his reputation. Yet, his achievements are so closely tied to his character that they cannot be understood without looking at Mazzini as a person.[1]

The "family years" covered in this chapter are the ones in which Mazzini's home was his universe, before he established other close relationships and before political agitation became the obsession of his life. In these years he was known as Pippo, the affectionate diminutive used by family members, and later by others who were intimate or claimed intimacy with him. Mazzini the adult seldom dwelled on his early years, and then only in generalities. He questioned the appropriateness of public disclosures of personal matters, even for people who gain public prominence. If that complicated the task of the biographer, so much the better. He had doubts about biography as a genre, questioning its value as a medium for the discussion and understanding of history. The individual was not the proper object of attention, he claimed.

Mazzini's tastes reflected this philosophy. Some credit him with anticipating Richard Wagner's theories on the social role of music. In opera, which was his favorite form of public entertainment, he preferred the chorus to the solo aria. In history, too, he listened for the chorus. He would not look at history through the eyes of prominent and powerful figures, unlike his friend Thomas Carlyle, with whom he argued the issue. Concentrating on leaders distorted the message of history, which was revealed by what the people did collectively. For him, heroes were individuals who understood and worked with the forces embodied in the people; those who thought they could dominate history were its dupes.

Perhaps this stance accounts for the defensive tone that surfaces in the introductory pages of his own autobiography. Yes, Mazzini did succumb to the temptation to write about himself, all the while protesting that he was not really doing so. In his Autobiographical Notes (1861) he insisted that his subject was his political life, not his personal life. While the former was of public interest, the latter was a private affair between himself and the few people with whom he was intimate. A life was of public interest only to the extent that it reflected the progress of an age; he felt his political biography should be read because it offered "a general sketch of the whole Italian movement since 1821."[2]

Only in that larger context was his life significant, and only to the extent that he had succeeded in expressing a collective longing could he claim any place in history. "My voice was often the voice of many, the echo of an idea shared by the young."[3] The rest belonged to the private sphere. He urged one would-be biographer to stay away from his private life: "About my private life . . . you ought to say as little as possible; what is sufficient to prove is that I was not altogether bad and that there was not an absolute want of unity between what I preached and what I did. What Italy and Europe at large may care about is the *Italian*: the *man* must remain dear to the few who know me and will survive me."[4] He wanted neither "hymn-singing biographers" nor indiscreet ones: "Do what God inspires you to do, but stay out of my letters and intimate affairs."[5]

Mazzini was fifty-five years old and living in London when he wrote his Autobiographical Notes. He had spent most of the previous twenty-four years in London and he stayed there off and on for another eleven, almost until his death. Although London was his base, his work was directed elsewhere. He spoke of brotherhood and sisterhood, yet he spent much of his time hatching plots that ended tragically for others. He claimed to understand the course of history, yet he also feared that history might be passing him by. At fifty-five he considered himself old, yet he addressed himself to the young, just as he had done thirty years before, when he had taken up political agitation.

Years were not the issue, he claimed. It was the old in spirit that he could not abide, those who turned cautious with the passage of time, who forsook the ideals of their youth. *Ora e sempre* (Now and always) was the motto that he adopted for himself and his movement. Most of his former companions either were dead or had dropped out of the struggle. There were times when he felt lonely and depressed, and times when he relished the solitude. Not many people called themselves his followers, yet when he spoke he was heeded by those who admired him and by those who detested or feared him. Power and weakness were intimately intertwined in his life. His life was as paradoxical as the passage from one of the letters of Paul of Tarsus that he paraphrased: "When I am weak, then I am strong."[6]

That was a comment on the life of Zacharias Werner, a German poet and playwright of questionable character, whom Mazzini admired for struggling against his weaknesses in pursuit of spiritual perfection. Mazzini's similar compulsion in pursuit of ideals put drama enough in his life. During thirty years of political activity he came to be regarded as Europe's most troublesome agitator. His enemies vilified him as a conspirator, murderer, and corrupter of the young. They called him a coward, charging that he was reckless with the lives of others but cautious with his own. After all, did he not live in the comfort and safety of London while many who followed him were strewn in jails across Europe, or blew themselves up making bombs, or died on the scaffolds and barricades?

For those who had died he felt sadness, but no remorse. They died for national independence, unity, liberty, and democracy, on the right side of history; their sacrifice raised them to the status of heroes and martyrs. What he admired most was moral courage, which he claimed for himself. Many who were drawn to him regarded him as a moral teacher, called themselves his disciples, and thought of his politics as the "religion of republicanism." That phrase was coined by Emilie Ashurst Venturi, an Englishwoman married to an Italian, who considered herself his most devoted disciple. Only "some powerful moral cause worthy of serious study," she argued, could explain the disparity between the slender means at his disposal and the results of his apostolate.[7]

The paeans intensified after Mazzini's death as part of a deliberate effort to purge his memory of undesirable connotations and include him among the other, less controversial founders of the nation. It was the poetry of an Englishman, George Meredith, that transfigured him into a member of a holy trinity:

> . . . we think of those
> Who blew the breath of life into her frame:
> Cavour, Mazzini, Garibaldi: Three:
> Her Brain, her Soul, her Sword; and set her free
> From ruinous discords, with one lustrous aim.
>   *George Meredith,*
>   "The Centénary of Garibaldi" (1907).

Mazzini had mixed feelings about his life's work. He saw the revolution of nationalities with which he identified sweeping through Europe. Italy was unified when he wrote his Autobiographical Notes, and other nationalities were moving toward the same goal. Yet, the results were not as he had expected. Italy was unified under a monarchy, not as the popular republic that was his ideal. If he hated monarchy, he feared socialism, which was gaining momentum in the later years of his life. He was caught in the middle, fighting against the relics of the past and the intimations of the future.

His few successes had been costly, both to himself and to people he loved. Most of his conspiracies had failed, his ideas had been distorted, and his efforts to open people's minds had been misunderstood. There had been moments of utter despair when he had contemplated suicide; his life was full of dark recesses, private passions, and tragedies he could not reveal. Not that he feared for his personal reputation, for he claimed to have long ceased caring about what others thought of him; but the cause to which he had devoted his life was something else, and he would not have it tarnished. He was the Apostle, the Martyr, the Prophet, and he felt the constraints of his mission. His story had to be presented in such a way that it would not obscure the role of the People, who were the protagonists of history.

The word People he always capitalized, as he did all other terms to which he attached particular significance. In his century, as in earlier times, it was the Italian People who bore the burden of propelling History along the road of Progress. God charged the Italian People with a Mission. To them belonged the historical Initiative of revealing the word of God to the rest of Humanity, and it was Mazzini's role to remind them of their Duty to seize that Initiative. Against this sweeping, inspiring historical backdrop, his life story was as puny as a "torch against the rising sun."[8] In this manner of thinking he began writing his Autobiographical Notes, warning readers not to look for specifics in his narrative, because his recollections of particulars were faulty. He had never saved notes or correspondence and had a poor memory for dates. Moreover, he was not writing an autobiography at all, but merely a set of introductions to the first comprehensive collection of his political and literary writings, which he anticipated would fill ten to twelve substantial volumes.

THE UPBRINGING

For Mazzini, individual lives took on meaning when they rode the tidal wave of history. He remembered the precise moment when this wave seized him. It happened, he wrote in an often-quoted passage, on a Sunday in April of 1821. He was strolling along Genoa's broad, palace-lined Strada Nuova with his mother and an old family friend when they were approached by a man soliciting donations for those who were being banished from Italy. Mazzini remembered the mute grief and stubborn pride of the patriot who held out a kerchief in his hands. In the Kingdom of Sardinia, of which Genoa was the principal seaport and major point of escape, and elsewhere in Europe where revolution had failed that year, the defeated sought safety in flight. The memory of those men haunted him during his own forty years of exile, when, like them, he was unwilling to concede defeat. In retrospect, that chance encounter looked like the decisive moment in his life: "That was the first day of my life in which I sensed, perhaps confusedly, not the ideals of Homeland [*Patria*] and Liberty [*Libertà*], but the thought that one could, and that therefore one should, fight for the liberty of one's homeland."[9]

He did not discount the earlier years of childhood and adolescence, however, for in his Autobiographical Notes he acknowledged the importance of parental influence, which he reduced to one fundamental lesson: "The democratic habits of my two parents and the identical ways with which they treated both patricians and commoners (*popolani*) had unconsciously educated me to the cult of equality. In the individual they looked only for character and honesty."[10] One inspiration that he mentioned was his father's republican past. Many a family gathering had been enlivened by his father's stories of the turbulent, exciting years following the outbreak of revolution in France in 1789. In 1796 the young general Napoleon Bonaparte, of Italian ancestry, had brought the revolution to Italy at the head of an army. Genoa's turn came in June of 1797, when the French were welcomed by sympathizers who felt no loyalty for the ancient republic ruled by a few aristocratic families. Although foreigners, the French were welcomed because they came in the name of liberty, equality, and fraternity, the watchwords of the French Revolution. The Italians who welcomed them were called Jacobins.

Giacomo Mazzini, Pippo's father, was a Jacobin. Born in the provincial town of Chiavari in 1767, Giacomo came from a family that in the course of four generations had risen from quarry work, through commerce, to the professions.[11] His was the fourth generation, and with a degree in medicine he was eager to establish himself in the capital, which, though no longer the thriving mercantile and financial emporium of centuries past, still bore the imprint of its past glories and remained a place of opportunity for an ambitious young man from the provinces. In 1794, at the age of twenty-seven, he married Maria Drago. Nearly seven years younger than her husband, Maria was attractive, vivacious, well-educated, and assertive. She read widely and was a good conversationalist. At a time when most women spoke only the local dialect, she was fluent in French and Italian. Like her two sisters, she married a young man who was poised for professional success.[12]

At about the time when their first child was born three years later, they moved into rented quarters about midway up the Via Lomellina, a narrow street that runs uphill from the popular quarters of the city toward the affluent suburbs on higher ground. The street was a metaphor for Giacomo's career. The new Democratic Republic of Liguria had just been created, sustained by the power of French arms, the progressive ideals of the French Revolution, and what seemed to be the irresistible momentum of history. In the euphoria of the moment Giacomo turned to politics. He sat on the editorial board of *Il Censore Genovese*, a radical democratic publication for which he probably wrote unsigned articles of patriotic content; he even served briefly as a republican vigilante, a potentially compromising and dangerous position to which he brought more tact than vigor. A sense of personal dignity had made him pull back, as he explained to his son: "Although I was a member of the police, I never persecuted anyone who was against the government. I must say that it would have been difficult to get ahead in government and at the same time retain one's honor and virtue . . . for which reason I left my post."[13] The difference between father and son was that the former kept his political convictions firmly under control, while the latter let them govern his life.

Giacomo took little interest in politics after that episode. He accepted Genoa's incorporation into the French Empire in 1805 and its annexation by the Kingdom of Sardinia in 1814, after the defeat of Napoleon. A police report of 1816 described him as an "independent democrat," suggesting that he was still politically suspect but disengaged.[14] By that time, his strongest longing was for quiet and security. It was perhaps then that he adopted the maxim that showed him to be a man of moderation: *Neque divitia neque paupertatem* (Neither wealth nor poverty).[15] His advancement in the medical profession proceeded regardless of changes in government and regime. At successive moments in his life Giacomo accepted without complaint the aristocratic and democratic republics, the French Empire, and the rule of the House of Savoy. The republic appointed him to the board of examiners for applicants in medicine, pharmacy, and surgery (1801), and the monarchy appointed him to the position of resident physician at the University of Genoa (1814), to the university's chair of Pathology and Hygiene (1823), and to the chair of Anatomy and Physiology (1830). He retired near the end of his life, the faithful servant of three Piedmontese monarchs not known for their liberal views: Victor Emmanuel I (1814–1821), Charles Felix (1821–1831), and Charles Albert (1831–1849).

Giacomo was a good example of the new bourgeoisie, which was born of the revolution but made peace with the monarchy when the tide turned. He was not an unprincipled careerist, however. He remained distrustful of the nobility, a feeling shared by other members of the family. A lingering nostalgia for the republic, which may also have been nostalgia for his youth, made him keep copies of *Il Censore Genovese* hidden behind rows of books in his personal library, where his inquisitive son found and read them.[16] Giacomo's work was his vocation; he healed the sick, improved his skills, and engaged in research and experimentation to increase medical knowledge. When cholera struck in 1835, he was the only one of the city's physicians who did not run in fear for his life. Convinced that cholera was not contagious, he examined patients carefully and urged others not to abandon them. In seeing no incompatibility between his self-interest and doing good for others Giacomo was a typical product of the Enlightenment. The substantial assets that he accumulated were the tangible signs of success, while the intangible parts were status and influence. The assets freed his son from financial need, and the influence helped mitigate the rigors of the law for his son's political infractions on more than one occasion.[17]

Giacomo and Maria's children were born at intervals that suggest planning: Rosa in 1797, Antonietta in 1803, Pippo in 1805, and Francesca, in 1808. That all the newborns survived suggests either exceptional good fortune or, more likely, extraordinary attentiveness. Perhaps because the Mazzini family was not large by middle-class standards of the time, the children received special attention—no one more so than Pippo, who was the only male descendant and Maria's unquestionable favorite. He was born into a world of political change. A few weeks before his birth on June 22, 1805, Genoa had become part of the French Empire, which made the newborn Giuseppe Giovanni Maria Mazzini technically a French citizen. Technically only, for toward his accidental motherland he would harbor sentiments that ranged from ambivalent to decidedly hostile.

Maria was thirty-one years old when her son was born. He was immediately sent to a nursemaid in the outlying village of Bavari, where the Mazzinis spent their summer months and where they later bought a cottage. Pippo remained in Bavari longer than expected. Whether because he had a delicate constitution or, as Maria claimed, because the nursemaid's milk was "spoiled," his health deteriorated during the first months. He spent the first two years of his life in the country, away from the miasmas of the city, in the care of a nursemaid, Benedetta, who later followed him to Genoa. With her status as *mamma di latte* (milk mother), Benedetta was an important figure in Pippo's life. She and

Maria were the only two people whom he saw regularly in the three years after his arrival in Genoa, when he was confined to his bed for health reasons. While Benedetta looked after his physical comforts, Maria engaged his mind and his emotions. Their combined ministrations shaped his sense of the centrality of women and his dependence on them, which became permanent traits of his adult personality. When he saw Lorenzo Bartolini's statue representing charity as a woman breastfeeding an infant while simultaneously pointing to the letters of the alphabet, he thought it was the most impressive sculpture he had ever seen.[18]

Pippo's upbringing was stern, but he was never starved for affection. He carried a special burden as the male heir who was expected to carry on the family name and fortune, but Giacomo and Maria showed concern for all their children's upbringing by exercising parental strictness, as was the rule in those days. Strictness aimed at fostering both self-discipline and self-expression, the former to harness natural abilities and the latter to develop the skills of communication that were prerequisites for success. If it is true that republican independence and personal autonomy were related attitudes that first flourished in nuclear families where ties of affection replaced traditional respect for parental authority, then the Mazzinis exemplified the "new conjugal family" that nurtured a sense of personal worth.[19]

That affection did not mean indulgence seems clear from the strict schedules and high expectations that prevailed in the household. Activities were structured and organized, private instruction occupied the better part of the day, Maria took time out to read to the children, and the children's eating habits and recreations were carefully regulated. Maria would sometimes bake an almond cake that was Pippo's favorite, but meals were generally simple, sweets were rare treats, and alcoholic beverages were consumed sparingly and only on special occasions. No pets were allowed. For pastimes Pippo was taught to play chess, read music, and strum the guitar. In the Mazzini household time was a commodity not to be wasted in aimless diversion. There was a compulsive element to the family ethic that echoes in Mazzini's abiding distaste for inactivity: "There is, therefore, no rest. Rest is immoral."[20]

A dislike of frivolities became part of Pippo's personality. Food, clothing, and diversions held even less attraction for him than for his father. Giacomo complained about the plain food prepared by the family cook under his wife's supervision, and sometimes escaped the spartan regime by dining at a nearby monastery, where the cooks dished out portions of succulent macaroni. That was the only transgression that he allowed himself in all his years of marriage. Pippo's cravings were few and simple; he liked vegetables and fruit, ate meat only if it was grilled, and in England he developed a taste for beer and potatoes. In adolescence he began to drink strong black coffee and smoke cigars, very much against the advice of his father, who warned him repeatedly about the dangers of smoking. At the age of thirty-three he would boast "I have won over medicine, the cigar does not dominate me, I dominate it."[21] Under the jesting tone there was still the defiance that had characterized much of his youthful behavior.

Those were the only physical "vices" that Pippo was unable to shake. Austerity would be too strong a word for the Mazzinis' life-style, for the home was comfortable and welcoming, but they did dislike displays of wealth, which they associated with the frivolous life-style of the nobility. "There were four servants," Pippo recounted of an evening spent in an affluent London home, "dressed in a way that made me feel inclined to rise and bow to them."[22] There were political reasons for his resentment of social pretensions, but the egalitarianism he displayed was also rooted in the sense of propriety typical of middle-class families like his own.

Only at the age of five was Pippo allowed outdoors. The event may have coincided with the family's move in 1810 from the cramped quarters in Via Lomellina, which Mazzini remembered as "certainly not large, but in which we lived rather well after all."[23] Either at that time or shortly thereafter, they rented, and later purchased, a more spacious dwelling near what is now the Salita San Nicolosio in the Zecca quarter of the city, on the climb to Castelletto. In that home, long since demolished and whose precise location is in doubt, Pippo lived a life revolving around his private room, which became a favorite gathering place for his circle of friends. Roaming the streets was not for children of respectable families, and in Pippo's case there was also little personal inclination to venture outdoors. In his sheltered environment he never developed a taste for the outdoor life or the resistance to physical hardship that one associates with the kind of political militancy he advocated. Yet, in other ways his experience of physical confinement did prepare him for a life lived in hiding. Physical confinement actually stimulated his imagination and shaped his sense of reality. The life of the mind mattered more to him than physical space and freedom of movement. "Small bedrooms are actually to my taste; I seem to live in them in a more concentrated way," he wrote to his mother from exile.[24]

Giacomo and Maria did not see eye to eye when it came to Pippo's upbringing. Maria began to dote on him as soon as he was brought home from Bavari, seldom left his room, and kept close watch on who came near him. That did not sit well with Giacomo, who had a reputation for wanting to exert paternal authority. He thought Pippo should lead a more active life; she wanted him to stay at home. He prescribed physical exercise; she nurtured his imagination by reading and telling him stories. He believed in rules applied across the board; she was sensitive to his special needs. The special relationship that developed between mother and son endured in life and beyond, when by their expressed wishes mother and son were buried near one another, far away from Giacomo's meddling presence.[25]

Maria was the first to notice Pippo's precocious intelligence and lively imagination. She sought advice for his education, not from her husband but from friends and relatives of her choice. Family tradition had it that Pippo learned to read by eavesdropping on the lessons being given to his sisters by private tutors. His sisters called him The Mute Ox, because he learned to speak late yet managed to get his way most of the time.[26] There was no denying his persistence and stubbornness. Sensitive to everything around him, he was mercurial, quick to laugh or throw a tantrum, to show affection or withdraw it. Giacomo attributed his son's behavior to excessive imagination, and reproached Maria for stimulating it further. She did so by reading to him from the only kind of children's literature she could find: illustrated literary classics that recounted tragic situations and heroic feats of arms, leaving the impression that the clash of extremes was a normal part of life. In those stories, life was a struggle between good and evil and the choice between the two was the test of morality. From this dualistic premise it followed that the good (those who shared your ideals) were locked in combat against the bad (those who denied the truth), and that the struggle must result in victory or defeat, never in compromise: "Indifference is the immorality of the mind."[27]

When Pippo was five or six his education was entrusted to Luca Agostino De Scalzi, one of the many Jansenist priests who had been attracted to Genoa by the old republic's policy of sheltering religious dissenters. None were more welcome than the Jansenists, who in the eighteenth century represented the liberal current within the Roman Catholic Church. Founded in seventeenth-century France as a movement to reform the Church, Jansenism took on a distinctly political tone in Italy. The Republic of Genoa welcomed the Jansenists because they were considered promoters of republican virtues, and therefore likely to instill in the faithful a sense of loyalty to the government. In the words of one republican tract, "Evangelical truths are those of republican patriotism. To form good citizens devoted to the republic one must form first of all good Christians who are endowed with a sense of duty, for the duties of the citizen coincide with those of the good Christian."[28] According to the teachings of Jansenism, good citizens had religion in their bones, like Saint Paul and Saint Augustine, who put their faith to the service of society after experiencing conversion.

Jansenists seemed to flock to the Mazzini family. A maternal uncle, Giovanni Maria De Albertis, and Giacomo's old Jacobin crony, Andrea Gambini, who was also Marias and Pippo's companion on that fateful

Sunday walk in March of 1821, were both Jansenists. Maria herself was strongly drawn to Jansenism, without professing its theology in any formal way. Both she and her husband were sincerely religious but in different ways. Giacomo's religiosity did not exclude the observance of formalities according to the theology of his favorite religious order, that of the Padri Filippini, whose monastery also dispensed the macaroni he liked so much. Maria's convictions were equally deep, but less formal. Except for attending church on Sundays, she avoided the ritual aspects of worship. Her son was surprised to learn in 1844 that she had gone to church on a weekday: "Have you then become more devout? Do you go to church every day?" he inquired.[29]

The spirit of religion permeated the household and shaped the education of the children. The oldest, Rosa, entered a religious order. Antonietta married into a very devout family and eventually distanced herself from her brother, in part because of his religious attitudes. Like his mother, and unlike the other members of the family, Pippo distinguished between faith and observance. His religiosity was unorthodox by all standards, even the Jansenist, but it did incorporate strands of Jansenist belief, including the importance of personal conversion and personal responsibility, a belief in the fundamental unity of reality, the right to challenge authority on grounds of conscience, and the social obligation to act on one's beliefs. The path to faith was by no means steady or uninterrupted for Pippo, but it took him toward a form of religiosity that strengthened the bond between mother and son.

What De Scalzi taught him is unclear, but we know that he learned Latin by reading directly from Cicero, Livy, and Tacitus, as was the custom at that time. Such readings were thought to develop both intellect and character. Their grammar and structure taught form and logic, while their accounts of brave deeds and sacrifice for the public good provided models of civic virtue. Perhaps Pippo also took some fencing lessons, probably at Giacomo's insistence, but this was not a skill he chose to cultivate. Maria was so impressed with the child's capacity to learn, and probably so eager to broadcast her son's talents, that in 1812 she asked her cousin Giuseppe Patroni for advice on his education. On the basis of her description of the child's gifts, Patroni, an artillery colonel stationed in Pavia, called Pippo "a star of the first magnitude," an "unlimited genius," and prescribed a heavy diet of geography, history, arithmetic, science, modern languages, music, dancing, and physical exercise. Then, remembering perhaps that Pippo was only seven years old, he advised that he should also "be forced to be himself, to behave like a *child* at some hour of the day for the sake of his health."[30] Maria called the letter "prophetic" and kept it as a precious possession.

Relations between father and son deteriorated as Pippo approached adolescence. Giacomo expected obedience, only to encounter resistance and headstrong behavior. Reprimanded, his son would run to other members of the family, especially to his mother and his younger sister. Confined to his own room, he would escape through a window. Later in life he would regret the eccentricities of his youth, the introversion and self-seclusion, the desire to isolate himself, and the reluctance to be seen in public.[31] There were compensating sides to his personality, however, which that brought out his spontaneity, affection, and sense of humor. From his correspondence we learn of moments of closeness that were every bit as real as the moments of tension: joyous family celebrations, pleasant outings, and leisurely vacations at the family's summer cottage in Bavari.

Like all families, the Mazzini family developed its own emotional dynamics and configurations. The dominant trait of family life was the close bond between mother and son. For Maria, Pippo's demands were never excessive; in fact, she encouraged them as signs of his superior capabilities. There is no question that she treated him differently, perhaps partly because he was her only son. She insisted that her daughters receive an education, but she held out to them conventional women's roles, which contrasted sharply with her own demeanor as a "very intelligent woman [*donna di gran testa*], that few men could stand up to in society."[32] She was closest to her youngest daughter, known in the family as Cichina. Maria, Cichina, and Pippo were the trio in the family, usually ranged against Giacomo, whom they perceived more as a nuisance than as a villain. Cichina was an anti-feminist at heart, who accepted the home-bound role instilled by her mother much more readily than did Pippo, whom she often chided for expecting too much of women.[33]

The other sisters were the least integrated members of the family. There is at least one hint that Rosa may have taken the veil in part to escape from a tense family situation. Apparently at her father's insistence, she was sent to a convent not of her choice, where she did not have to take vows, which would have given the convent the right to claim a dowry.[34] Antonietta's relationship with Maria was strained on account of her religious beliefs. Her marriage to Francesco Massuccone in 1829 made matters worse. Maria opposed the marriage at first, relenting only after Pippo interceded on behalf of his sister. Antonietta felt immediately at home in her husband's religious and patriarchal family, where several generations lived under the same roof, individuals expressed their opinions only if asked, and the oldest male consulted everyone out of consideration but spoke for the whole family. According to Maria, the Massuccones had to "hold a state council before deciding to eat out."[35] The Massuccones were communal, the Mazzinis individualistic.

In 1814 Maria again sought advice on Pippo's education from an outsider, her friend Giacomo Breganze. Breganze, a lawyer, had been a militant Jacobin under the democratic republic and was a friend of Ugo Foscolo, the poet whose writings captured the imagination of a whole generation of Italian romantics. Their acquaintance dated from 1799, when the Austrians and the British had tried to suppress the democratic republic and Foscolo had called on "Napoleon the Liberator" to relieve the besieged city. That appeal may not mark the beginning of the Risorgimento, as some historians claim, but it did contribute to Foscolo's reputation for patriotism. Some of Foscolo's glamour rubbed off on Breganze, and Maria may have been attracted to him because he still professed his liberal convictions, unlike her now sedate husband, who appeared to have given up on the ideals of his youth.

"That lawyer Breganze, whom you knew, is he still alive?", Mazzini asked his mother in 1836, when he was planning an edition of Foscolo's writings.[36] The colonel had just died, but the inquiry reminded Maria of still another "prophetic letter" she had received and preserved. Breganze's advice was much more *au courant* than Patroni's in urging that Pippo study modern Italian literary classics, engage in strenuous physical exercise, and develop his moral faculties in addition to his mental ones. Breganze acknowledged the child's exceptional gifts, but thought he might also be hypersensitive and melancholy. He felt Pippo needed regular physical exercise because "in children who are very studious and wise beyond their years the cerebral faculties gain at the expense of their animal life, unless directed toward useful diversions." He also urged that the boy be taught some practical skills such as music or drawing, for one who has such skills "will find a fatherland [*patria*] in any part of the world."[37]

In 1817 the family hired another private tutor, Stefano De Gregori, a Jansenist more learned than De Scalzi, who for the next two years instructed his pupil in advanced Latin, rhetoric, humanities, philosophy, and literature. Pippo profited enough from this curriculum to qualify for university admission two years later, but he never developed the affection for De Gregori that he felt for his first tutor, whom he credited with opening his mind more by his love than by his teaching. He counted De Scalzi among the few adults who had truly influenced him in his youth, and remembered him fondly in a letter to his mother written at a particularly difficult moment in his life, when he was oppressed by a sense of utter loneliness: "My life now consists of nothing more than loving: loving you, father, the sisters . . . Don Luca De Scalzi. . . . It consists of loving not the current generation, which, with a few exceptions, is corrupted by egoism and fear . . . but my land [*il mio paese*], which will bear the generations of the future."[38]

His love for his *paese*, he later felt, was unrequited; but it endured and became the obsession of his life, owing perhaps to his experience of family life. He explained to his mother that the experience of love in the home had opened his mind to the larger possibilities of love, a feeling, he lamented, that was seldom sought or appreciated in public figures: "I have never met someone who says: how that man loves, how he feels and fulfills all his duties."[39] It was through love rather than intellect that the Individual could stretch out toward Family, Country, Humanity, and God. The family was an obligatory stepping stone on that continuum of love, and the woman was a privileged presence within the family. "The family is the fatherland of the heart," and "woman is the angel of the family, as mother, wife, and sister."[40] Women would play a role in his political movement and he would be among those who raised the "woman question," but he always stressed the role of woman as educator within the family. Society suffered when the family had failed to fulfill its educational role. His own generation lapsed, he claimed, because the family failed the child: "His imprudent mother has murmured in his ear, with a kiss, *be happy!*, his father has said to him *be rich!* Wealth and happiness! . . . Thus begins temptation."[41]

Mazzini had been saved because his family was different. But how was it different? Mazzini remembered the love by which *he* felt surrounded, a love not shared equally by all. It was the extraordinary bond between mother and son that set the Mazzini family apart. It would continue after he left home, when distance separated them physically but not emotionally. Her letters to him are outpourings of passion. She lives only for him (*vivo del tuo respiro*), who is God's chosen (*benedetto e prediletto di Dio*). She is the only person who understands him "because I am one with you [*essendo immedesimata teco*] in every tiny fold of your soul." When he lies in bed he must think of her, "for it is at that time that your mother is most truly with you and wishes for your happiness." But she also gives him practical advice. "Spare no expense for your needs," she urges, "do it for my peace of mind." She advises him to write his requests for money at the bottom of his letters, where she can cut them out so that his father will not see them: "Do not forget, you little bone head [*testina che sei*]," she adds playfully.[42]

He did not share everything with his mother, but there was no other person with whom he was so consistently candid. She earned his confidence with her love and support, becoming the guardian of his name and reputation and the obligatory contact for those who wanted to reach him abroad. It was she who provided his first biographers with information about his early life, his delicate health, sweetness of character, precocious intelligence, and generous impulses. She was the filter through which all the information passed that became part of the legend of her son's life. For her loyalty and protective love, historians put her in the pantheon of great Italian mothers. She was Mary, and her son was "the One, the Chosen of the Lord."[43]

NOTES

Works frequently cited in the notes have been identified by the following abbreviations:

BDM   *Bollettino della Domus Mazziniana*

EN   *Edizione Nazionale. Scritti editi ed inediti di Giuseppe Mazzini* (1906–90), 106 vols.

1. The most recent biography, Dennis Mack Smith's *Mazzini* (New Haven, Conn.: Yale University Press, 1994), deals with these early years on pages 1–3. See also A. Biondi, *Mazzini uomo* (Milan: Edizioni Tramontana, 1969), 9–14; and Gwilym O. Griffith, *Mazzini: Prophet of Modern Europe* (London: Hodder and Stoughton, 1932), 17–29. The most thorough coverage of the early years appears in Arturo Codignola, *La giovinezza di G. Mazzini* (Florence: Vallecchi, 1926); and Gaetano Salvemini, "La giovinezza di Mazzini," in his *Scritti sul Risorgimento* (Milan: Feltrinelli, 1963), II, 285–307, but first published in 1911 as part of a projected study of Mazzini's youth that Salvemini never completed.

2. EN, LXXIII, 332–33.

3. EN, LXXVII, 4.

4. EN, LIII, 44.

5. EN, XLII, 221–22; LII, 131.

6. The biblical reference is to Paul, 2 Cor., 12: 9–10. Mazzini's paraphrase appears in an essay on the Prussian poet Zacharias Werner, probably written in 1836. See Alda Manghi, "Mazzini e Werner," *Convivium*, 6 (1952), 873–95. See EN, VIII, 235.

7. Emilie Ashurst Venturi, *Religious Republicanism. Joseph Mazzini As a Religious Teacher* (Bath, U.K.: Wilkinson Brothers, 1871), 6.

8. EN, LXXVII, 4.

9. EN, LXXVII, 6.

10. EN, LXXVII, 6.

11. See Lorenzo Caratti, "La genealogia di Giuseppe Mazzini," BDM, XXIV, 2 (1978), 151–89.

12. See Bianca Montale, *Maria Drago Mazzini* (Genoa: Comune di Genova, 1955), 1–13.

13. *Appendice Epistolario*, EN, VIII, 685. On Giacomo Mazzini's political activities, see Achille Neri, "Il padre di Giuseppe Mazzini," *Rivista Ligure di Scienze, Lettere ed Arti*, XXXVII (May–June 1910), 138–43.

14. Enrico Guglielmino, *Genova dal 1814 al 1849. Gli sviluppi economici e l'opinione pubblica* (Genoa: Atti della R. Deputazione di Storia Patria per la Liguria, 1939), 19.

15. *Appendice Epistolario*, EN, VIII, 480.

16. EN, XX, 54.

17. *Appendice Epistolario*, EN, VIII, 685.

18. EN, XVI, 21–22.

19. See Maurizio Barbagli, *Sotto lo stesso tetto. Mutamenti della famiglia in Italia dal XV al XX secolo* (Bologna: Il Mulino, 1984), 520.

20. EN, LXXXIV, 244.

21. EN, XV, 176.

22. See *Mazzini's Letters to an English Family, 1861–1872* (London: John Lane, 1922), III, 83. Also, EN, XV, 117–18; XXIII, 133.

23. EN, XIX, 304.

24. EN, XIX, 51.

25. On the special bond between mother and son in these early years, see Itala Cremona Cozzolino, ed., *Maria Mazzini e il suo ultimo carteggio* (Florence: La Nuova Italia, 1939), xviii–xix. Also, Stringfellow Barr, *Mazzini, Portrait of an Exile* (New York: H. Holt, 1935), 1–12.

26. EN, X, 135. The nickname was applied later to Mazzini's friend, Filippo Bettini, who was also known for his reticence. See *Appendice epistolario*, EN, VII, 4.

27. EN, VII, 284.

28. Quoted in Francesco Landogna, *Giuseppe Mazzini e il pensiero giansenistico* (Bologna: Zanichelli, 1921), 54n.

29. EN, XXVI, 167. References to Jansenism are frequent in the correspondence between mother and son. See, for example, EN, X, 113, and *Appendice epistolario*, EN, VIII, 203, 217, 220, 281, 430, 529–30.

30. The letter, dated August 12, 1812, appears in Piero Cironi, *Giuseppe Mazzini. Notizie tratte dalle carte di Pietro Cironi* (Florence: Lumachi, 1901), 130–36. Cironi, a close friend of Mazzini, copied the letter from the original shown to him by Maria Mazzini. After Maria's death, the original passed into the hands of Aurelio Saffi, another close friend and collaborator, and was later turned over to the Istituto Mazziniano in Genoa. See the catalog edited by Leo Morabito and Giovanni Spadolini, *Museo del Risorgimento* (Genoa: Comune di Genova, 1987), 152.

31. EN, XV, 192–93. Also, P. A. Colletti, *Giuseppe Mazzini: l'uomo, l'opera* (Genoa: Fassicone, 1905), 14. This work betrays a strong hostility to Mazzini, but also contains information gathered from the last surviving acquaintances of the Mazzinis.

32. EN, XV, 35.

33. EN, XIV, 294; *Appendice epistolario*, EN, VIII, 401, 407, 454. Also, Anna Errera, *Vita di Mazzini* (Milan: Casa Editrice E.S.I., 1932), 241.

34. *Appendice epistolario*, EN, VIII, 500. According to Piero Cironi's *Giuseppe Mazzini*, 13–14, which relies on Maria Mazzini's account of her son's life, it was her brother who insisted that Rosa take no vows, perhaps because he did not wish to see his sister commit herself irrevocably to living in a convent.

35. *Appendice epistolario*, EN, VIII, 499, 551, 570. Also, Carlo Cagnacci, *Giuseppe Mazzini e i fratelli Ruffini* (Porto Maurizio: Tipografia Berio, 1893), 196–97.

36. EN, XII, 239.

37. Breganze's letter, dated December 8, 1814, appears in Codignola, *La giovinezza di G. Mazzini*, 19–21, and in Cozzolino, *Maria Mazzini*, 223–27.

38. EN, XIV, 64.

39. EN, XIV, 289.

40. EN, LXIX, 70–78.

41. EN, XCIV, 72–73.

42. *Appendice epistolario*, EN, VII, Tome 1, 13, 101, 106, 107, 111, 129, 133; VIII, 436, 449, 451, 471–73, 484, 494–95, 587.

43. Michele Saponaro, *Mazzini* (Milan: Garzanti, 1945), 11. Also, Ettore Rota and Silvia Spellanzon, *Maternità illustri* (Milan: Vallardi, 1948), 87–119.

CHAPTER 2

Fantasio: The Years of Apprenticeship (1819–1831)

Fantasio is Mazzini's name in a novel written by a fellow student, which portrays him as a born leader among fellow students. How he acquired that status and what he did with it is the story of this chapter of his life, which, though better documented than his childhood, is still obscure in many respects. The opening event is an incident that Mazzini never mentioned and that biographers neglect, but which was important enough leave a paper trail: his arrest for disorderly conduct on June 21, 1820. The culminating moment is Mazzini's second arrest ten years later on the more serious charge of political conspiracy. In the intervening decade the figure of Fantasio gradually eclipsed that of Pippo, yielding the Mazzini known to posterity. To better understand the transition from the child to the young man, we must first look at the adolescent who became a first-year student at the University of Genoa in November 1819, at the age of fourteen.

Student status was an ambiguous one in Restoration society, which was beginning to recognize the practical utility of education but suspected students of harboring subversive designs. Accountants, scribes, and statisticians were needed to keep track of the business of government, surveyors and engineers to build roads, medical doctors to look after the growing population, and lawyers to deal with increasingly complex codes. Students were needed to fill these professions, but governments did not trust students as a group. Universities were expected to keep out or weed out the most suspect. Applicants had to submit certificates of good conduct from the police and of religious

Pencil sketch of Mazzini at age 25, by Giuseppe Isola. From Leo Morabito and Giovanni Spadolini, eds. *Museo del Risorgimento* (Genova: Istituto Mazziniano, 1987. Courtesy of the Comune di Genova.).

observance from the clergy. Such certificates were issued routinely, but young men eager to assert their independence resented a process that put them at the mercy of priests and bureaucrats; the first impression was that the university was a place of regimentation. University students were expected to be part of the elite, but they were also reminded that they must be obedient subjects. Not surprisingly, many found it difficult or impossible to be both. "Confused youngsters who have everything laid out in front of them while everybody else has to scrounge for a living," is how one observer described Genoese students in the 1820s.[1]

Mazzini and most of his friends looked upon the university as an opportunity to pursue interests that would not necessarily make them good servants of the state. Mazzini never dwelled at length on his university experiences (the Autobiographical Notes all but skip over the years from 1822 to 1827), and it is not even clear whether he first attended the preparatory Royal College. Scattered references in his writings suggest a tortured young man. That may have been a pose prompted by the pervasive influence of romanticism, which made it fashionable for sensitive young people to despair at their own lack of freedom and at the human condition in general. Mazzini, a confessed romantic, claimed that he despaired to the point of contemplating suicide. Other evidence suggests a less dramatic experience, one more typical of student life then and now. He was no stranger to pranks, played billiards, smoked cigars, drank a lot of coffee, and made fun of professors. The problems that he experienced had causes other than romantic angst. That he was intellectually precocious is suggested by his admission to a literary society on the strength of certain compositions in verse, which have not survived. But at fourteen, the minimum age for admission, he was younger than most first-year students, and by his own admission his academic preparation was uneven. The language, trappings, and ceremonial of higher learning intimidated him; he felt like a dolt at a gathering of the wise.

People saw a serious and studious young man who eschewed frivolous behavior and seemed wrapped up in his studies. This image lives on in countless biographies in spite of evidence to the contrary. It appears in the university notebooks that he kept and that his mother preserved for posterity. The notes do attest to the breadth of his intellectual interests, which encompassed literature, history, philosophy, law, and the sciences; but the variety of topics, the presentist tone of the comments, and the long lists of authors also suggest impatience and superficiality. These traits, both the good and the bad, are typical of the adult Mazzini, who read and wrote furiously, but was never able to complete the great novel or the profound philosophical work that he aspired to write. The talents that he had in abundance and that sustained his life's work were those of the political journalist and pamphleteer.

Breadth of interests did not make for an easy choice of career, and the system did not allow much delay. He declared his intention to study jurisprudence at the beginning of his freshman year, but later that same year changed briefly to medicine, perhaps to satisfy his father. The change meant that he had to take courses in chemistry and natural science in addition to those in philosophy and fine arts that were required of all first-year students. The absence of instructor signatures for the science courses suggests that he did not complete them.[2] Stories were later told that Mazzini forsook medicine because he could not stand the sight of blood or cadavers.[3] Squeamish he was, but according to Filippo Bettini, a fellow student who knew him well, the reason he switched back to law was that he wanted to distance himself from his father; as professor of anatomy, Giacomo would have been uncomfortably close had the son studied medicine. According to Bettini, the young Mazzini deplored his father's obsequiousness toward patients—not the humble ones, whom he treated free of charge, but the wealthy ones, on whom he fawned because they paid generously. Such servility offended the young man's sense of dignity. Mazzini's admiration for democratic behavior was not unrelated to adolescent rebelliousness.[4]

It was Mazzini's defiant disposition that got him into trouble with administrators who acted *in loco parentis*, enforcing ordinances against frequenting theaters, coffee-houses, and places of ill repute. Every two months students had to submit certificates of good conduct or be subject to disciplinary proceedings.[5] Mazzini's behavior left much to be desired. There is no evidence that he was attracted to houses of ill repute, which was a heinous offense, but he loved the theater and was too fond of coffee not to frequent the cafés. One administrator noted that he received holy sacraments only four times in his first year, which was considered a bare minimum. He was reprimanded for ignoring school regulations and creating disturbances, preventing other students from attending classes, leaving the school premises without permission, loitering in the courtyard, and being "very dissipated."[6]

THE FIRST SCRAPES WITH THE LAW

Minor incidents escalated into larger protests, because students were good at extracting large issues from small crises; it took relatively little to confirm the student's suspicion that administrators, police agents, and clergy acted in concert as minions of the same oppressive system. Thus we come to the events that led to Mazzini's arrest on June 21, 1820. The incident that caused the arrest occurred on the feast day of Saint Louis, patron of the young, in the church dedicated to that saint, which was frequented by students from the university and the nearby Royal College. A shoving match developed over precedence and seating as students from the two schools filed into the church. It was a common enough occurrence among adolescents, but this one escalated into something bigger when members of the Jesuit order sided with the students from the college.

The Jesuits' intervention exacerbated matters, because it was no secret that they were trying to wrest control of higher education from lay teachers, whom they suspected of harboring liberal tendencies. The most vociferous defenders of the rights of university students turned out to be young Mazzini and his friend Andrea Castaldi, who were arrested for disorderly conduct. They were detained only briefly, perhaps because the entire student body walked out in protest, the faculty supported the students, and the police wanted to avoid further tumult. The students were also backed by many Genoese notables, including Giacomo Mazzini, who were former Jacobins and disliked clerical influence. Whatever the reason for their prompt release, Mazzini and Castaldi were greeted by students and faculty as heroes of the hour.[7]

This minor incident earned Mazzini a reputation for courage and brought him to the attention of the public; it may also have taught him a lesson about power. In their confrontation with the might and majesty of the state, the students had prevailed. It was perhaps no coincidence that several of Mazzini's professors were Jansenists who preached social engagement. Did the outcome not confirm what they preached, that divine providence comes to the rescue of those who act according to conscience? The larger issue was the control of education and the direction of the university, and the powerful Jesuits had been beaten back by powerless students armed only with their faith, enthusiasm, and vigor. Jesuit efforts to gain control of the university continued into the late 1830s, when they finally gave up and decided to establish their own school. Mazzini followed the struggle to the very end, without ever mentioning the incident in which he had played a major role, for reasons that can only be surmised.[8] Perhaps he did not consider it significant, or his sense of drama told him that highlighting it would have detracted from the significance of his later encounter with the fugitive patriots, which he wanted people to see as the decisive moment of conversion. Nevertheless, it was his role in the events of June 21, 1820, that brought him recognition; one day before his fifteenth birthday Mazzini became a political agitator.

That first arrest marks the beginning of the transition from the life of Pippo to that of Fantasio, the name under which he appears in a documentary novel published in 1853 by a fellow student who knew him well. The novel, entitled *Lorenzo Benoni*, is by Giovanni Ruffini, who cast himself in the role of narrator. Two years younger than Mazzini,

Ruffini was a student at the Royal College in 1820. He probably already knew Mazzini, for Mazzini and Giovanni's older brother, Jacopo, were the same age and became inseparable friends after entering the university in 1819. Jacopo and Giuseppe were both bright young men with a promising future, and their respective families, particularly the mothers, encouraged the friendship, which was dominated by Giuseppe. He was the one others looked up to, a born leader, as he is described in the novel:

> His head was well proportioned, the forehead large and prominent; there were times when his jet-black eyes sent forth flashes. His complexion was olive dark; black, wavy hair, which he wore rather long, framed his features. The facial expression was serious, almost stern, but softened by gentleness and by some indefinable quality that hinted at a rich vein of humor. He was a polished and accomplished speaker. In the heat of a discussion, his eyes, gestures, and voice, his whole being, exerted an irresistible charm.[9]

Fantasio's first appearance in the novel is as a veteran of school battles, composed, cordial, and judicious toward his fellow students, but never hesitant to challenge authority in the name of justice. He leads fellow students to demand justice for one of their group who has been wronged, only to be silenced and threatened with jail. The message is that student solidarity was born of such encounters with unbending authority figures, and was sustained by the unjust behavior of those in power. The appeal to justice, rather than to concrete economic interests or class resentments, would always dominate Mazzini's political message. The bonds of solidarity that kept his political movement together later on were always intensely personal, strongest in the immediacy of daily contact and diminishing with distance. Those in whom the fire burned were disciples, while those who felt only its warmth were mere collaborators. If Fantasio is an accurate representation, then we can say that the appeal to conscience and leadership by example were characteristics of the adult already evident in the personality of the young agitator.

The disturbances of 1820 were eclipsed by what happened a year later, when agitation for constitutional government and civil rights spread through southern Europe, from Portugal to Greece. The movement reached Turin in January 1821, with student protests that activated secret political societies. In Piedmont the lead was taken by the Carbonari, the best organized of the secret societies, which brought together students, military officers, middle-class professionals, and members of the liberal nobility. The revolution broke out on March 10, 1821, when troops rebelled, demanded the constitution, and set up a provisional government.

Disturbances broke out in Genoa on March 20–23, with militant students abandoning classes and taking to the streets. Mazzini's role is not clear. The police, who were keeping an eye on him, did not name him as a participant, although he claimed to have joined the protesters. He may have been part of a student delegation that went to see the governor of the city. The spokesman for the group, apparently someone other than Mazzini, opened his speech with the question "Are we slaves or men?" The governor listened and dismissed them without comment. On April 20, Good Friday, troops occupied the university, which was shut down indefinitely.[10]

We are now very close to the legendary encounter with the defeated insurgents. By April the government was cracking down on the insurgents, forcing into flight abroad those who wanted to avoid arrest. It was to escape jail or an even worse fate that the desperate men flocked to Genoa, where the local authorities issued passports in a hurry and outfitted two ships to speed on the unwelcome guests. Private citizens protected them, gave them food, money, and shelter for perhaps more generous motives. Years later, an exile who had sailed from Genoa on that day in late April remembered, or imagined, seeing a young man of sixteen at his mother's side waving farewell to the expatriates.[11]

Popular support for the insurgents expressed widespread anti-Piedmontese sentiments. Genoa still smarted over the decision of 1814 to make it part of Piedmont, a state that the Genoese considered backward and indifferent to the commercial needs of their port city. Military service, obligatory under Piedmontese law, was an unreasonable imposition on people who had never been subjected to conscription. Also resented were the large numbers of troops stationed in the city (8,600 in 1819, on a population of 78,414). Trade, shipping, and banking, the city's traditional sources of wealth and employment, languished under Piedmontese tariffs designed to protect the agricultural and manufacturing interests of the interior provinces. The government was aware of the problem, but its measures to help the city were barely beginning to have an effect in 1821.[12]

Mazzini certainly shared these anti-Piedmontese sentiments, which he would never shed entirely, but his sympathy for the rebels probably had other and more personal causes. The insurgents forced from their homeland personified the civic virtues praised by his mother and his Jansenist teachers. In his memories of those events, Mazzini always placed his mother at his side. Their companion in that fateful stroll along the Via Nuova was Andrea Gambini, a Jansenist sympathizer. Even though father and son shared some political sentiments, Mazzini never mentions his father as an ally. Giacomo stood for authority within the family, just as the king stood for the authority of the state. The teenage son and the rebels had that much in common, that they challenged the personifications of authority in the private and public spheres. Mazzini saw the tensions of the household played out and replicated in the streets, blurring those lines between public and private that the mature Mazzini would condemn as artificial and immoral. Thus, his whole being resonated to the encounter in the Via Nuova, which he remembered for the rest of his life as a political epiphany.

During the two and a half years that the university remained closed (it reopened in November of 1823) classes met informally, usually in the homes of professors. Punishments for students were light, and most managed to graduate on time. Mazzini was shown particular considera-tion, either because he had played a small role in the events or out of respect for his father, who was a member of the faculty. Leniency did not make him change course, however, and it was after 1821 that he emerged fully as the character that Giovanni Ruffini portrayed as Fantasio. The group that he led was small but cohesive. Beside his closest friend Jacopo Ruffini and his brother Giovanni, it included others whose names are worth mentioning because they remained at his side in more important ventures later on. Elia Benza (1802–82) was an older student of great talent and promise, who helped Mazzini overcome the first of several emotional crises in his life; Mazzini called him the "Prophet," probably because of his deep religious faith. There was Filippo Bettini (1803–69), the least politically inclined of the group, who helped Mazzini in many personal ways throughout his life; to Mazzini he was the "Ecstatic," probably because he was notoriously absent-minded. Federico Campanella (1804–84) was an anti-clerical rowdy, who became less rowdy but not less anti-clerical and secular as he grew older.[13]

By far the most important connection that Mazzini established in these years was with the Ruffini family. Their fathers, Giacomo Mazzini and Bernardo Ruffini, had both been Jacobins in their youth, but their paths had diverged, Bernardo becoming a lawyer and pursuing a fairly modest career as a local magistrate. In 1798, at the age of thirty-two, he had married the nineteen-year-old Eleonora Curlo. He came from a prosperous family of bourgeois landowners, had a good head for business and a good sense of humor, but was also authoritarian and stubborn. Eleonora came from impoverished nobility; she had lost her mother at the age of seven and spent the next ten years of her life in a convent. Her impulsive and romantic temperament made her an improbable partner to Bernardo, whom she married on the rebound from a broken romantic liaison with a cousin.[14] Eleonora appreciated the financial security of marriage to Bernardo, but she could not forget that she was an aristocrat and he a mere commoner—and a demanding one at that. Scurrilous gossip dogged her, and Bernardo blamed her for besmirching his reputation and ruining his career.[15]

If their marriage was not entirely happy, it was prolific: twelve children were born between 1799 and 1815, of whom ten survived birth. Seven of these died before their parents, three by suicide. There was an air of tragedy about the Ruffinis, which they ascribed to unspecified personality disorders: "The flaw in our family is that we are extremists; we have some very fine qualities, but they are not well balanced."[16] Eleonora's pride was her fourth-born son, Jacopo, who was born on the same day of the same year as Mazzini. The two met at the university, which they also entered the same year. Parallels are evident even when their decisions were different: Giuseppe, whose father was a doctor, studied law; Jacopo, whose father was a lawyer, studied medicine. They resembled one another, Jacopo only slightly taller, both dark-complexioned, lean, intense, and fastidious about appearance and attire. People saw them as outgoing, enthusiastic, and impetuous, but Mazzini also remembered pensive and melancholy moments spent together, and their yearning for solitude. Their strongest bond was an intense interest in religion, music, art, and literature, which meant much more to them than either law or medicine.[17]

LITERATURE AND POLITICS

The period from 1822 to 1829 was one of intellectual preparation and development for Mazzini, who documented it in broad outline in his notebooks. The undated entries do not tell the story chronologically, but they do throw light on what he read and how he studied.[18] The notes deal mostly with art, history, philosophy, religion, and above all literature. They show him following developments in the then fashionable areas of linguistics, phrenology, spiritualism, popular education, and poor relief. The patriotic motif is present but not dominant. His notes are in English, French, Italian, and Latin, usually in the form of extracts from texts, in a tradition of study that dated from medieval times. Initially, he seemed more at home with French, but his Italian improved enough for him to aspire to a career as a writer in that language. The notebooks contain long lists of authors, including Diderot, Boccaccio, Rousseau, Dante, Richardson, Madame de Staël, Voltaire, Alfieri, Genovesi, Byron, Scott, Paine, Ossian, Foscolo, Monti, Cuoco, Schiller, Goethe, Manzoni, Machiavelli, and Vico. It is hard to tell how many of these he actually read, but if nothing else the lists do attest to his eclectic interests.

Not everything in the notebooks is literary and learned. There is the summary of an erotic tale, written in the style of the Thousand and One Nights. There are entries that deal with the physiology of sex; one asserts that wives who refuse to perform the conjugal act at least four times a month commit a mortal sin, and another that Sodom was destroyed because women assumed the dominant position in the act of sex. A composition in verse casts doubt on the virtue of Roman women, the celibacy of priests, and the sexual orientation of Tuscan men. References to sexual matters appear even in his legal notes, where he registers arguments in favor of allowing sex between unmarried consenting adults and accepting cohabitation as a legally valid union.[19] He may have lived as a revolutionary ascetic, but he was not prudish or narrow-minded.

This concern with sexual matters was not unrelated to his own romantic attachments, two of which we know of from his own testimony. The first was to an Englishwoman, Marianne Thomas, who was his neighbor; the second to Adelaide Zoagli, a Genoese noblewoman a few years older. Mazzini made light of both attachments, describing them as childish infatuations. But he was interested enough in Marianne to track her down in England twenty years later. As for Adele, he was twenty-two when she disappointed him by marrying a naval officer. When Goffredo Mameli, the son born of that marriage, died defending the Roman republic in 1849, Mazzini, who headed the government, resumed contact with her. Estranged from her husband and flattered by Mazzini's attention, she gravitated toward him emotionally and politically. Her son became a republican martyr and hero, and she was absorbed into the pantheon of great Italian mothers, along with Maria Mazzini and Eleonora Ruffini. Her elevation linked the sexual passions of Mazzini's youth with the political passions of his maturity.[20]

The indifference to sexual passion that is often attributed to Mazzini was more apparent than real. Sexual matters entered into Mazzini's politics in many ways, starting with his political apprenticeship. Several notebook entries suggest bonds of homoerotic friendship among adolescents. Among notes on ancient Roman civilization, Mazzini writes that it is possible to love a man and a woman simultaneously and with equal intensity. A young man who is a "hot lover of women" (*caldo amatore di donne*) will be drawn to love a male friend with equal intensity because love is a passion capable of infinite expansion: "The passions of love and friendship are related, and may be considered to be one and the same passion."[21] To the Tuscan novelist Gian Domenico Guerrazzi he wrote, before meeting him personally, that his writings inspired in him a sentiment that was "strikingly similar to that of love inspired by beauty; I mean beauty not of appearances, but intimate and profound. It seems to me that I would kiss Foscolo, Byron, and you with the same feeling and enthusiasm with which I would put the seal of love on the lips of Canova's Venus, if she could return my kiss."[22]

Mazzini used the language of love to call on his generation: "Let us love one another," he wrote, "for all living beings are born to love. Let us unite and we shall be the strongest."[23] Expressions such as these, which recur frequently in his writings, suggest a particular notion of what lies at the basis of association. Just as his experience of family life predisposed him to extend the bond of love beyond the family, so did his experience of male bonding inspire him to extend ties of affection to the political realm. The language of his correspondence points to the presence of homoerotic bonds, without implying the existence of homosexual relations. At a time when custom, parental strictness, and relationships determined by family interests made it difficult for young people to establish spontaneous relationships with members of the opposite sex, erotic language between members of the same sex served perhaps as a substitute. It shows up with such frequency in nineteenth-century correspondence as to suggest that it denoted something quite different from homosexuality, but still sexual in nature. One who worked closely with him thought that "the impatience to do something that keeps Mazzini in a constant state of physical eroticism [*erotismo d'azione materiale*]" had an element of repressed sexuality.[24]

Literature, not sex, however, was the secret political weapon of the young. More precisely, it was literary criticism that intellectuals of Mazzini's generation chose as their battleground. They were brought up on classics that paraded before them ideals of civic virtue, but while they adopted the ideals of citizenship that classic literature inspired, they rejected its literary forms. Mazzini saw it as the task of his generation to propagate those ideals in a style that appealed to the emotions. That was the central issue that he saw in the literary polemic between the classicists, who worshipped form, and the romanticists, who believed in free expression. Italians came late to that debate, but they infused it with political fervor. The conflict, for that is what the debate became in Italy, was also between generations: youth was romanticist, age classicist.

Mazzini's first literary essay, "On Dante's Love of Country" (1826), claimed for the poet and for literature in general a social role that, he argued, literature had lost under the influence of classicism. In Dante's time "literature was, as it should be, part of the institutions that sustained society; it was not seen as a mere convenience, but rather as a useful ministry, and the poet was seen not as compiler of metered syllables, but as a free being, inspired by the Gods to show man the truth disguised as allegory."[25] It was to Dante's eternal credit that he had tried to cure his contemporaries of the social vices and political divisiveness that had plagued Italian history since Roman times.

Mazzini misread Dante, as scholars were quick to point out, and he was embarrassed when the article was published years later without his consent, but it is of interest as his first statement about literature's social significance. Dante, he wrote, was a a great writer because he voiced and acted on his vision of a just society; he had been a "witness to the century," a "prophet to the age," and an "initiator," the real prototype of the modern artist, whose mission was not to amuse or console, as the classicists would have it, but to incite to action. This was the Germanic concept of literature as a form of social expression, which Mazzini interpreted dynamically: the function of literature was to change society, and the great writer was a social reformer in disguise.[26]

Such a view of the writer's role anticipated Mazzini's later concept of the nature of political leadership. In politics as in literature innovators emerge who fulfill their mission by anticipating, interpreting, and shaping the collective will. What that will might be Mazzini did not say in his essay on Dante, but he argued that it was to the credit of his generation that it believed in the social mission of literary criticism. As he put it in the Autobiographical Notes, "No one in Italy had said that romanticism stood for liberty against oppression, that it battled against every construct or norm that we had not chosen freely through individual inspiration or the deep, collective aspirations of the country. We were the ones who said it."[27]

Mazzini's development from the temperamental rebelliousness of 1820–21 to the more considered radicalism of 1826 is hard to trace. The lack of opportunity for public protest in the repressive atmosphere that developed after 1821, and the pressure of police surveillance and worried parents made it a time for private pursuits. The parents, especially Bernardo and Giacomo, kept a close watch on their troublesome offspring, demanding that they be home early in the evening, giving them no spending money, and forbidding them to attend the theater or to leave the city unaccompanied. For someone as resourceful as Mazzini, however, covert forms of protest were not hard to devise. During these years he developed his lifelong habit of dressing in black, to mourn the oppression of his country, he claimed, but also perhaps to protest his own. Wearing black was not an indictable offense; it also signified a coming out of sorts, because the black-clad youth who appeared in the streets of the city with a retinue of followers was clearly not the shy youngster who had not wanted to be seen in public.

Sometime between 1822 and 1825 Mazzini experienced an emotional crisis; later on he remembered it as religious, but it may have involved more than his religious beliefs. Maria worried about his propensity for sarcasm, which she interpreted as lack of faith. Traces of a disturbed state of mind appear in random notebook jottings: "There are days when I feel inert, as if struck dumb," he writes, "when I feel as if I do not belong to this world, even as events parade themselves before my eyes." He resumes his notes in Latin, but a few pages later we have what looks like the incomplete rough draft of a letter to a friend: "they are like dreams perceived through a veil, which prevent me from concentrating; at such times you may have seen me as if stuck to a chair, unable to answer your prayers and entreaties."[28] A letter he wrote to Benza in 1825 attests to his troubled state. In it Mazzini described his feelings of pent-up anger and the wild projects he contemplated while lying awake at night, "cursing chance, or whatever power exists, which has flung us down here, with this unrequited longing in our hearts, with this immense love for a country that is denied to us, giving us tyrants instead. I have often thought of escaping from them, and denying them the pleasure of seeing me suffer. Hope for revenge, love of family and, underneath it all, perhaps the cowardice with which I constantly reproach myself, prevent me from doing so."[29]

Mazzini remembered coming out of the crisis stronger in faith, but it was a faith that conformed to no standard canon. It was not traditional Christianity, for he rejected the sacramental aspects and the fundamental dogmas of original sin, the divinity of Christ, resurrection, and trinity as "absurd."[30] He read Condorcet surreptitiously while attending mass, perhaps reflecting that Condorcet's theory of unlimited progress clashed with Christian notions of human fallibility. Emotionally, he found himself drawn to Foscolo's *Last Letters of Jacopo Ortis*, a novel inspired by Goethe's *Sufferings of Young Werther*, in which the protagonist is driven to suicide by love of woman and country. Reading Foscolo's novel "fanaticized" him, he said later, but he resisted the temptation to commit suicide. There is a rumor that he and his friends plotted to assassinate various heads of state on the occasion of an international conference in Genoa in May of 1825.[31] It is unlikely that the dignitaries were in any real danger, but if the rumor is true, it marked the first time that private anguish predisposed Mazzini to commit an act of mayhem.

He made steady progress in the study of law, some aspects of which absorbed him. Capital punishment was one, and he expressed his disapproval by spelling out in his notebooks the means of recourse. He looked into ways of protecting the accused from false testimony, noted the need for prison reform, and outlined arguments in favor of the right to bear arms, which he would always defend as a safeguard of democracy and for individual self-protection. This was not disinterested advocacy, for he and his friends were now surreptitiously manufacturing ammunition in the cellar of the family cottage in Bavari.

He was also interested in family legislation, including inheritance laws, and he wrote his thesis on the juridical nature of the marriage contract. This controversial issue had been the subject of debate ever since the government had abolished the Napoleonic legislation that sanctioned divorce. Mazzini's position was that the civil contract and religious contracts were separate and distinct, and that the provisions of the civil contract took precedence over the religious sacrament. It was a secular view at odds with the law, which accorded legal validity to the religious function. He did not bother to rebut that view with legal arguments. Showing his penchant to go for the throat when important issues were at stake, he swept aside technical considerations with the argument that no law is valid when it does not have the consent of the people.[32]

In the spring of 1827 Mazzini passed his law exams, and for two years thereafter "attended to the law just enough to fulfill the commands of duty."[33] It is not clear whether that meant duty to his father for the money he had spent on his education, or duty to the mostly poor clients whose cases he is said to have handled *pro bono*, although no record of such cases has been found. What he did pursue seriously after gradu- ation was literary criticism in the columns of a local publication. The first issue of the weekly *L'Indicatore Genovese* came out in May 1828.

At first it specialized in business announcements, but then it turned into a literary journal right under the censor's nose.[34] Mazzini and his friends were the driving force behind the publication, but others sup- ported it financially and politically. Its publisher was Luigi Ponthenier, who had doubts about transforming the paper into a literary journal. He allowed Mazzini to do so perhaps to improve its flagging circulation. The journal and a reading society were located in a bookshop owned by a member of the prominent Doria family. Antonio Doria came from an aristocratic family, but he was also a businessman and a liberal at heart. His name and his family connections provided good cover for activities that skirted the margins of legality. While the reading society dissemi- nated forbidden or hard-to-find publications, the journal addressed the hottest literary issues of the moment through reviews of recent publi- cations. It sided with the romanticists against the classicists, discussed the relationship between popular culture and literature, as well as the merits of historical fiction, and polemicized with prominent figures.

Mazzini took on Carlo Botta, who had accused young writers of betraying Italy's cultural heritage by imitating foreign models. The real traitors, replied Mazzini, were the classicists, who kept Italy culturally isolated while the rest of Europe embarked on an exciting intellectual journey. The polemic brought into the open the patriotic theme, with Mazzini trying to appropriate what until then had been the classicists' ace in the hole. For the first time he also sounded the theme that Italy's cultural destiny had to be fulfilled in the larger European setting. Other contributors to *L'Indicatore*, which included Benza and Bettini, could be relied on to be kind to authors whose works exuded patriotism. Foscolo, Guerrazzi, and Manzoni were praised, but so was the classicist Vincenzo Monti, who had burnt incense at every political altar since the French Revolution; his politics were not above suspicion, but he was one of the glories of Italy.

The journal was suppressed by the government in December of 1828. Its tone of rebelliousness could not have pleased the authorities, but what is clear is that they responded to pressure from influential individuals and groups who were the target of the journal's attacks. Giovanni Battista Spotorno, a priest in charge of a rival publication, led the attack, but behind him were other members of the clergy and several university professors with whom Mazzini may have been trying to settle old scores . After the last issue appeared in December of 1828, someone was impudent enough to petition that it be revived as an explicitly literary journal.[35] If it was Mazzini, he did not wait for a reply: by the time the petition was denied, he was already in contact with a group of writers who planned to launch a similar journal in the Tuscan port city of Livorno.

The first issue of *L'Indicatore Livornese* came out in January of 1829. The similarity of names appears to have been coincidental; there never was full cooperation between the Genoese and Tuscan writers, but the Livorno journal did publish articles by Mazzini, Benza, and Bettini before it was shut down by the Tuscan government for being too inflammatory.[36] Mazzini's Tuscan contacts extended to Florence, where he was in touch with the editors of *L'Antologia*, a prestigious publication familiar to Mazzini since his student days. Its editors had turned down his first submission, the essay on Dante's patriotism, but accepted others, including an important essay on European literature that affords a first glimpse of Mazzini as Europeanist. The essay argued that national styles of literary expression were in no way threatened by international dialogue, that governments did a great disservice to the development of European culture by creating artificial barriers to communication, and that the national styles of the literatures of Europe shared common interests and traditions and moved toward the same goal.[37] He did not elaborate on what the goal was, but he concluded hopefully that a common European literature would eventually emerge from the diversity of national styles. There was no discussion of politics, but the political implications of the argument were clear.

MAZZINI AS CARBONARO

Only Mazzini's closest friends knew that while he waged his literary battle he was also engaged in much more compromising secret activities. Secret political societies were rumored to exist everywhere, but in Genoa they were maddeningly elusive, even though by the mid-1820s the city was reputed to be an important center of Carbonari activity. Mazzini searched, spied, and questioned for months, until a former classmate put him in touch with the right people.[38] Sometime in 1827, he was summoned to appear at a secret location to be initiated. The initiator was Raimondo Doria, a long-time Carbonaro with a questionable past who claimed membership in the Doria family. Raimondo was curt; there was no time for the usual ceremonies, he said, because the police were on their trail. Mazzini kneeled, swore loyalty on a drawn dagger, received the secret signs and passwords, and was sent on his way. To Mazzini's disappointment, nothing was said about ideals and goals, only about the inexorable retribution that would follow if he betrayed secrets or failed to obey instructions. As an apprentice he had to prove himself before being entrusted with anything important.[39]

The fact that it was a former classmate who put Mazzini in touch with the Carbonari reveals that he sought them out after leaving the university. Why then? The decision to join a secret society is usually explained politically, and political considerations were obviously important for Mazzini. Other motivations were also involved, however. What secret societies provided to all their members regardless of rank was a sense of belonging. That was the primary function of the oath, which along with obligations also conferred rights and power over other members of the sect.[40] Membership in the Carboneria, with its reputedly large and powerful network, compensated for the loss of identity and power as a student leader that was the unavoidable result of Mazzini's graduation.

Success in the Carboneria required patience and perseverance. Like all secret societies of the time, the brotherhood revealed itself by degrees. Members, who addressed each other as *buoni cugini* (good cousins), belonged to local cells called *vendite*, composed of about twenty members; local cells took their orders from regional committees called *vendite centrali*, which in turn answered to a high command (*alta vendita*). Members recognized each other through secret passwords and handshakes, but the organization was tightly hierarchical, orders came down from above, and direct contacts between local cells were discouraged. The goals of the society were disclosed gradually as members rose through successive levels of membership. Starting at the first level with promises of strict secrecy and obedience, and vague professions of brotherhood, the objectives became increasingly radical, from commitment to institutional reform and constitutional government to national independence (in the case of Italy), republicanism, and finally perhaps "communism," which meant shared ownership of material possessions.[41]

Mazzini may have understood that the Carbonari's greatest source of power was the aura of mystery that surrounded their activities, but he was also interested in the power of numbers and guns. He became a Carbonaro to start the revolution, only to discover that most of the *buoni cugini* did not share his zest for action. Professionals often joined to advance their careers, officers and enlisted men to rise through the ranks, and sailors to find cheap lodgings and diversions in ports of call. The local leaders with whom Mazzini was in contact relished the hocus-pocus of their fraternity. Fewer oaths and more action, he is said to have demanded of the Genoese Carbonari. When they hesitated he circumvented them, seeking to win over his superiors and reaching out to others further afield who shared his way of thinking.

Thus Mazzini caught the attention of an old Carbonaro who was said to be a chief of the order. Francesco Antonio Passano took a liking to the zealous young man whose literary skills were attracting public attention and who was so well-connected in Genoa. The son of Doctor Giacomo Mazzini was worth cultivating. Passano made him his personal secretary, and commissioned him to write an open letter to Charles X urging the French monarch to grant a constitution. The letter appeared with Raimondo Doria's signature, however, perhaps to allay the older man's sense of suspicion and jealousy.[42] Greatly impressed by the young convert, Passano sponsored his promotion to the second level of membership, probably in 1829. At the second level members were permitted to recruit, which Mazzini proceeded to do zealously, starting with his friends Benza and Jacopo Ruffini. Genoa was a good recruiting ground. The Genoese who still resented Piedmontese rule no longer thought about local independence; instead, they hoped to transform Piedmont into a constitutional, representative monarchy responsive to the special needs and interests of their city. The aims of Carboneria answered those needs.

Antonio Doria's bookshop became headquarters for the Carbonari, Antonio joined along with most members of the reading society, and Mazzini's importance grew with the size of his following. If what an informer reported is true, that the Genoese cell of the Carbonari was by that time in charge of operations for all of Italy, then Mazzini played a much more important role in Carboneria then he admitted to in his Autobiographical Notes.[43] His contacts extended to other parts of Italy. He visited Tuscany in August of 1830 to establish new cells, starting with Livorno where he enrolled Carlo Bini, a merchant with literary aspirations and a kindred spirit. They got along well and traveled together to visit Guerrazzi, who was serving six months of detention in Montepulciano for a seditious patriotic speech. Admirable from a distance, up close Guerrazzi seemed vain and conceited, and Mazzini did not invite him to join the Carbonari. It was the first of several unpleasant encounters between two often intolerant individuals.[44] The trip to Tuscany convinced Mazzini that there were other people who like himself were eager for action. He announced triumphantly to his Genoese friends that he had found the Italian Hetairia in Tuscany. That reference was to the Greek patriotic society that Mazzini admired; unlike the Carbonari, who seemed content to wait, Hetairia called on the Greek people to sacrifice their lives for the liberty of their country; that was the kind of language Italians ought to hear.[45]

Mazzini's initiator, Raimondo Doria, kept a close watch on Mazzini. Doria had worked his way up since becoming a Carbonaro in 1812, at the age of eighteen. He sported the illustrious name of the Doria and thought of himself as an aristocrat, but found himself rubbing shoulders with riffraff and young upstarts who did not know their place. Doria turned against secret societies in general and against Mazzini in particular. That he recognized Mazzini as a person of principle only made things worse. When he started to inform on him he was careful to point out that Mazzini was particularly dangerous precisely because he lived what he professed. Doria was clever, too; he took Mazzini aside as he was about to leave for Tuscany and reminded him sternly of the dire fate that awaited traitors.

Mazzini stepped up his conspiratorial activities after his return from Tuscany. In Tuscany he had met two Milanese conspirators who proposed to assassinate Metternich.[46] The police knew of the plot, but they worried about compromising their source if they used the information. They therefore decided to obtain evidence by entrapment. Doria was careful to leave town before the trap was sprung, and it was the guileless Passano who sent Mazzini to initiate a new member at a supposedly secret location. While Mazzini officiated, a stranger peered into the room seemingly by mistake, then quickly withdrew. That was the eyewitness whose testimony was needed to make a case that would stand up in court. Three weeks later, in the early morning hours of November 13, 1830, the police arrested Mazzini on the doorstep of his home, as he returned from an all-night meeting. In his room he had compromising papers, and on him ammunition, a sword-stick, and an encoded letter from Bini, but the arresting agents managed to miss this incriminating evidence. Others were also arrested that morning, including Passano and Doria the bookseller.[47]

After being detained and questioned for a few days in Genoa, Mazzini was whisked off in the middle of the night to a jail in Savona. It was a shock for him to sit in a rumbling carriage, flanked by guards who sneered at his elegant clothes and refined manners. The protective environment of family, friends, and familiar places was slipping by him in the dark that night. Then, suddenly, while being moved from one conveyance to another, he heard a familiar voice and caught a glimpse of his father in the darkness. He barely had time to grasp his hand and hear the few words of encouragement that his father whispered in his ear before the guards hustled him into the waiting coach and they were off again. It was an instant, but it changed the way he felt about his father. The sound of his father's voice that night was something he would never forget.[48] That moment made up for all the tensions of their relationship, and made it possible for them to communicate from a distance as they were never able to do in proximity.

The warden who took charge of Mazzini advised him sardonically to catch up on the sleep he had lost attending so many late-night meetings. The prisoner was either disoriented or impudent enough to ask for a cigar. The request was ignored, but the hard-boiled jailer was not allowed to gloat over his captive. Within days he was replaced by a much more accommodating warden who treated the young man like a member of the family, providing him with books, inviting him to take tea in his own suite, introducing his wife and daughter, and allowing his parents to visit him. The experience was not at all unpleasant, he reminisced years later.[49]

The imprisonment is enshrined in patriotic legend, put there by Mazzini himself. According to his recollections, the design to break with the Carbonari, start a new political course, and establish an organization that fought openly for independence and unity was conceived in his prison cell in the fortress of Savona. Few historians today accept that account as an accurate description of what happened. In the short run, the imprisonment actually solidified his position as a Carbonaro. It was in prison that Passano conferred on him the full powers of a Grand Master. Mazzini later made light of the event, describing it as an *opera buffa* in which a befuddled Passano promoted him hurriedly by tapping him on the head during a brief encounter in a corridor.[50] Nonetheless, Mazzini continued to capitalize on his Carbonaro status and connections long after his release, and Young Italy, the revolutionary organization he would found, resembled the Carboneria more than he was willing to admit.

The Carbonari were by no means finished. One historian has even suggested that the slipshod search of Mazzini's person and home that failed to turn up incriminating evidence and the lenient treatment he received in jail and at the hands of his judges were due to the influence of his Carbonari connections.[51] There may be some truth to this. The proceedings against him and the other suspects were conducted in an unusual manner. Instead of being subjected to criminal proceedings as the law allowed, their cases were referred to a committee of magistrates in Turin. Their findings impugned the credibility of the sole eyewitness in Mazzini's case, even though he was a policeman. As for Passano, the judges let him go expressing disbelief that a person of such limited intellectual capabilities could be the head of a dangerous organization. Their report of January 9, 1831, recommended that all seven suspects be released.

Giacomo and Maria came to collect their son, but the case was not over. The police were still convinced of Mazzini's guilt, and he had Jesuit enemies at court who did not want to see him get off scot-free. Leading the Jesuit charge was Antonio Bresciani, a member of the order who knew all about Mazzini's activities in Genoa and who pursued a lifelong

campaign against him. King Charles Felix looked into the affair personally; although he did not question the findings of the magistrates, he
decided to teach the young man a lesson. A royal decree of January 28,
1831, gave Mazzini the choice between expatriation and temporary
confinement in some remote locality of the kingdom.

Mazzini chose expatriation and left for France before the end of the
month. It seemed like the right decision. Revolution seemed imminent,
and the Carbonari were on the move in Bologna, Modena, and Rome.
The ultraconservative but ambitious duke of Modena, Francis IV,
seemed ready to join the revolution. The revolution of July 1830 had
brought Louis Philippe to the French throne, and the Carbonari expected great things from this member of the supposedly liberal Orleans
dynasty. Rumor had it that the real power behind the throne was none
other than the Marquis de Lafayette, George Washington's old collaborator, who was reputed to be the real head of the international Carbonari
movement. France might even send its revolutionary armies into Italy,
as it had done in 1796.

Mazzini left Genoa not as a political exile but as a private traveler,
equipped with a legal passport and in the company of a maternal uncle
who was a French citizen and who owned property in France. Parting
therefore was not the wrenching experience that it might have been had
he and his parents known what was in store. He carried boundless
enthusiasm and a limited baggage of ideas culled more from the general
intellectual climate of the time than from any specific thinkers. Certainly, he had no systematic creed or philosophy. He had a concept of
Italy as a cultural and historical entity, blamed foreign rule and the
political division of the country for the ills of Italian society, and perhaps
from the Neapolitan commentator Vincenzo Cuoco he had picked up the
notion that leadership must come from individuals of intellect and
education and that the people would follow.[52] Society was divided
between young and old; the old were hopelessly conservative, while the
young were open to change but paralyzed by the spirit of skepticism.[53]
Italy lagged behind the rest of Europe, but could close the gap because
culturally it was part of Europe: "We believe that all Italy needs is the
will to do it."[54]

His tendency to think in terms of will was already set, as was his
practice of treating abstractions as if they were corporeal entities. He
spoke of God, Italy, and the Italian People as if they were realities
waiting to manifest themselves in the material world. Perhaps he owed
this belief to German philosophy; although it is doubtful that he had
read Hegel, Hegelian philosophy was part of the zeitgeist. Mazzini's
belief in the spiritual nature of reality separates him, then and now,
from those who think that reality is a social construct. National identity,
for instance, for him was a reality of the spirit not to be measured

scientifically, but a reality nonetheless, which would be brought out by the power of example and education.

When he spoke of Italy and the Italian People he meant those few who shared his vision and resolve. The few would become a people when the rest were educated in the heart and in the intellect. The people must be taught love. *Amor patrio* (love of country) was precisely that, a form of love that drew individuals outside themselves. The opposite of love was egoism; egoists understood only "the filthy language of the senses. . . . Nature has inscribed on their foreheads, thou shall not love."[55] Italians must overcome the isolation that made them weak, by moving toward each other and toward the rest of Europe. Only then would they gain a sense of their own collective identity: "Political independence and spiritual unity are the highest values of civilization to which nations can aspire. Time will tell whether Italy will benefit or be harmed by that aspiration."[56] That final sobering thought disappeared in the excitement of the moment. Fantasio left Italy imagining a quick and triumphal return in the vanguard of a liberating army.

NOTES

Works frequently cited in the notes have been identified by the following abbreviations:

EN   *Edizione Nazionale. Scritti editi ed inediti di Giuseppe Mazzini* (1906–90), 106 vols.

SEI   *Scritti editi ed inediti di Giuseppe Mazzini* (1861–91), 18 vols.

1. Quoted in Walter Maturi, *Il Principe di Canosa* (Florence: Le Monnier, 1944), 200. For the reminiscences of one student born in 1803, see Giovanni Spano, *Iniziazione ai miei studi* (Sassari: Tip. Azuni, 1884).

2. Gaetano Salvemini, "La giovinezza di Mazzini," in *Scritti sul Risorgimento* (Milan: Feltrinelli, 1963), 291–92, and Itala Cremona Cozzolino, *Maria Mazzini e il suo ultimo carteggio* (Florence: La Nuova Italia, 1039), xxvii–xxix.

3. Jessie White Mario, *Della vita di Giuseppe Mazzini* (Milan: Sonzogno, 1885), 38; the source for these stories was probably Maria Mazzini.

4. Bettini's comment appears in a letter of recollections that is reproduced in *Epistolario di Giuseppe Mazzini* (Florence: Sansoni, 1902–4), I, SEI, XIX, xxix.

5. Friedrich von Raumer, *Italy and the Italians* (London: H. Colburn, 1840), I, 291–94.

6. Alessandro Luzio, *Giuseppe Mazzini carbonaro* (Turin: Bocca, 1920), 34.

7. See Emanuele Celesia, *Storia della Università di Genova dal 1814 fino a' dì nostri* (Genoa: Tip. Sordo-muti, 1867), II, 302–3, and Alessandro Levi, *Mazzini* (Florence: Barbera, 1955), 13–14.

8. References to the Jesuits' designs on the university appear in *Appendice epistolario*, EN, VIII, 448, 708.

9. Giovanni Ruffini, *Lorenzo Benoni, ovvero, Pagine della vita d'un italiano* (Milan: Luigi Trevisini, 1908), 175. First published in English as *Lorenzo Benoni, or Passages in the Life of an Italian* (London: Hamilton, Adams, 1863).

10. Arturo Codignola, *La giovinezza di Giuseppe Mazzini* (Florence: Vallecchi, 1926), 114–24. Also, Salvemini, *Scritti sul Risorgimento*, 301–2, and Leo Morabito and Giovanni Spadolini, eds., *Museo del Risorgimento* (Genova: Comune di Genova, 1987), 152.

11. Silvia Pelosi, *Della vita di Maurizio Quadrio* (Sondrio: Arti Grafiche Valtelli, 1921–22), I, 55–58.

12. Giulio Giacchero, *Genova e Liguria nell'età contemporanea*, I: *La rivoluzione industriale, 1815–1900* (Genoa: Sagep Editore, 1980), 43–44, and Enrico Guglielmino, *Genova dal 1814 al 1849. Gli sviluppi economici e l'opinione pubblica* (Genoa: Atti della Regia Deputazione di Storia Patria per la Liguria, 1939), 54–55.

13. Federico Donaver, *Vita di Giuseppe Mazzini* (Florence: Le Monnier, 1903), 25.

14. Giovanni Faldella, *I fratelli Ruffini; storia della Giovine Italia* (Turin: Roux e Viarengo, 1900), 86–91.

15. Adolfo Bassi, "La vita familiare dei Ruffini e dei Curlo durante la loro dimora in Genova," in *Giovanni Ruffini e i suoi tempi* (Genoa: Comitato per le onoranze a Giovanni Ruffini, 1931), 14–40.

16. Quoted in Carlo Cagnacci, *Giuseppe Mazzini e i fratelli Ruffini* (Porto Maurizio: Tip. Berio, 1893), 55n.

17. See Mazzini's comments on the interests that he and Jacopo shared in EN, XXXIV, 71–75. Also, W. J. Linton, *European Republicans* (London: Lawrence and Bullen, 1892), 167–73.

18. The notebooks have been published in four volumes as a new series of the national edition. The reference here is to the third volume, which covers the years 1822–29. See *Zibaldone giovanile*, EN, III. The law notes appear clustered near the beginning and end of the volume, on pages 3–31 and 218–68. An excellent analysis of the content of the notebooks appears in Francesco Luigi Mannucci, *Giuseppe Mazzini e la prima fase del suo pensiero letterario* (Milan: Casa Editrice Risorgimento, 1919), 10–25.

19. *Zibaldone giovanile*, EN, III, 34–37, 48, 90, 104–5, 218–42; IV, 310–15.

20. Arturo Salucci, *Amori mazziniani* (Florence: Vallecchi, 1928), 73–79. For later references and correspondence with Adele, see EN, XX, 251; XL, 167; XLII, 306–7; LXXVIII, 301.

21. *Zibaldone giovanile*, EN, IV, 303–4.

22. EN, V, 4.

23. From an essay of 1829 on European literature, in EN, I, 214.

24. Mauro Macchi, *La conciliazione dei partiti* (Genoa: Moretti, 1856), 4–5.

25. From Mazzini's "On Dante's Love of Country," in EN, I, 3.

26. See Anna T. Ossani, *Letteratura e politica in Giuseppe Mazzini* (Urbino: Argalia, 1973), 8–10. Also, Otto Vossler, *Il pensiero politico di Mazzini* (Florence: La Nuova Italia, 1971), 19–27.

27. EN, XXVII, 88.

28. *Zibaldone giovanile*, EN, IV, 6, 14.

29. Ibid., III, 274–75.

30. Ibid., III, 90.

31. See Luzio, *Giuseppe Mazzini Carbonaro*, 385, 397, and Cesar Vidal, *Louis-Philippe, Metternich et la crise italienne de 1831–1832* (Paris: E. de Boccard, 1931), 8.

32. *Zibaldone giovanile*, EN, III, 6–21, 95–99, 119–37. On Mazzini's legal studies, see also the observations in Lucrezia Zappia, "Temi giuridici nello Zibaldone giovanile," in *Mazzini. Tra insegnamento e ricerca* (Rome: Edizioni dell'Ateneo, 1982), 61–65.

33. Mario, *Della vita di Giuseppe Mazzini*, 40.

34. EN, LXXVII, 11–13. Mazzini's contributions to the paper appear in EN, I, 27–124.

35. Achille Neri, *La soppressione dell'"Indicatore Genovese"* (Turin: Fratelli Bocca, 1910), 26–38. Also, Renato Carmignani, *Storia del giornalismo mazziniano* (Pisa: Domus Mazziniana, 1959), I, 39–80.

36. Arturo Linaker, *La vita e i tempi di Enrico Mayer* (Florence: Barbera, 1882), I, 123–25, 133.

37. EN, I, 215.

38. EN, LXXVII, 15.

39. Luzio, *Mazzini carbonaro*, 39–46.

40. See the comments in George Simmel, "The Sociology of Secret Societies," *American Journal of Sociology,* XI (June 1906), 464–66.

41. See J. M. Roberts, *The Mythology of the Secret Societies* (London: Secker & Warburg, 1972), 316–40.

42. EN, XCIV, 107–71.

43. Luzio, *Giuseppe Mazzini Carbonaro*, 399–401. Also, Giovanni La Cecilia, *Memorie storico-politiche dal 1820 al 1876* (Rome: Artero, 1876–78), I, 77–78; Ersilio Michel, "Carlo Bini cittadino e patriotta," in *Carlo Bini, nel centenario della morte* (Livorno: Stabilimento Tipografico Toscano, 1943), 10.

44. EN, LXXVII, 19–23.

45. *Zibaldone giovanile*, EN, IV, 459. Also, White Mario, *Della vita di Giuseppe Mazzini*, 79.

46. Mazzini's Milanese contacts were the Marquis Camillo d'Adda, whom he had enrolled as a Carbonaro in Livorno, and Felice Argenti, who had fled abroad after 1821. Argenti may have been an agent provocateur in the service of the Lombard police. See EN, V, 39–41.

47. Mazzini's account of his arrest appears in SEI, LXXVII, 23–26. He gives the impression that the arrest occurred shortly after he returned from his first trip to Tuscany. In reality, it happened more than a year later, probably after he returned from a second trip that he does not mention.

48. EN, XV, 336.

49. EN, XXVIII, 232.

50. EN, LXXVII, 80.

51. See Luzio, *Giuseppe Mazzini Carbonaro*, 75–77. Emilio Faldella (*I fratelli Ruffini*, 58) suggests that the lenient treatment may have been due to

the personal intervention of the king himself, who may have realized that Mazzini had been entrapped.

52. *Zibaldone giovanile*, EN, III, 189.

53. From "Frammento d'un libro inedito intitolato: Due adunanze degli Accademici Pitagorici," published in 1839 but written around 1830, in EN, XVI, 403.

54. EN, I, 71.

55. EN, I, 141.

56. EN, I, 219.

CHAPTER 3

In Love and Anger: France (1831–1833)

France was a haven for political refugees when Mazzini reached it in 1831. Neither Louis Philippe, who owed his throne to the July Revolution, nor his liberal ministers could afford to turn their backs on revolutionists from other lands. The official policy, therefore, was to keep the door open to thousands of political refugees arriving from other parts of Europe. They were received most warmly by French republicans, who objected to Louis Philippe and were eager to show Europe that France cherished its revolutionary traditions. Italian and Polish refugees came in great numbers, and Mazzini had much in common with them. Like himself, they were mostly young men on their own for the first time, impatient of delay, hopeful, and eager to test their wings. The pain, the petty quarrels, and the deadly enmities would come later. *Santi d'amore e di sdegno* (saintly in love and anger) is how Mazzini described them.[1] In their company he ceased to be an apprentice and became a full-fledged political agitator.

LEARNING ON THE ROAD

After leaving Genoa, Mazzini and his uncle traveled north through the regions of Piedmont and Savoy, crossing the Alps through the Mont Cenis Pass on February 10, 1831, headed for Paris. At Mazzini's insistence they made a short detour to visit the Swiss city of Geneva. There were many Italian expatriates in the city, which was also home to the distinguished historian Jean Charles Sismondi. Mazzini admired Sismondi's monumental *History of the Italian Republics in the Middle Ages* (1809–18), in which he saw proof that republican traditions were indigenous to Italy and monarchy was a foreign import. One of Sismondi's regular guests was the aloof and reserved Count Pellegrino Rossi, abroad since 1814, who warned Mazzini to weigh his words carefully because they were surrounded by spies. Another exile, the wealthy Milanese Giacomo Ciani, abroad since 1821, was also helpful. Figuring that the lean and mercurial young man was not traveling for pleasure, he whispered to him one evening that if he was looking for a certain kind of action he should go to a certain café in Lyons.[2]

The *Caffè della Fenice* in Lyons attracted a motley clientele of idealists, confidence men, and spies. Italian exiles met there to plan the liberation of Italy, starting with an expedition to liberate Savoy from Piedmontese rule. Savoy was a French-speaking region with more in common with France and the French-speaking cantons of Switzerland than with Piedmont and its other Italian provinces. It was a matter of faith in radical circles that Savoy was ready to revolt. What was even more exciting was the prospect that a revolt in Savoy would trigger a war among surrounding powers. War was what radicals of various descriptions banked on to destabilize the system of alliances and collective security put in place in 1815 to keep revolution in check. That seemingly far-fetched scenario was made barely plausible by the fact that France and the Swiss cantons had territorial designs on Savoy, and that Austria could not remain indifferent to territorial changes that would affect the balance of power in the region.[3]

Expatriates also counted on the support of French republicans, who were eager to show that they were more patriotic and decisive than the cautious Louis Philippe. What they did not take into account was that the alliance between republicans and monarchists was fragile. As Louis Philippe moved cautiously but steadily toward the conservatives in an effort to make himself more acceptable, the likelihood diminished that the French government would support revolution. That was the situation in February 1831. The expatriates who were planning a move on Savoy were caught between the shifting policies of the French government. All they could count on was support from the opposition and from a group of wealthy Lombard exiles willing to risk their money in a venture that would make it possible for them to return home. Recruits were found among exiles and unemployed workers, of which there were several thousand in Lyons by the beginning of 1831, as a result of a crisis of production in the silk industry.[4]

By the time Mazzini made contact with the organizers at the *Caffè della Fenice* in late February recruits were ready to march. By then revolution had broken out in Italy, and the move on Savoy would not be an isolated event. Just as the columns were ready to move on February

26, they were surrounded and disarmed by regular French troops. That, in a nutshell, was the inglorious course of the event that history books call the First Savoy Expedition. Its quick end threw consternation among the two thousand Italian exiles who had gathered in Lyons expecting a quick march to victory. Hundreds were arrested and detained, or shipped off to England and America. No one bothered Mazzini, who was protected by his legal status as visitor. His freedom was not complete, however, for his uncle was there to remind him that he was still accountable to his family in Genoa. There was nothing to do but give him the slip, which Mazzini did by joining a group of Italians headed for Toulon and Marseilles, from where they went on to Corsica. The plan was to mount another expedition, this one to support the revolts in the Po Valley, which were already spluttering.

Corsica made a favorable and lasting impression on Mazzini. He was enchanted by those "rough but very kind mountaineers, almost all armed." They loved a good fight and, with their strong sense of honor, they would let no offense go unpunished.[5] They also seemed to love Italy, and talked of little else but going off to liberate its fertile lands. The presence of many Carbonari on the island made him feel right at home. The islanders looked up to them as the natural leaders, and Mazzini remembered that he was a chief, thanks to Passano's hurried transfer of powers. The hope of liberating Italy from Corsica was cut short in mid-March, when an Austrian army marched into the Po Valley and put down the local revolts. For Mazzini there would be no triumphant return; in fact, there would be no return at all for the next seventeen years. When he did go home in 1848, it would be to a country very different from the one he had left. In exile he lost touch with the changing realities of his country, which in his mind existed frozen in 1830. Distance no doubt made it easier for him to persist in an endeavor that most would have dismissed as hopeless.

Mazzini's parents tracked him down in Corsica and urged him to rejoin his uncle, who was waiting for him in Marseilles. He was happy enough to do so, for Marseilles was a hotbed of political intrigue and home to thousands of political refugees, who arrived daily mainly from Italy and Poland. Government efforts to scatter the refugees to other parts of France had limited success. Forced to subsist on a meager government allowance or herded into crowded camps and makeshift lodgings, the refugees were a turbulent and disturbing presence. Precisely for that reason, they were like putty in Mazzini's hands. His rhetoric, too passionate for normal times, was just right for the surcharged atmosphere of Marseilles. Vehemence, self-confidence, and endurance made him stand out. His uncle, who owned property in Marseilles, decided to go back to Genoa. We do not know what he reported, but Mazzini's parents promised to continue their financial support. If they thought it would be only a temporary arrangement until their son could return home, they were wrong: the arrangement would last for the rest of their lives and his. The substantial estate of the parsimonious and cautious Doctor Giacomo was destined to subsidize the revolution.[6]

Mazzini's feverish state of mind is documented in the first of several articles that he wrote while in Marseilles. "Une nuit de Rimini en 1831" appeared in May 1831 in the opposition paper *National*. It was a diatribe against the government of Louis Philippe, which Mazzini charged with duplicity for its failure to help the insurgents, some of whom were said to have been massacred by Papal troops while a French task force simply stood by. Describing the alleged massacre in macabre detail, Mazzini evoked visions of corpses with staring eyes and mangled limbs, exhorting Italians to take revenge. That kind of writing appealed to the romantic taste for the horrific; the piece made Mazzini a figure to reckon with in refugee circles.[7]

The article is important for its content as well as its tone, for in it Mazzini voiced his critique of liberal monarchy as an insidious form of government. It was the liberal monarchy of Louis Philippe in particular that he chastised, but the argument had broader implications. Liberal monarchy was insidious because it gave people false hope that meaningful change could come about by means of moderate, constitutional reform; liberalism, whether à la Louis Philippe or as it would be practiced later by the Piedmontese monarchy, was particularly dangerous because its moderate discourse blurred the clash of principles and deadened sensibility to moral issues. As a student he had admired Victor Cousin and François Guizot as the voices of a new generation; he rejected them now as servants of the July Monarchy, blaming their eclectic philosophy and search for the *juste milieu* for the government's policy of nonintervention in support of revolution outside France.[8]

This new stance meant that Mazzini was rejecting the tactics of the Carbonari, who favored cooperation with moderate monarchs. In April of 1831 he joined the secret society of the Apofasimeni ("those who have vowed to die"), whose stated aim was to "make Italy one, independent, and free." Terrorist designs lurked under this rhetoric, as the Apofasimeni secretly endorsed killing prisoners and poisoning wells and food supplies, and advocated guerrilla warfare. It was an exciting prescription that appealed to an impatient Mazzini. Italians should be prepared to torch their own cities, he commented, rather than endure piecemeal reforms under foreign rule.[9]

Mazzini's decision to join the Apofasimeni underscores his continuing taste for conspiracy. He was a zealous recruit who rose quickly through the ranks, as he had done in the Carbonari. The chief Apofasimeno was Carlo Bianco di St. Jorioz (1795–1843), whom Mazzini had met in Lyons.

Bianco was a Piedmontese officer from a distinguished family who had been implicated in the revolution of 1821. He had fought on the liberal side in Spain, and then in Greece, and had settled for a while in British Malta. The prospect of revolution brought him to Marseilles, where he wrote a military tract that gave him a reputation as a guerrilla warfare expert. His tract *Of National Insurrectionary Warfare by Bands Applied to Italy* had just been published when he and Mazzini met in 1830. The older man steered Mazzini through the treacherous world of secret societies in France. Although he was too self-effacing to play a major role in the revolution, his military thinking proved influential and had a lasting impact on Mazzini. Mazzini's ringing endorsement of guerrilla warfare *(insurrezione per bande)* as the "war of all nations striving to emancipate themselves from foreign rule" obscured Bianco's authorship of the tract, to the point that the book was often attributed to Mazzini.[10] The book was not Mazzini's, but the language that publicized guerrilla warfare certainly was. He urged his followers to bring to the people the "cross of fire" that makes them invincible: "Multitudes and weapons! There is the secret of future revolutions."[11]

It was probably Bianco who put Mazzini in touch with Filippo Buonarroti (1761–1837), the grand old man of revolution. An indirect descendant of Michelangelo, Buonarroti's career as a subversive began with the French Revolution in 1789, when he left his native Pisa for France. He opted for French citizenship and sided with the most radical political elements of his generation. Rousseau and Robespierre were his idols. In 1796 he was at "Gracchus" Babeuf's side in the fabled Conspiracy of Equals, an ephemeral event that was destined to achieve legendary status as the first modern communist insurrection. For his role in that debacle he spent ten years in prison. Released in 1806 by Napoleon, who seems to have had a weakness for this unrepentant Jacobin, he supported himself in Geneva and Brussels by giving music lessons, while still conspiring with Masons and Carbonari.

Mazzini made contact with him after the July Revolution, when Buonarroti took up residence in Paris. There he lived quietly and plotted tirelessly to make himself head of an international insurrectionary network, looked after by an elderly domestic whom he called his Official, out of respect, he said, for the dignity of man. He was less patient with his young correspondent from the provinces, who was inclined to question his authority. Even at a distance their differences proved to be irreconcilable. Buonarroti identified with France and with the French mission in Europe. He retained a sentimental attachment to Italy and sympathized with the movement for Italian independence, as he did with other revolutionary movements, because of the cosmopolitanism that he had absorbed from the culture of the Enlightenment. He was convinced, however, that the revolutionary initiative must come from

France.[12] His plan was to reform the Carbonari, giving that association a truly international character and centralizing it in his own hands. He was cordial to Mazzini at first because he saw him as a promising recruit who might help him rejuvenate the Carbonari, and Mazzini went along with him for a while because he did not wish to pick a quarrel with someone so influential. But he did not commit himself to Buonarroti's views or tactics, and bided his time. The world of political refugees was split by factions and personal jealousies, and he had to learn to navigate its treacherous waters before striking out on his own. It is quite possible that Mazzini chose Marseilles as his base of operations precisely because Buonarroti dominated the Parisian scene.

At the *Caffè degli americani*, where Italians gathered in Marseilles, there were endless arguments over the principles, organization, tactics, and goals of revolution. The arguments often degenerated into quarrels that turned personal, violent, and loud. Spies frequented the café. One informer noted that the exiles "share a powerful desire to sacrifice their lives for the redemption of their country, but nobody has a deep sense of national unity, nobody shows attachment to others."[13] It was an observation that Mazzini could have endorsed. In deciding to strike out on his own, it was not his intention to introduce still another faction.

MAZZINI ON HIS OWN

Young Italy (*Giovine Italia*) emerged in July of 1831 as an instrument of unity and renewal. Mazzini signaled his desire to cooperate with other societies by calling Young Italy a federation, encouraging its members to join other societies. It was not intended to exclude but to reach out and build on the work of others. As head of Young Italy he even retained his Carbonaro pseudonym of Strozzi.

In his Autobiographical Notes Mazzini traced the origins of the idea of Young Italy back to the days of his imprisonment in Savona. It was there, he claimed, that he had first conceived of a new type of revolutionary organization committed to waging its fight in the open, to influencing public opinion, and to reaching out to the people, without whose support no revolution could hope to succeed.[14] The idea may indeed have come to him in his prison cell, but Young Italy was forged in the turbulent world of refugee politics, where Mazzini felt most at home. However early he may have thought of it, Young Italy was not an original organization. It owed much to the example of other organizations that combined conspiracy with public activity out of necessity, for not even the July Monarchy could tolerate militantly republican associations. In the case of Young Italy, the fear was not so much that it might unleash revolution, but that its conspiracies against foreign powers would create diplomatic complications for the French government.

Young Italy stood out because Mazzini was a tireless and resourceful organizer who took the high road and appealed to ideals rather than to material interests, stressed the need for unity and discipline, expressed political concerns in the emotional language of religion, demanded principled behavior from its members, spoke of duties as well as rights, and delivered a positive message of victory through action and education.

For a while, Mazzini was more interested in consolidating his position in the movement than in challenging the great powers. "Do not trust Paris," he wrote to a wavering supporter shortly after the founding of Young Italy, "there the best people get lost among so many inimical groups."[15] He made a half-hearted attempt to challenge Buonarroti on his home ground when he invited Pietro Giannone, an older exile residing in Paris, to promote Young Italy in the capital city; but Paris would always be Buonarroti's stronghold.[16] Mazzini's objective was to elevate Marseilles at the expense of Paris, while avoiding an open break with Buonarroti and the Carbonari.

Like most revolutionists, Mazzini was reluctant to admit that revolutions fail for lack of support. The reasons for failure had to be external, hence his public reproaches to liberal monarchs, whom he accused of sponsoring and then betraying revolutions to serve dynastic interests. If internal to the revolution, the causes of failure must be wrong leadership, flawed tactics, or lack of revolutionary fervor among the leaders. His remedy was to encourage young people "from twenty to thirty-five years old who have grown with the revolution" to trust in their own powers and seize the initiative.[17] That was a quote from Victor Cousin, whom he had admired as a student in Genoa, but it also reflected Mazzini's conviction, born of personal experience, that the political conflict was generational. Young Italy was to admit no one who was forty or older. The rule was never applied rigidly (it was only meant to flatter the young, Mazzini explained when he invited the older Giannone to join), but the intent was clear: Only those born and raised in the climate of revolution were mentally and emotionally equipped to envision and carry out the renewal of society.

The generational argument was tailored to the struggle that Mazzini was fighting at that moment against Metternich and conservatism and against the revolutionary culture personified in Buonarroti. The "errors of the fathers" included relying more on words than on weapons, loving peace and quiet, and denying the young their moment in history.[18] Here was the germ of Mazzini's broader attack on the culture of the Enlightenment and on the political legacy of the French Revolution. But that was still to come. In Marseilles he had not fully developed his critique of the French revolutionary tradition and did not want to offend the national susceptibilities of French republicans, on whose open support he counted until they were forced underground by the government crackdown of June 1832. He called on the youth of Europe, however, to rally under the banner of Young Italy: "My young brothers, have courage, aspire to greatness. Have faith in God, in what is right, and in us. That was Luther's call, which stirred half of Europe. Raise that call and go forward."[19]

Young Italy was part modern political party, part traditional secret society. Its party character stemmed from its commitment to agitate openly, which it did mostly through publications, especially through its journal *Giovine Italia*, which began to appear in March of 1832. It was the first paper that was truly Mazzini's. Although the money for it came largely from exiles wealthier than him, Mazzini controlled the paper with an iron hand. "The press is today the arbiter of nations," he wrote, "the ink of the wise is a match for the sword of the strong."[20] He would rather spill ink than blood, he pointed out, but blood was needed where repressive governments prevented the free circulation of ideas. Young Italy waged its fight peacefully and publicly where it could, or violently where it was forced underground. Hence the need for secrecy, the oaths, passwords, and symbols of traditional secret societies.

Members swore to defame (*infamar colla voce*) and snuff out (*spegnere col braccio*) tyrants, to proselytize, and to keep ready a dagger, a gun, and fifty rounds of ammunition. The ritual of the organization was accordingly replete with the symbolism of brotherhood and violence, alternating avowals of love and peaceful intentions with threats of retribution. No criminals, embezzlers, drunkards, or womanizers were to be admitted, for their crimes and immorality would discredit the whole movement. Members were to be like brothers toward one another; for traitors there would be infamy and death.[21] Better to be few but good (*pochi ma buoni*) than many and untrustworthy. For Mazzini, it all boiled down to will, which could move mountains all by itself: "Believe me, he who really wants to can attain anything, as long as he does not overlook details. . . . So long as he has faith in himself he is omnipotent, as we will be if we love one another and remain self-confident."[22]

Most secret societies relied on an inner core of true believers, but Young Italy also called out to the people. The sons must correct the errors of the fathers by mobilizing the moral force inherent in the people. This could be done by invoking a new principle that could be "generalized and believed in by the majority."[23] The mobilizing principle was to be that of faith in the irresistible power of the people, but Mazzini was careful to explain that the people (*popolo*) of which he spoke was not necessarily the same as the masses. He defined *popolo* as "the universality of those who compose the nation," arguing that a people existed only as a nation. Italians, therefore, were not a people because they were not one nation. Until they emerged as a nation, they would be a mere throng (gente).[24] Nations were necessary links in the great social chain that drew individuals out of their private spheres, gave them a collective identity, and connected them to larger and larger entities. The attainment of human solidarity required the prior transformation of *gente* into *popolo*.

It was through association that *gente* became *popolo*. The emergence of a sense of nationality depended therefore on the capacity of individuals to come together purposefully. The problem was that in Italy association faced all sorts of historical, political, and social obstacles. Repression, foreign domination, regional loyalties, dynastic attachments, class divisions, antagonism between city and countryside, illiteracy, ignorance and superstition, and the inadequacy of governments, all conspired to prevent Italians from becoming *popolo*. Mazzini did not expect popular support for Young Italy for precisely those reasons. Its purpose was not to represent the *gente* that populated the Italian peninsula, but to promote the idea of nationality. Mazzini's frequent appeals to democracy should not mislead us as to his intentions. The distinction he made between *gente* and *popolo* makes it clear that he was indifferent to the will of the majority as long as that majority was made up of mere *gente*. He saw the majority as part of the problem, and sought to speak only for that minority that considered itself *popolo*. The Italian *popolo* would emerge from the struggle for liberation, but for the time being it was nothing more than an idea. Hence the need to appeal to those who were willing to suffer martyrdom for an idea and to present the struggle as an essentially religious enterprise.

Avowedly elitist in calling on the educated, the journal *Giovine Italia* made few concessions to the masses in its language, style, and substance. Mazzini was enough of a journalist to understand that it would appeal to the educated few who formed "the invisible Italy, the underground Italy, the chain that ties the past to the future in a secret unity of beliefs, hopes, works, a brotherhood of the strong who sharpen the sword of vengeance on their own chains."[25] If those were the real *popolo*, what about the rest? He had no clear answer, except that the revolution he had in mind had to be for the people before it became of the people. Initially, he seems to have been willing to leave the task of reaching out to what he sometimes called the *bassa gente* (multitudes) to Bianco's Apofasimeni, which claimed a following among sailors, dock workers, and peasants.[26] When the Apofasimeni merged with Young Italy, he set up an affiliate called the Society for the Propagation of Lights (*Società di propagazione de' lumi*), whose task was to bring light to the unenlightened in the spirit of eighteenth-century educational reform. Their support would be needed to wage the kind of guerrilla warfare conceptualized by Bianco, for Mazzini hoped to replicate in Italy the feats of popular resistance seen in the Spanish war of liberation against Napo-

leon.[27] He argued that if ordinary Spaniards, including large numbers
of peasants, could fight against the French, why could not Italians do
the same against the Austrians? If revolutionary warfare could be waged
successfully by bands of Catholic peasants, then France lost its place as
the natural home of revolution and Buonarroti lost his claim that the
revolutionary movement had to be directed from Paris. Italians could
claim an autonomous revolutionary tradition of their own, based not on
French Jacobinism, but on popular resistance against Napoleon. Not
only would Italy owe nothing to France, but France might learn something from Italy, for in Italy and Spain those strata of the population
that were least touched by the ideas of the Enlightenment and the
French Revolution had fought for liberation.[28]

There was a great deal of wishful thinking in these reflections. For
one thing, while there had been instances of popular warfare in Italy,
the Italian and Spanish situation in Napoleonic times was hardly
analogous to the Italian situation after 1815. Spaniards had fought
against an alien presence that was generally resented, while Italians
had to contend with Austria, whose rule in Lombardy and Venetia was
not unpopular, and with native governments and the Catholic Church,
both of which enjoyed popular support. Italian wars of liberation inevitably took on the character of civil wars, with Italians ranged on both
sides. Young Italy did its best to fan hatred for the *tedeschi*: "A national
dislike, a deep, mortal hatred, suckled with mothers' milk, sanctified by
ten centuries of oppression, plunder, and blood makes implacable enemies of Italy and Austria."[29] Many Italians, however, saw their situation
in more complex and realistic terms; popular support was the missing
ingredient in Mazzini's prescription for revolution.

For reasons that were as much political as military, Mazzini continued to advocate guerrilla warfare as a means of forming an Italian
people. Thought and action meant doing by learning and learning by
doing. Popular warfare would form patriots and citizens and establish
a basis for democracy, for only those who play an active role in the
making of the nation can claim a role in its governance. Ideologies of
national liberation owe much to Bianco and Mazzini, because of the
connection that they made between popular warfare on the one hand
and democracy on the other. While Marx and Lenin tied wars of national
liberation to the struggle against colonialism, it was Bianco and Mazzini
who rooted them in the notion of national identity and republican
democracy.[30]

"The people means everyone. The most rich, the most noble, the most
powerful are also part of the people, because that term encompasses all
wealth, all nobility, all power," wrote Enrico Mayer, an early and wealthy
supporter of Mazzini.[31] That formulation was shared up to a point by
Mazzini, who wished to exclude no one from the struggle for liberation

on the basis of class. A comprehensive definition of the people to include all classes had the undeniable advantage of not scaring away the people of means who were the financial backers of Young Italy in these years. But Young Italy, however, did not aim its message at people of wealth. It was elitist because it addressed itself to the educated; its rank-and-file members were overwhelmingly young professionals, officers, students, writers, and literate urban workers.

Most members shared Mazzini's perception that social problems could be solved by political means, and specifically by a political revolution that would put power in the hands of those who took to heart the interests of the people. For this political approach Mazzini and Young Italy have been criticized by the Left for paying scant attention to economic and social issues. It would be wrong to suggest that the decision to promote a political agenda was due to ignorance of or indifference to social issues. Members were instructed in capital letters to "Proclaim the SOCIAL intent of the revolution, announce it to the people; call on the multitudes, who are omnipotent. . . . Inscribe on one side of your flag EQUALITY and LIBERTY, and on the other GOD IS WITH YOU."[32] Mazzini warned the *apostoli* (apostles) who were to carry the word to the masses that it was time to "delve deeply into the social question . . . to tell those fighting for the liberty of their country that they must not only help the people . . . but that they must proclaim their intention loudly and work for results."[33]

This was not the language of someone unaware of or indifferent to social issues. Mazzini saw them etched in the urban landscape of Lyons and Marseilles. He chose a political course for other reasons. His language makes it clear that his intent was not to address the social question directly, but rather to establish a cadre of political activists (the apostles) who would instruct the people by word and action. Their message was that liberty and equality were of equal value, a position substantially different from that of other political activists, including Buonarroti, who preached that economic equality was the ultimate goal of revolution. Tactically, the emphasis on the equal value of liberty and equality helped to differentiate Mazzini's message from Buonarroti's at a time when they were in a tight race to build up their respective organizations.

Mazzini's concern for liberty and equality should also be seen in the light of his definition of liberty. His definition came from Sismondi, who traced its origins to the history of republican medieval communes, where it was understood as the collective liberty of the group rather than as the freedom of individuals within the group. Individualism was the creed of materialists who could not see beyond particular interest. It corrupted Jeremy Bentham's utilitarianism, with its calculus of pain and pleasure, and infected British culture, in which Mazzini at this

stage of his life saw the fullest expression of egotistical materialism—
although he also believed that Orleanist France was equally infected by
materialism and self-seeking individualism. His definition of liberty left
room for reciprocal obligations among members of the group and was
the basis of his notion that the concept of liberty must not be separated
from that of duty. He gave the idea of liberty a modern twist when he
urged that the commune (*comune*) be preserved as the smallest unit of
administration in the national state, with administrative autonomy and
real power over local affairs. Such was the importance that he attached
to Sismondi's ideas and intellectual reputation, that he could not contain
his disappointment when the older man refused an invitation to write
for *Giovine Italia*. The tone of the journal was too militant, replied
Sismondi, and Mazzini too involved in theoretical speculation. The poor
and ignorant for whom Mazzini claimed to speak, warned Sismondi,
were their own worst enemies: They could not transcend their lack of
education and would always be the first to betray their brothers in
misfortune.[34]

Henri de Saint-Simon, the proponent of a new society based on
association, progress, and religious faith, was another important influence on Mazzini. Saint-Simon called on *Dieu et l'humanité*, Mazzini on
God and the People. Mazzini's God, like Saint-Simon's, bore little resemblance to the God of traditional Christianity. Mazzini continued to
profess belief in the immortality of the soul to the end of his life, and
even spoke of a continuing relationship between the living and the dead,
but he rejected the basic Christian doctrines of the resurrection and
divinity of Christ. He consigned Christianity's promise of individual
salvation to the waning age of individualism, along with the secular
philosophies of the Enlightenment.

The new age would be one of association, governed by the principle
of solidarity, expressed as love among individuals. While some Saint-Simonians carried that notion to an extreme by experimenting with free
love and communal living arrangements, Mazzini continued to look on
the conventional family as an essential social building block. His understanding of Saint-Simon was perhaps idiosyncratic, in that he seemed
to search for its intellectual origins in the murky world of eighteenth-
century mysticism and secret societies, but what attracted him to
Saint-Simon was precisely its religious afflatus. He liked the idea of God
as a principle of unity, for without unity there could be no civil society:
"Unity is the law of the moral world just as it is the law of the material
world. Without unity there is only anarchy, uncertainty, and arbitrary
will, and force rules alone: Thence comes despotism, which is nothing
more than arbitrary will protected by force."[35] In effect, Mazzini was
trying to locate himself between Buonarroti, the eighteenth-century
materialist, and Saint-Simon, the prophet of a new society based on the

"universal association" of all individuals. In such a society the spirit of association would temper class differences, there would be unity in diversity, and faith in progressive improvement. Through Saint-Simon Mazzini hoped to achieve a synthesis of opposites, for which the idea of God was a necessary premise. If the philosophical synthesis that he sought eluded him, the balancing act was enough to give his movement an intellectual basis of its own that set it apart from its competitors.

Mazzini borrowed, but borrowed creatively. He took the notion of national primacy from Saint-Simon, but bent it to make Italy rather than France the initiator of the new historical epoch of the people. France, a nation formed over the centuries, could not be the model for modern nations struggling to emerge by revolution. France had failed to sever its historical tie with monarchy and was not moving toward democracy; its culture was materialistic in the spirit of the Enlightenment, and lacked the principle of universal association that was needed to bind citizens into a whole "on the basis of civil and political equality, for the common purpose of developing and perfecting progressively the social forces at their disposal."[36] Paradoxically, it was Italy that met this definition precisely, because it was a melting pot of all those who had gathered and mingled there in the course of centuries to produce a people "who combined southern vivacity and spontaneity with the seriousness and steadfastness of the northern races."[37]

As Mazzini conceived it, Italian nationality was real because it represented a triumph of the spirit over matter. Educated Italians spoke the language of Dante, the uneducated spoke dialects closely related to it, and all shared republican traditions that went back to the Middle Ages. Italian identity rested also on a special relationship with the Roman Catholic Church, which Mazzini did not yet see as the enemy of national unity. In Marseilles he articulated his dream of seeing the new Italy and the Catholic Church march together into the new era of nationalities. The Church was a vital body because it combined the spiritual message of Christianity with the secular legacy of classical Rome. The Church had transformed the Rome of the Caesars into the Rome of the Popes; it had also transformed Christianity from a religion of personal salvation into a social religion capable of changing the world. The Protestant Reformation had tried to turn the clock back by restoring the spirit of primitive Christianity and its message of individual salvation. In so doing it had given Protestantism a new spiritual charge, but had deprived it of the power to bind. Luther's challenge to the Church was an inspiring act of conscience (Mazzini would often invoke Luther's words "Here I Stand, so help me God," when cornered by his critics), but it condemned Protestantism to social impotence because it expressed only individual conscience. Roman Catholicism avoided that fate and could change the world because it retained the sense of public mission embedded in ancient Roman civilization. The Rome of the People would also change the world by retaining the ecumenical spirit of the Rome of the Popes.[38]

What stood in the way of Mazzini's vision was not the Roman Catholic Church, but the papacy and papal absolutism, which he regarded as anachronistic. The papacy was nothing more than an outmoded theocracy seeking to survive by making an alliance with absolute monarchs. Sweeping away the papacy by revolution was part of the mission that God entrusted to the Italian people. Just as the Rome of the Popes had absorbed the Rome of the Caesars, so the Rome of the People would transcend the Rome of the Popes: "The papacy will endure until a reborn Italy overturns the seat in which it sleeps. It is in Italy that the European knot must be untied. To Italy belongs the high office of emancipation; Italy will fulfill its civilizing mission."[39]

Mazzini's anticlericalism stemmed from this view of the intertwined fate of the Church and the Italian people. His was a selective anticlericalism that spared the lower clergy and lashed out at the papacy. Recalling the Jansenist priests who had educated him, he would always regard the lower clergy as a potential source of support for the revolution: "Priests of my fatherland, take your place at the head of the people and lead them on the road to progress."[40]

It did not embarrass Mazzini to admit that these were not original ideas. The point of his intellectual efforts, he insisted, was not to elaborate new social theories, but "to apply to Italy truths that today are diffused throughout Europe."[41] His style was suited to his goal, which was to arouse enthusiasm for ideas already in circulation. His writing is turgid and reveals its power only if read aloud with the passionate emphasis that animated its author, which is how it would often be heard in a society with high levels of illiteracy. It was the language of a young man confident of his powers, who was coming into his own.

The changes that became apparent at this time were also physical and emotional. The beardless, round-faced youth with the complacent expression shown in a sketch depicting him at the age of twenty-five became the bearded, brooding figure familiar to posterity. Attired in black velvet, wearing a large "republican hat," curly black hair falling to his shoulders, gaunt face elongated by the dark beard, he exuded mystery and masculine appeal. Charming and amusing in friendly conversation, he showed heat and anger when crossed. Part prophet and part conspirator, he impressed those who met him by what he said and how he said it.

In this period for the first time in his life he experienced passion, not the abstract passion of political principles, but the searing passion for another being of flesh and blood. The brief reference to the "woman of rare purity and constant principles" that appears in the Autobiographical Notes barely does justice to the role that Giuditta Sidoli played in his life.[42] When he met her, Giuditta was the rare single woman in the mostly male world of political expatriates. Born Giuditta Bellerio into a titled Milanese family, she had married Giovanni Sidoli at sixteen. He was a Carbonaro from Reggio Emilia, and she followed him to Switzerland in 1823, when he fled there to avoid arrest. Widowed in 1828, she returned to Reggio Emilia with the four children born of the marriage to live with her in-laws. It was not a happy arrangement. In 1831 she settled in Marseilles with a brother who was also a political exile, without her children. The family did not abandon her, and she was able to live in relative comfort with their financial support. An attractive and unattached woman of independent means, she became the focal point of social life among exiles. She declaimed Mazzini's writings in her informal salon; he became her most attentive visitor.

In August of 1832 Giuditta gave birth to a boy who was almost certainly fathered by Mazzini. The baby, named Joseph Démosthène Adolphe Aristide after members of the Ollivier family with whom Mazzini was living in Marseilles, was registered as "fils de parents inconnu." That the child was not acknowledged should come as no surprise. Giuditta's influential and conservative in-laws would have disapproved of her marriage to someone like Mazzini and would have barred access to the other children. The scandal of bearing an illegitimate child would have had the same consequences.[43] Mazzini had less to worry about personally (Maria actually encouraged him to marry, without knowing about the child), but the revelation would have damaged him politically by tarnishing the image of incorruptibility and revolutionary fervor that he cultivated. He had also at the time been ordered to leave France. We know little about the infant, who may have been left in Montpellier, where he was born, in the care of acquaintances. This would explain the mysterious trip that Giuditta and Mazzini took there in June of 1833, probably to retrieve the baby and bring him to the Olliviers in Marseilles, just before they left for Switzerland. The abandonment, and the child's death in February of 1835, left both with a sense of guilt that surfaces in cryptic references to a mysterious "A" who is never identified in the correspondence.

The sense of guilt and the fear of the consequences of disclosure resulting from the birth of an illegitimate child give us a better understanding of Mazzini, his desire for privacy, his cultivated image as a man immune to human passions, and his self-imposed isolation that became a shield in the later years of his life. He was not immune to passion, whether personal or political. The mask he wore in public was meant to disguise the warmth of his nature, which often betrayed him, as it did in his affair with Giuditta. The passions he feared, however, lived on inside the revolutionary ascetic, propelling him into actions that he then rationalized on moral and philosophical grounds.

A TIME TO ACT

The start of the relationship with Giuditta coincided with a period of intense political activity following the death of Charles Felix on April 27, 1831. The death of this last direct descendant of the House of Savoy brought Charles Albert to the throne, reviving hopes that this man, who had intrigued with the Carbonari in 1821, could be relied on to advance the cause of liberal reform. Mazzini later claimed that he had no faith at all in the new king, and that may have been true, for in private he called him a "coward or worse."[44] But he still thought like a Carbonaro when Charles Albert came to the throne and may have hoped to influence or pressure him into making concessions. As he had done earlier with Charles X, he now addressed an open letter to Charles Albert.

Mixing flattery and not-so-veiled threats, the letter credited Charles Albert with good intentions, but warned him that the struggle between liberty and despotism was nearing the culminating point. Charles Albert could choose to prop up his throne with terror, concessions, and compromises, or he could fight for liberty, independence, and national union on the side of history, the young, and the educated. If he chose the latter he would save his throne and fulfill the will of God; people would say that "God is to heaven as Charles Albert is to earth," and would follow him as a savior. The injunction *Se no, no!* (Otherwise, no!) summed up the peremptory message of the letter.[45]

The letter sounded like an ultimatum, laced with threatening phrases that must have caught the attention of the police: "Blood calls for blood. Every victim calls forth its own avenger . . . the dagger of the conspirator is never so dreadful as when it is sharpened by the blood of martyrs." It was signed "An Italian" and circulated in pamphlet form before being published in *Giovine Italia*. The police must have suspected that Mazzini was the author, because in October 1831 his parents were told that their son should consider himself permanently banished from the kingdom and subject to arrest should he return. That made him a genuine political refugee, one marked as particularly dangerous. It was now important, more for those who corresponded with him than for himself, that the courts not be able to prove the existence of any communication. Thus, when the police began to intercept his correspondence in 1834, they found him addressing his parents as uncle and aunt, and signing off as their niece Emilia. The ruse did not fool the police, but it did make it more difficult to prove culpable correspondence in court, should the government decide to prosecute or attach the Mazzinis' property. Charles Albert had shown his true colors as far as Mazzini was concerned: "Let's conclude," he wrote in March 1832, "Charles Albert is neither virtuous enough nor criminal enough to rank high among Italian tyrants."[46]

Nowhere was Mazzini entirely safe. Spies had already infiltrated Young Italy (one was Raimondo Doria, Mazzini's old nemesis, who hastened to leave Marseilles after the French press began to question his background). There were rumors that the Piedmontese police planned to spirit Mazzini back home. The Austrian, Papal, and Piedmontese governments demanded his expulsion from France, and the French had no desire to compromise good relations with these powers to protect him. His image as a diabolically clever conspirator was beginning to take shape, based on the fears of governments and the reports of spies who had an interest in magnifying his powers. Metternich called Young Italy the cutting edge of a vast subversive movement and defined Mazzini as the most dangerous man in Europe. Metternich and Mazzini were like two antagonists who needed each other, Metternich to justify his own role as the policeman of Europe, Mazzini to have a target worthier than Louis Philippe or Charles Albert.[47]

What spies and Metternich exaggerated was Mazzini's power, not his intentions, which were indeed grandiose. It was Mazzini's intent after founding Young Italy to effect a gigantic merger of secret societies that would give unity and direction to the European revolutionary movement. Bianco's Apofasimeni merged with Young Italy soon after its founding, but then Mazzini's drive ran into opposition from Buonarroti in Paris, who countered by encouraging the Veri Italiani (True Italians), whose program, though similar to Young Italy's in many respects, stressed the goal of social equality, reflecting the Jacobinism of Buonarroti and most of its members. There was conflict between the two, followed by an agreement that Mazzini interpreted as relegating the Veri Italiani to the role of theorists, while leaving Young Italy to carry out the revolution. That was not the way Buonarroti saw it. He hastened to recruit in Italy, which Mazzini considered to be Young Italy's exclusive preserve. Rather than concede, Buonarroti preferred to inform on Mazzini by revealing to the Piedmontese what he knew of Mazzini's plans.[48]

In June of 1833 Mazzini broke with Buonarroti in Paris. Marseilles was his base of operations, and he had an organization in place as well as money to back up the operations that he had in mind. He never hesitated to put into his political operations what money he had at his disposal, but most of the funds came from wealthy émigrés from Lombardy, who subsidized the movement to overthrow Austrian rule and reclaim the rest of their fortunes. Backers included Gaspare Rosales, Carlo Bellerio, the brothers Camillo and Francesco d'Adda, Emilio

Belgioioso and his estranged wife, Princess Cristina Trivulzio Belgioioso, all belonging to the Lombard nobility, and the brothers Filippo and Giacomo Ciani. The Ciani brothers funded the publication of the journal *Giovine Italia*, but Mazzini relied most heavily on Rosales, who had left Milan for political and personal reasons, being suspected of political disloyalty and living openly with a married woman who had left her husband. Rosales not only subsidized and participated in Mazzini's political ventures, but he also supported Mazzini's literary projects and provided for his personal needs when he ran out of money from home.

Beside the Lombards, his closest collaborators were Giuditta's many friends and acquaintances, many of them exiles from the Duchy of Modena, including the brothers Angelo and Emilio Usiglio, Giuseppe Giglioli, Giuseppe Lamberti, Nicola Fabrizi, Giambattista Ruffini, and Luigi Amedeo Melegari, and the actor Gustavo Modena, a Venetian. The initial core of Young Italy was heavily northern, but others from various parts of Italy floated in and out, making it hazardous to guess at the size and geographical distribution of its membership, which had to be secret out of necessity. Mazzini made special efforts to recruit in different regions, but the organization was strongest in Liguria, Lombardy, Tuscany, and Romagna (the northern provinces of the Papal States). It was weakest in Rome and most of the South, except in Naples where Mazzini had some personal contacts.

The education requirement cut down on the number of workers who were members of Young Italy. There were some, and others were connected unofficially, as was the case with many artisans and port workers in Genoa and Livorno. Sailors and itinerant workers who shuttled frequently between Italy and France were occasionally recruited to smuggle messages and leaflets. *Figurinai* from Lucca hid these inside hollow plaster figurines. Recruits were found in the Piedmontese army and navy, and even among priests. One clerical sympathizer was Vincenzo Gioberti, chaplain at the court of Charles Albert, who wrote a letter of support published in *Giovine Italia*.[49] Women were also members, particularly in Genoa, where Young Italy attracted young women mainly from the aristocracy. Young Italy did represent a cross section of society.

Spies reported wildly inflated membership figures of 70,000 for southern Italy, 40,000 for the Papal States, and over 30,000 for Piedmont. A probably more realistic figure puts Young Italy's total membership at 50–60,000 in 1833. Members paid or were expected to pay dues, but we have no records of receipts; they were required to be equipped and fit to fight, but no one inspected them for their state of preparedness. Although Mazzini insisted on unity of command and uniformity of belief, because the network was dispersed over many regions there was no

effective way to enforce discipline. It cannot therefore be assumed that
Young Italy was Mazzinian in anything but name. It was too loosely knit
to live up to Mazzini's exalted view of it as a phalanx of true believers
prepared to "found a nation and create a people."[50]

Governments feared Young Italy both for the ideas it ventilated and
for its suspected secret activities. Both fears were confirmed in July of
1832, when customs officials discovered compromising literature and
messages in the false bottom of a trunk meant for Elia Benza and Jacopo
Ruffini in Genoa. On orders from the police, the inspectors resealed the
trunk and sent it on to its destination. From then on they were able to
monitor Mazzini's contacts and correspondence. The French were also
on Mazzini's trail since May, when an Italian exile stabbed and killed
two Italians in Thorez who were suspected of spying for the police. The
widow of one of the victims accused Mazzini of having ordered the
execution and produced what she claimed was a copy of the death
sentence signed by Mazzini as head of a secret revolutionary tribunal.
The charge was probably false, but the press seized on the incident to
demand Mazzini's expulsion from France.

The order to leave France was issued in August of 1832. With Giuditta
about to give birth and political conspiracies about to come to fruition,
it could not have come at a worse time. The conspiracy that was under
way was directed at Piedmont, but had ramifications in other parts of
Italy. Jacopo Ruffini was responsible for the Piedmontese part of the
plan, while Benza was to coordinate events in the rest of the peninsula.
Mazzini envisaged a vast movement sweeping from the Alps to Sicily.
Unable to resist the temptation to send in his own agents, he may have
unwittingly created confusion by overlapping with and overriding
Benza's efforts to coordinate the movement. His *viaggiatori* (traveling
salesmen), as he called his agents, targeted the Piedmontese army and
navy, wining and dining the conscripts and officers who joined the
revolution and promising rewards and rapid advancement. The results
were just beginning to show when Mazzini received the order to leave
France.

He spent the next ten months in hiding, disguising his appearance
when he went out, and changing residence every few weeks to keep
ahead of the police. They were traumatic months, during which he
experienced wild swings of mood, buoyed by the prospect of success one
moment, despairing at his personal problems and political complications the next. The plaintive tone that crept into his letters during these
months hinted at the martyr's stance he adopted in his later years. He
felt dispirited, complaining that he heard only recriminations from the
people who were closest to him and declaring that only his will power
and sense of duty kept him going. He said he wanted to abdicate his
responsibilities in the movement, live a private life, and expect less of

people, particularly the Italian people, who could not rise to the occasion. Indeed, he was under personal attack as never before in his life, from governments, from Buonarroti (whom Mazzini suspected of being behind the campaign to expel him), and from his own collaborators, who accused him of being a hard taskmaster, willful, and dictatorial. What they did not understand, he complained, was that conspiracies could not be kept secret indefinitely.[51]

It was indeed a race against time, and Mazzini lost it. On April 28, 1833, two army sergeants who were part of the conspiracy came to blows over a woman and were arrested in Genoa. Questioned separately by the police, they revealed what they knew, hoping for personal clemency. The police were already on the alert, but were alarmed to discover that the conspiracy extended to Turin and Chambery and reached into the army and navy, where it involved some highly placed officers, including a general. Step by step, the police worked their way to the organizers. Still in France, Mazzini was beyond their reach. On the night of June 13, however, they arrested Jacopo Ruffini in his home. During his interrogation the investigator dropped information gleaned from intercepted correspondence that should have been known only to Jacopo and Mazzini. Perhaps they hoped to convince him that he had no reason to hide anything, or perhaps they had the more sinister intent of making Jacopo believe that he had been betrayed by his best friend. Alone that evening, Jacopo pried a sliver of metal from the door, sharpened it on the stone walls of his cell, and severed his jugular vein. The guards found him in the morning, dead in a pool of blood.

Mazzini did not learn the particulars of his friend's death until years later, and it may be a patriotic legend that Jacopo wrote "My brothers will avenge me" with his own blood before dying. There is no doubt, however, that Mazzini was overwhelmed by feelings of guilt and a craving for revenge when he learned of Jacopo's suicide. From his mother he also learned that all his friends and relatives were under suspicion. When Maria read Cesare Cantù's novel *Margherita Pusterla*, she thought that all the horrors described in that tale of oppression set in medieval Milan described the mood that prevailed in Genoa after the discovery of the plot.[52] She and her husband endured their own public ordeal when charges of high treason against their son were announced outside their home. Giovanni Ruffini fled immediately, followed by his mother Eleonora, his younger brother Agostino, and Federico Campanella. Benza was mysteriously spared from arrest; officially confined to his native Porto Maurizio for many years, he never again meddled in politics. Eleonora, her two sons, and Campanella joined Mazzini in Marseilles, burdening him with the additional responsibility of looking after people for whom he felt responsible.

Too much was happening for Mazzini to give the Ruffinis the undivided attention that they expected and that he felt he owed them. They were affronted when Mazzini left them alone in Marseilles for no other apparent reason than to go away with a woman. The probable reason for that mysterious journey was that he and Giuditta had to retrieve their infant son in Montpellier and find a more permanent home for him in Marseilles before leaving France. It was no longer possible to delay the departure, for the police were closing in and he needed freedom of movement to strike back at the Piedmontese government. His organization had suffered a severe blow. He thought he still had cards to play, but he could not play them from where he was. Leaving Luigi Amedeo Melegari behind to look after the affairs of Young Italy in France, he, Giuditta, and the Ruffinis left Marseilles in the first days of July 1833 bound for Geneva.

The French sojourn was over. Although Mazzini left France embittered and seemingly defeated, the two and a half years he had spent there left a lasting legacy, much of it positive. The European cast of his thinking took shape in the international milieu of Marseilles, where French, German, Hungarian, Italian, and Polish émigrés mingled freely. In France he saw for the first time how the conditions of modern production affected workers, he familiarized himself with the ideas of Saint-Simon, and he conceptualized a strategy of revolution that tied the political movements for national liberation to the struggle for economic justice. In that regard he was more revolutionary than most socialists of his time, particularly Saint-Simon, Charles Fourier, and Robert Owen, who hoped to direct social change peacefully either through the power of the state or through the example of model communities. Mazzini's answer to such optimism was that there could be no meaningful social reform without a prior revolutionary seizure of the power of government, for there could be no political equality, no social improvement, and no economic justice without the elimination of monarchy. His condemnation of monarchy was total and without exception. He reserved his sharpest criticism for liberal monarchies like those of Louis Philippe in the early 1830s and of Charles Albert later on, when that monarch also began to experiment with limited reforms. His resentment of liberal monarchy as he saw it in France colored his views of almost everything French, including the French Revolution of 1789, Napoleon, and François Guizot's pragmatic liberalism and policy of the *juste milieu*, which looked for the middle ground. He did not spare even the French republicans, whom he suspected of being more nationalist than the royalists, or the followers of Saint-Simon, whom he accused of betraying the teachings of their master with their practice of communal living, sexual promiscuity, and attacks on the family.

Mazzini usually couched his criticisms of French culture in philosophical terms, but his abiding resentment of France was also based on personal experience and his understanding of recent history. From family tales he remembered the disillusionment with Napoleon and the French Revolution; from his own experience he had learned to distrust the liberal monarchy of Louis Philippe. His rivalry with the Francophile Buonarroti and his hostility toward the communal theories and practices of the latter-day Saint-Simonians made him equate French radicalism with materialism and communism. He left France believing that France had exhausted its historical mission and that the revolutions of the future would begin elsewhere. He believed in the world mission of the Rome of the People. Barred from Italy, he was headed for Switzerland, the only major republic in Europe, where he hoped to find republican zeal and courage. With others who heeded his call to gather in Geneva, he would launch his strongest challenge yet to the monarchs of Europe.

NOTES

Works frequently cited in the notes have been identified by the following abbreviations:

BDM	*Bollettino della Domus Mazziniana*
EN	*Edizione Nazionale. Scritti editi ed inediti di Giuseppe Mazzini* (1906–90), 106 vols.
GI	*La Giovine Italia* (1902–25), 6 vols.

    1. EN, XXIX, 148.

    2. EN, LXXVII, 35–37.

    3. See Carlo di Nola, *La politica degli Stati europei dopo la Restaurazione e le spedizioni di Savoia negli anni 1831 e 1834* (Rome-Naples: Albrighi-Segati, 1952), 28–31.

    4. See Salvo Mastellone, *Mazzini e la Giovine Italia, 1831–1834* (Pisa: Domus Mazziniana, 1960), I, 63, and Cesar Vidal, *Mazzini et les tentatives révolutionnaires de la Jeune Italie dans les états sardes* (Paris: Boccard, 1927), 10–14.

    5. EN, LXXVII, 41–42.

    6. Paul Harro-Harring, *Memorie sulla Giovine Italia e sugli ultimi avvenimenti di Savoia* (Milan: Società Editrice Dante Alighieri, 1913), 106–8.

    7. EN, II, 5–8.

    8. Mastellone, *Mazzini e la Giovine Italia*, I, 133–37.

    9. Quoted in Franco Della Peruta, *Mazzini e i rivoluzionari italiani. Il partito d'azione, 1830–1845* (Milan: Feltrinelli, 1974), 23–52.

    10. On Carlo Bianco, see Vittorio Parmentola, "Carlo Bianco, Giuseppe Mazzini e la teoria dell'insurrezione," BDM, V, 2 (1959), 5–40. Also, Enrica Melossi, "Documenti sulla diffusione in Italia del Trattato di Carlo Bianco di

St. Jorioz," in *Mazzini e i repubblicani italiani* (Turin: Istituto per la Storia del Risorgimento Italiano, 1976), 45–53.

11. EN, II, 53–54, 221.

12. See Alessandro Galante-Garrone, *Filippo Buonarroti e i rivoluzionari dell'Ottocento, 1828–1837* (Turin: Einaudi, 1951), 153. For an overview of Buonarroti's life, see Elizabeth L. Eisenstein, *The First Professional Revolutionist: Filippo Michele Buonarroti, 1761–1837* (Cambridge, Mass.: Harvard University Press, 1959).

13. Giovanni La Cecilia, *Memorie storico-politiche dal 1820 al 1876* (Rome: Artero, 1976–78), III, 182–83.

14. EN, LXXVII, 33.

15. EN, V, 44.

16. EN, V, 106–7.

17. GI, I, 3.

18. GI, II, 3–19, 71–94.

19. GI, I, 36.

20. GI, I, 129–30.

21. EN, II, 59–63.

22. EN, V, 17.

23. EN, III, 58.

24. EN, III, 61–62.

25. EN, I, 387.

26. EN, V, 50.

27. EN, II, 53–54.

28. GI, I, 5–25.

29. GI, II, 181.

30. Mazzini's faith in guerrilla warfare was shared by many other democratic patriots, including Giuseppe Garibaldi and Carlo Pisacane. Probably the best treatment of the topic appears in Egidio Liberti, ed., *Tecniche della guerra partigiana nel Risorgimento* (Florence: Barbera, 1972), 95–105, 120–225.

31. Arturo Linaker, *La vita e i tempi di Enrico Mayer* (Florence: G. Barbera, 1882), I, 185.

32. GI, II, 88.

33. EN, II, 194.

34. GI, II, 228, 248–51; V, 209–29; EN, III, 3–23, 69–73. Mazzini's 1832 essay on the history of liberty in Italy appears in EN, II, 147–221.

35. GI, IV, 10.

36. EN, III, 62, 64.

37. EN, III, 299.

38. EN, X, 79.

39. EN, XCIV, 213.

40. EN, III, 157. Mazzini's ideas on the relationship between the Roman Catholic Church and the body of the faithful bear a striking resemblance to those advocated by the liberal priest Félicité Robert de Lamennais (1782–1854) in his journal *Avenir*, which began to publish in 1830. Mazzini mentioned Lamennais in 1822 (*Zibaldone giovanile*, EN, I, 4, 161), but it was only ten years later that he became familiar with Lamennais's writings on Catholicism

and democracy. See Livio Pivano, *Lamennais e Mazzini* (Turin: Associazione Mazziniana Italiana, 1958), 51–52.

41. GI , IV, 38.

42. EN, LXXVII, 43. On the Sidoli family, see Rossana Maseroli Bertolotti, *I Sidoli* (Reggio Emilia: Magis Books, 1994).

43. See Alessandro Galante Garrone, "Il figlio di Mazzini," *Il Ponte*, VII (1951), 467–75, 603–11, and "Ancora il figlio di Mazzini," *Il Ponte*, XVII (1961), 711–28. Also, Livio Pivano, *Mazzini e Giuditta Sidoli* (Modena: Guanda, 1936), 198–221.

44. EN, V, 9.

45. EN, II, 17–41.

46. GI, II, 191.

47. Richard Blaas, "Metternich, Mazzini und die Gründung der Giovine Italia," in *Mitteilungen des Österreichischen Staatsarchivs* (Vienna: Ferdinand Berger, 1972), 595–616.

48. EN, V, 114–15n, 130–31n, 153n, 173, 206, 238–40, 298–300, 303, 308–12, 501–6. On Buonarroti's contacts with the Piedmontese, see Eugenio Passamonti, *Nuova luce sui processi del 1833 in Piemonte* (Florence: Le Monnier, 1930), 100–101.

49. GI, VI, 183–84, and *Carteggi di Vincenzo Gioberti* (Rome: Vittoriano, 1937), IV, 7. Gioberti signed himself Demofilo (Friend of the people).

50. EN, LXXVII, 190–91. On Young Italy's early network, see Blaas, "Metternich, Mazzini und die Gründung der Giovine Italia," p. 614; Romualdo Bonfandini, *Vita di Francesco Arese con documenti inediti* (Turin: L. Roux, 1894), 16–17; La Cecilia, *Memorie storico-politiche*, III, 155–57; Dora Melegari, *La Giovine Italia e la Giovine Europa dal carteggio inedito di Giuseppe Mazzini a Luigi Amedeo Melegari* (Milan: Treves, 1906), 60.

51. EN, V, 263, 272.

52. *Appendice epistolario*, EN, VIII, 665, 668, 674–75.

CHAPTER 4

Arms and War: The Swiss Years (1833–1837)

Geneva's attractions were both political and geographic: As a free republican city, it was beyond the jurisdiction of France, and it was close enough to Savoy to serve as a base for another attempt at insurrection in that region. What Mazzini and his companions contemplated was a variant of the 1831 armed incursion, with the significant difference that Mazzini was now the principal organizer. Others trusted him because he had demonstrated talent as an organizer and had a network of contacts in Italy, but the more influential backers insisted on certain conditions and limitations of his authority. He was to consult with them regularly and find an experienced commander for the military part of the plan. He certainly did not have the military experience; his heart was full of fire, but he had never faced gunfire in battle.

As in 1831, the objective was not merely to stir up Savoy, but to ignite a larger conflagration. Mazzini thought that he could assemble a force of five thousand, but more than on numbers he counted on the lessons of past failures and on the repressive policies of governments to help the revolution. If the lesson of prior failures was that revolutions required strong leadership, he was there to provide it; if governments thought they could repress revolution, they would learn differently: "All is well whenever oppression rages in Europe."[1]

There was a personal side to Mazzini's commitment. Far from calculating dispassionately like a professional conspirator, he was driven by anger and fury. Jacopo's death and the reign of terror visited on his family, friends, and followers were not forgotten. The fact that Charles

Mazzini during his Swiss stay, 1833–1837. From *Edizione Nazionale*, vol. XIII (Cooperativa Tipografico-Editrice Paolo Galeati of Imola, 1912–1924).

Albert stood behind the government responsible for these actions made it easier for Mazzini to personalize the issue and see it as a duel between himself and the king. His visceral hatred of monarchs was never as sharp as it was in these months of frantic activity. When he learned that King Ferdinand VII of Spain had died, his comment was that he wished every day would bring him similar good news. "Right now," he wrote shortly after reaching Geneva, "my only desire is to seek revenge, to act, and to strike."[2]

The timing was less propitious than in 1831, when revolution had been in the air, but Young Italy was no figment of the imagination. With converts in the armed forces of Piedmont, and cells in Lombardy, Parma, the Papal States, Tuscany, and Naples, it was capable of doing damage. In France and Switzerland there were several thousand Polish exiles and even greater numbers of unemployed workers who were ready to serve for honor or pay. Some remembered the provision of the Treaty of Vienna that promised Savoy to the Swiss federation if the Piedmontese government could not keep the peace there. That provision wetted Swiss appetite for territorial gain: An uprising in Savoy would demonstrate that Piedmont could not fulfill its obligation.

The council of the canton of Geneva was on record as opposing the entry of political refugees if they threatened to become an economic burden. Therefore, "five or six Modenese who were financially independent" were admitted on July 8, 1833.[3] That is probably how Mazzini entered Geneva, traveling with Giovanni Ruffini's passport to disguise his own identity, accompanied probably by Eleanora Ruffini, Agostino, Giuditta, and some of her friends. Giovanni remained in Marseilles joining Mazzini and the others in Geneva in January of 1834. As for the inevitable protests by the great powers, the Genevans were a free people, and proud of their independence. Calvinist Geneva was proud to shelter the victims of political repression, especially when the oppressors were Catholic countries such as Austria, France, and Piedmont. The conflict between Catholicism and Protestantism was something that Mazzini understood very well, and not just from a theological standpoint. In Switzerland he would find opportunities to turn religious animosities to his advantage.

THE CONSPIRATOR

Mazzini and his friends took lodgings at the Hotel de la Navigation, a walled, isolated, and tree-shaded structure that they rented in its entirety and transformed into their political headquarters. It was expensive, but initially they were not pinched for money. Behind its well-tended lawns and placid exterior some one hundred and fifty excited refugees slept, dined, and plotted. The authorities closed an eye on what was going on behind those walls and in the streets where the spirited guests often took their celebrations and their quarrels; the youngsters were loud and unruly, but they broke no laws and paid their bill. Life at the Hotel de la Navigation settled into a routine that seemed anything but revolutionary. Agostino Ruffini, the youngest of the Ruffini brothers, took note of the idleness of the residents, who were "getting up late, smoking here and there, drinking coffee, gossiping."[4] Eleonora Ruffini could be seen promenading along the shore of Lake Geneva, clad in black for the death of her Jacopo and flanked by Agostino and Mazzini, who had become her "other son." She was striking because of her still youthful appearance and her aura of martyrdom. The role of heroine appealed to her far more than that of wife and mother, to the chagrin of her husband Bernardo who called her back home. She had lost her Jacopo to the cause, but had gained the admiration and respect of these young men who were there to vindicate his death. The role she took on that summer is immortalized in the sculpture that stands over her tomb in the town of Taggia where she died in 1856, which represents her as an eagle nurturing three eaglets, the sons that she offered to Mazzini's Italy. She embroidered a tricolor for Mazzini to carry at the head of his liberating army.

Shortly after the arrival in Geneva Mazzini received a letter from Melegari in Marseilles introducing a young refugee from Parma. His name was Antonio Gallenga, but as a member of Young Italy he took the name of Procida, who, as every patriot knew, had led Sicilians against the French masters of their island in the 1282 uprising of the Sicilian Vespers. The modern Procida's intended victim was Charles Albert, and Gallenga promised to assassinate him at the risk of his own life. There was more than a touch of vanity to the personality of the twenty-two-year-old volunteer, but Mazzini thought him a "young man worthy of veneration, holy and good."[5] Snuffing out tyrants was one of Young Italy's goals; if Gallenga was caught, he would still be useful as a martyr to the cause. Mazzini later claimed to have yielded reluctantly to Gallenga's entreaties, but the evidence leaves little doubt that he welcomed him, steered him, and counted on the success of his mission to aid the larger revolutionary movement.[6]

There were complications with Gallenga's plan from the beginning. The spies who were mixed in with the conspirators warned of an impending attempt on the king's life; Mazzini's contacts in Turin were shocked to discover that he expected them to aid a would-be assassin; Gallenga himself left much to be desired as a conspirator. The first time he came close enough to strike at Charles Albert he had no weapon. When he tried to procure one, nobody would help him. It seems incredible that no knife could be found in a city full of kitchens and butcher shops. Mazzini himself sent him a small stiletto, which was discovered and confiscated by guards at the border. In October, after two months of living in daily fear of being discovered, Gallenga slipped out of the city without telling anyone where he was going. Mazzini ran into him in London six years later.

Gallenga's failure meant that the plan to invade Savoy had to proceed without the political disarray that was expected to follow the violent death of Charles Albert. It was a cumbersome plan that required coordinating multiple initiatives over long distances. Until September, Mazzini counted on an uprising in Naples to spark a movement by French republicans against Louis Philippe. When nothing happened in Naples, he decided that his own incursion into Savoy would have to be the detonator of the revolution, aided by simultaneous land and sea incursions into Piedmont and Liguria from French soil. Melegari was in charge of a maritime expedition that was intended to land one hundred and fifty men near Genoa, where Mazzini expected the people to be worthy of their history. Savoy itself was to be invaded simultaneously at different points from Switzerland and France, with the main thrust to come from the force that Mazzini was assembling in Geneva. Young Italy had few contacts among peasants, but Mazzini expected the countryside to join in spontaneously.[7] He did not envisage protracted guerrilla warfare in this instance, because he expected a general uprising that would sweep everyone in its way, and not just in Italy, for France, Spain, and Germany would be caught up in the conflagration. The young would issue the call and Italians would provide the initiative: "we are attempting to liberate our country, but we are also attempting to seize the initiative in Europe. If we succeed, we will inaugurate a new era, the era of the People."[8]

Mazzini had a tendency to mix reality and wishful thinking, which was aggravated in 1833 by a personal crisis caused by the death of Jacopo, the abandonment of his child in Marseilles, and Giuditta's abandonment of him. Precisely what may have prompted her to leave for Italy is not known. There is some evidence that she may have gone on a political errand, but it is more probable that she went to reclaim her children. His passionate letters make it clear that the separation was intensely painful for him. "If only I could have you," he wrote in a typical outpouring, "hold you in my arms, sleep, rest my head on your knees just once." He was vehement with Melegari, who may have been the only one of his collaborators who knew of the relationship: "I am beside myself over *her*; I am still a man, *perdio*!" With his mother he was self-pitying: "I would have liked to make everyone happy, and I have made everyone unhappy, myself first of all. I don't mind that, I mind that in my life I will probably have to inflict more sorrow on those I love."[9]

Suffering energized him. Many who saw Mazzini that summer and fall remarked on his energy and apparent self-confidence. The Danish poet Paul Harro-Harring met him and found him electrifying.[10] Self-delusion played a role, but he had moments of lucidity when he doubted of success. "Tranquillity reigns supreme everywhere in the world," he wrote his mother on September 1, "the kings are taking their siesta, Spanish style; the populations are still, either because they are satiated or because they are afraid of the devil. Hence, universal peace." But he was too deeply committed, and quite ruthless with those who wanted to turn back. When his funds were running out, he threatened to expose his contributors if they did not come up with more. He authorized his followers to seize public funds from government offices and customs houses. If a few lives were lost in the process, so be it. "It is not enough to rise up, you understand," he wrote to Melegari, "we must also rise *youthfully*."[11]

Unfortunately for the insurgents, their plans were public knowledge. The Count of Cavour, the future prime minister of Italy, then a young officer in the Piedmontese army visiting relatives in Geneva, learned of Mazzini's plans from a police inspector. The Austrians had an inside source in Plinio Santarini, a Mazzini confidant who reported regularly to his contacts in Milan. The Papal government also had an informer, Michele Accursi, a member of Young Italy previously arrested, "turned," and released to spy on the conspirators. The Piedmontese government was warned in August that republicans were planning attacks on Savoy from France and Switzerland. Charles Albert called up nine thousand troops to meet the emergency and teach the bandits a good lesson.[12]

The plan ran into seemingly endless obstacles. Mazzini wanted a movement inside Italy to show internal support, but no one in Italy wanted to make the first move. First it was his friends in Genoa who demurred, then his contacts in Naples and Livorno who wanted to be sure that they would get help from France. The attack on Savoy was decided at the end of September, but Giacomo Ciani and Gaspare Rosales, who had contributed about half a million francs to the venture, insisted on having a commander of proven military expertise. That ruled out Mazzini, who may have hoped to lead the raid in person. Someone suggested a certain Damas, who passed himself off as a military officer. But he was French and insisted on fighting under the French flag, which was unacceptable to the Italians. Bianco was Italian, but he was more theoretician than field commander, and too unassuming to inspire confidence.

One Italian officer did have the requisite qualifications. Gerolamo Ramorino (1792–1849) was Genoese, said to be the illegitimate son of one of Napoleon's marshals, a graduate of St-Cyr, a captain in the French army under Napoleon, a Carbonaro after 1815, and a political refugee of 1821 who had fought for the revolution in Poland. He was fighting for the liberal side in Portugal when his name was mentioned as a possible commander for the Savoy expedition. He was a liberal, he claimed the rank of general, and he was reputed to be brilliant in the field. He was also at a loose end, for he belonged to the generation of unemployed Napoleonic officers who could not adjust to peacetime pursuits. Unable to land regular commissions, such men were available for irregular ventures like the one that Mazzini contemplated.

Mazzini later claimed that Ramorino was imposed on him by his backers. He may indeed have had reservations about him, but he pushed for Ramorino's appointment and defended him against his detractors in his eagerness to move quickly.[13] He may even have pressured him into accepting the command, perhaps to ward off Damas's candidacy and to make sure that an Italian was in charge. More than pressure, it may have been Mazzini's promise of 40,000 francs that persuaded Ramorino to accept the offer.[14]

Mazzini and Ramorino met in Geneva on October 10, and Ramorino promised to return with one thousand recruits by November 5. He then left for Paris, and a life of sudden affluence. He never delivered the recruits. Many Polish exiles in Paris did not trust him. They circulated unflattering accounts of his behavior in Poland, accused him of being a spy, and threatened to kill him rather than serve under his command.

Ramorino was probably not a spy, but he was certainly an accomplished procrastinator. Mazzini showed restraint as November and December passed without word from him, but he could no longer contain himself when January began to go by. By the end of January it was clear that the operation had either to be launched immediately or to be canceled. Recruits gathered in and around Geneva were coming down with influenza, the Swiss were getting ready to crack down on them in response to mounting pressure from foreign governments, and participants in Italy were in danger of being exposed and arrested. Responding to Mazzini's urgent pleas, Ramorino left Paris on January 20, 1834, and proceeded at a leisurely pace by carriage to the Swiss town of Rolle. He stopped there, just short of Geneva, where Mazzini was waiting impatiently, on January 30. He had with him an aide, two officers, and a medical doctor, but no volunteers. He reached Geneva the next evening just in time for dinner.

Mazzini was beside himself. By this time he may have suspected Ramorino of being in the pay of the French government. Nevertheless, a plan was concocted in which Ramorino was to play a major part. There were to be four separate thrusts into Savoyard territory, two from Switzerland and two from France. The Swiss columns, led by Ramorino, would constitute the principal thrust. He was to move south toward the Savoy town of St. Julien with a force of six hundred men, flanked on his

left by a column of 150 Polish volunteers, who were expected to make
their way down Lake Geneva from a bivouac area near Nyon. The
columns from France would enter Savoy from Seyssel and Grenoble. The
meeting point for all was the capital city of Chambery. Simultaneous
uprisings were expected elsewhere, including one in Genoa, where
sailors were to mutiny and join insurgents in the city. The action was to
begin the very next morning, with recruits mustering at a rendezvous
point outside the city and marching at 11:00 PM that same evening,
Saturday, February 1, 1834.[15]

Complications ensued almost immediately. The Polish column from
Nyon took an unexpected detour to avoid a confrontation with Swiss
gendarmes; Ramorino with only two hundred volunteers moved up his
departure time by two hours to give his force extra time to rendezvous
with the Poles. Instead of marching directly south toward St. Julien as
Mazzini urged him to do, Ramorino lingered for some hours on the Swiss
side of the border. When he finally crossed the border he did so in an
easterly direction, ostensibly to link up with the Polish volunteers, but
probably because he feared being lured into a trap deep into Savoy. There
were some desultory exchanges of fire with Savoyard border guards, a
raid on a customs house to appropriate its receipts, and the burning of
tax records in a few Savoyard villages close to the border. He completed
his revolutionary action by planting a liberty tree and issuing a fiery
proclamation promising liberty to the oppressed subjects of Charles
Albert.

The oppressed subjects seemed more worried about the bandits who
were disturbing the peace; there were no popular demonstrations, no
uprisings, and no defections from the army.[16] It was the volunteers who
felt oppressed and betrayed, for no one had made provision to pay them,
feed them, or keep them warm in the winter cold. Ramorino was furious
with Mazzini, who had been in charge of the preparations, and disappointed with the recruits he had been given, who were few, untrained,
and undisciplined. When someone stole his bedding straw, he announced
that he would dismiss everyone in the morning, which proved to be
unnecessary since most of the men disappeared during the night. He
ordered the few who were left to retreat into Swiss territory, which was
done with relative ease because he had been careful to march parallel
to the border rather than away from it. Finally settled at the end of a
hard day, he was rousted out of bed by several Poles who broke into his
room to mete out rough justice. He saved himself by jumping out of a
window and escaping into the night.[17]

The subsidiary operations also failed. In Genoa a twenty-six-year old
petty officer named Giuseppe Garibaldi deserted from the Piedmontese
navy after becoming implicated in the movement. He was an obscure
sailor who admired Mazzini from afar, and who continued to admire him

from South America, where he fought for various causes, including Uruguayan independence, always in the name of Mazzinian republicanism.[18]

Mazzini experienced the debacle as a simple soldier. He had taken his place in the ranks, keeping an eye on Ramorino from a distance, carrying the banner on which Eleonora Ruffini had embroidered the words Liberty, Independence, Equality, Humanity, and Unity. He was young and healthy, but his studious and sedentary habits had not prepared him for the hardships of life in the field. The physical and mental strain induced a high fever and delirium; at times he hallucinated. His friends thought that he might have poisoned himself to avoid the shame of defeat. When they shouted at him "What have you taken?" he thought they were accusing him of pocketing the funds of the expedition. Lamberti and Angelo Usiglio managed to carry him back to Geneva, unconscious. When he came to, Usiglio told him that they had suffered few casualties, but were now prisoners of the Swiss authorities.[19]

An avalanche of recriminations followed the debacle. Ramorino was an obvious target, but so was Mazzini. Nothing of what he had promised had materialized, not the uprisings in Italy, nor the mutinies in the Piedmontese army, nor help from French republicans. His detractors charged that he expected citizens to pour into the streets and peasants to take to the roads with their pitchforks as if it were 1789 instead of 1834.[20] He kept quiet for the most part, preferring to let others speak for him, especially when Ramorino, safely back in Paris, charged him with incompetence and bad faith. He did react when someone called for his resignation as head of Young Italy. "They must be kidding," he replied, "you would think that they put me in charge."[21]

Privately, he was hard on himself. To Melegari, he wrote that inept revolutionists are no better than traitors and that illness is no excuse: "There are moments when it is simply not permissible to be ill." With Giuditta he was perhaps less candid, blaming his physical state for the failure: "I was ill, very ill, completely delirious. I miscalculated my powers of physical and mental resistance. That is all."[22] Someone cut out the text that followed, but the confession of physical impotence was perhaps meant to salvage something that was much more vital to him than his physical pride: the notion that revolution was viable and the expectation of victory was realistic.

After being released because the authorities had no record of his involvement in the movement, he went into hiding, first in Geneva, where he stayed for about three weeks, then in Lausanne. His position was precarious both personally and politically. There was always a close correlation between his politics and his health, with political setbacks often triggering bouts of physical suffering. This time he complained of insomnia, severe toothaches, throat pains, and facial swellings. His problems were many, for France and Piedmont demanded his extradition, Buonarroti plotted against him, and his own collaborators questioned his ability to lead. He urged Bianco and Harro-Harring to speak up for him and tell the world that a few hundred insurgents, isolated and poorly led, had raised the banner of revolution against great odds and caused great alarm in Europe. A handful of Italian, Polish, French, German, and Swiss patriots had resurrected the prospects of revolution with one daring move. The raid on Savoy was really a victory that marked the start of a new phase in the struggle against oppression.[23]

YOUNG EUROPE

There was a reason for stressing the multinational nature of the effort. Even before the raid Mazzini had envisaged an international movement based on associations of Poles, Hungarians, Germans, Slavs, and Swiss patterned after Young Italy. Single defeats should not be allowed to obscure the larger picture: "The same calculating coldness that makes me feel the desperate state of our condition as individuals also makes me feel the silent progress of humanity. Would I be here otherwise? Progress is continuous, like the improvement of the majority, even when it seems otherwise."[24] That was the voice of Mazzini the Europeanist, who would even condone acts of conquest to enlarge the spiral of progress: "Europe is the lever of the world; Europe is the land of liberty; Europe controls the universe. Hers is the mission of progressive development that encompasses humanity."[25] It was therefore necessary to create in Europe "the *holy alliance* of Peoples who are constituted as great single aggregates according to the dominant moral and material attributes that determine their particular national mission."[26]

That was the mission of Mazzini's Young Europe, founded in Bern on April 15, 1834. Launched in the aftermath of defeat, it was a reminder that the revolution had many heads. The seventeen original signatories of its Pact of Brotherhood represented Young Italy, Young Germany, and Young Poland, but they were soon joined by representatives of Young Switzerland, France, Spain, Hungary, Scandinavia, and even Austria. Young Europe was conceived as a federation of autonomous national societies, but its constituent societies were tenuous bodies. The Germans constituted if not the largest, certainly the most militant element, chafing at Mazzini's predilection for Italy.[27] This predilection, however, was not in the statutes of Young Europe, which stressed that nationalities are different but equal, each having a mission to fulfill for the benefit of humanity. The brotherhood of nations was a safeguard against egoism, both individual and national.[28]

Mazzini also saw socialism as an antidote to the materialistic philosophies of French origin. The word socialism was a recent addition to the political vocabulary, which he and his contemporaries felt free to interpret and define. He first used the term approvingly in the context of Young Europe, where he took it to denote cooperation not only among individuals, but among nations as well: "The new epoch is destined to constitute humanity, which is socialism not only among individuals but among independent nationalities . . . associated in pursuit of a common goal, in the name of liberty, equality, humanity."[29] He took socialism to mean association pure and simple, and his socialism stressed the need for social cooperation across both national and class lines, rejecting as too divisive all class-based notions of social justice. He opposed independent organizations of workers, because he saw no sign that the workers themselves wanted them and because they would place workers is a social ghetto and deprive them of power. If the "association of labor" was merely premature, schemes of land redistribution and attacks on the institution of private property in general were misguided and immoral. Making property widely accessible would solve the social question without alarming property owners.[30]

Mazzini has been criticized for addressing nationalities at a time when they existed only in the imagination of a few. He heard that charge from many quarters, including his father, who argued with him by correspondence that there was no such thing as the Italian people, that there were only Tuscans, Venetians, Neapolitans, and so on. Mazzini granted that was true for the present, but pointed to the future. His mission was to foster the "association of all men who, united by language, geography, and their role in history, form a single group, and move under one law in pursuit of a shared goal."[31] That was the definition of nationality he elaborated in the months he spent in hiding. Nationalities, he reiterated, had to carry out the will of God on earth "so that the divine plan may be fulfilled."[32]

The religious character of Mazzini's political pronouncements intensified after the events of February 1834. Now he returned with renewed interest to the writings of Lamennais, saw him as a religious and social prophet calling on the Church to take up the cause of the disinherited, and initiated a correspondence with him.[33] He increasingly viewed his own mission in religious terms. Influenced perhaps by Adam Mickiewicz's vision of Poland as a martyred nation, Mazzini claimed that role for Italy. Italians were the *Cristo popolo*, he asserted, and he the *Cristo uomo* sacrificing for their redemption. In hiding, he fretted that he might have to carry his unheard message with him to the grave.[34]

The mystical tone and language played to the distrust of rational discourse that permeated European culture under the influence of romanticism. Mazzini shared the yearning for certainty felt by his contemporaries, especially by the young, a yearning that reason could not satisfy. To them, cool objectivity was not a virtue. To entertain all possibilities equally, to keep an open mind, to strive for neutrality, balance, and moderation was the American approach, said Mazzini, and he did not like it.[35] He felt that when the press adopted the "responsible" tone of moderation and objectivity, it showed complete disregard for its social responsibilities. The hunger for certainty could only be satisfied by faith. Here his message tapped into the need for reassurance that was felt by members of his generation. They lived at a time when ideas were being scrutinized and challenged like never before, and the intensity of the questioning produced an equally intense yearning for answers. That yearning led to the search for the Believer *(Il Credente)*. It was to such a mysterious figure, never identified, that Garibaldi attributed his political awakening. Mazzini also saw the Believer as the savior. In the midst of doubt, he wrote, "The Believer alone remains standing, like an oak beaten by the storm."[36]

Believers were to spread the gospel of nationality among the multitudes. That is why he called the bearers of his message the Apostles of the People. We might call them opinion makers, but in Mazzini's way of thinking the Apostles spoke incontestable truths, not mere versions of events. Far removed from any postmodernist concept of reality, Mazzini insisted that nationality was a spiritual reality waiting to manifest itself, something more permanent than anything material. His sense of nationality was not an "imagined community" built on transient expectations. He envisaged nationality as an intrinsic reality of the spirit, though not of the blood, dormant until awakened by education and by the example of the "Apostles of the People," as he called his followers. Like the apostles of old, they must move among the People bearing witness to their faith by their readiness to sacrifice. The People were to be won over by deeds, for they "never side with those whom they consider weak or inept. They love and fight alongside the strong. They are strong who in every circumstance, at every moment, readily bear witness in word and deed to the faith that fills their souls."[37] The apostles must reassure the multitudes afflicted by a "confused disquiet" *(confusa inquietudine)*; it was the task of the apostles to put others in touch with the truth.[38]

Mazzini thus put a heavy burden on both his collaborators, who were to announce a new gospel, and the People, who must be prepared to receive it. It is not without significance that he elaborated these thoughts at a time of enforced isolation, when for months at a stretch he was out of touch with the world for which he claimed to speak. The feelings of betrayal that he felt as a result of the personal and political attacks reinforced his image of himself as a Christ-like figure abandoned by all in his own Gethsemane. From the image of the betrayed redeemer he sought the strength to justify himself: The master had to be forsaken by the disciples and left with no other guide but the voice of God. But, unlike Christ, Mazzini was not resigned to his fate; his harsh judgments of others suggest that he was looking for ways to exculpate himself. It was not only his collaborators whom he judged harshly for not living up to the sacrificial role he envisaged for them. He was also unsparing in his condemnation of the People who had shown no interest in being redeemed, particularly the Italian people who refused to play the role of historical vanguard: "I love Italy, not Italians, with very few exceptions; I love humanity but not individuals. I carry on for the sake of my conscience, for religion, and to obey the impulse of the heart, not at all for others. Hence, we are *quittés* (even)."[39] Such comments were for private consumption; publicly, he would not admit that Italians were unequal to the task, and censured Lamennais for expressing lack of faith in them. That was not for a Frenchman to say, not even one whom he admired.[40]

REVIVED HOPES

In the months that followed the failure of the raid Mazzini found time to work on several writing projects. In 1835 he produced a complete statement of his creed in *Fede e avvenire* (Faith and the Future), a treatise in which he tried to bring together various strands of his religiosity. His elaboration can perhaps be criticized for its lack of logical rigor and originality, but the attempt to confront certain fundamental issues of belief, however unsuccessful on a philosophical level, reveals the tensions that kept the faith alive in him. In trying to reconcile divine omnipotence with human volition, design with chance, matter with spirit, and rights with duties, he restated his religious beliefs in a way that showed the synthesizing tendency of his mind.

He threw out materialism and chance, but managed to save just about everything else. The doctrine of rights he saved as the valuable legacy of the era of individualism, which was yielding to the era of association with its emphasis on mutual obligations. Association linked individual rights to duties in the interest of the collective good. Because modern society requires collaboration, the "doctrine of duties advances toward certain victory" without effacing the importance of rights.[41] Divine omnipotence and free will he saved by giving up on reason and logic altogether and appealing instead to the "unknowable" (*incognita umana*): "God eternal, your word is not fulfilled; your mind, your encompassing mind, is not revealed. You create, and will continue to create in the centuries unknown. . . . Our mission is not concluded."[42]

The *incognita umana* justified continuing the struggle; the outcome was uncertain, but without struggle there could be no progress.

It may have been precisely the absence of a satisfactory definition of the relationship between free will and divine omnipotence that kept him in a state of psychological tension and spurred him on. Mazzini did not give up hope after the Savoy setback. He continued to conspire in assassination plots directed against Louis Philippe and Duke Francis IV of Modena and in secret understandings with Prince Louis Napoleon, the future Napoleon III. The evidence for these activities is admittedly hard to evaluate, being mostly in the form of reports from spies, but his own writings suggest that something was indeed going on.[43]

Within Mazzini's own camp, critics multiplied. Perhaps the most troublesome, because he was the most articulate and outspoken, was Vincenzo Gioberti, who broke openly with Mazzini and his tactics in the aftermath of the Savoy fiasco. Gioberti's new slogan of "War and the People" redefined political activism in a most un-Mazzinian sense, for it meant that the people could not prevail unless the great powers destroyed themselves through war. When he called on the people, Gioberti was emphatic that they had to be the people *in Italy*, not bands of desperate political exiles who claimed to speak for the people. Before the people could play any role, they had to develop a religiously based awareness of their own identity; that meant a long wait, possibly of generations.[44]

Gioberti's temporizing was probably better suited to the moment than Mazzini's call to action, and Mazzini handled Gioberti with diplomatic restraint, agreeing that change could not be hurried and pointing out that the primary purpose of Young Europe was educational. He disagreed tactically, arguing that "the People had to be *constituted* before it could acquire its religious conscience [*formola religiosa*]. Therefore, the political revolution must precede the religious."[45] In other words, Mazzini defended his tactic of promoting political action not only for its possible results in the short run, but also, and more significantly, for its long-term educational value. Political action was worthwhile even when it resulted in defeat, because it was only through such action that the people developed political consciousness. Thought and action were related; participation was at the heart of political education. The choice at any one moment was not between thought and action, as Gioberti implied, but only among modes of action possible and appropriate to that given moment.

SWISS POLITICS

If Italy would not respond, there was Switzerland. Mazzini imagined Switzerland with a strong central government as a republican fortress in the mountainous heart of monarchist Europe, its armed citizens fighting for a worthwhile cause instead of selling their services as mercenaries to other governments. As such, Switzerland would be the fulcrum of revolution, and Italy and Germany would be the lever: "The flag that waves over our heads is a republican flag; it stands for all insurrections, guides the efforts of all Europeans who believe in progress and want to wage a war of principles."[46] He held out the bait of territorial gain for a restructured confederation: "Savoy, Switzerland, the Tyrol, etc., would form a confederate republic, a Confederation of the Alps, which, situated between us [Italy] and the North, would make use of both North and South."[47]

That first reference to a national entity based on topography shows the political Mazzini ready to revise definitions for the sake of expediency. In the case of Switzerland, he was willing to forgo language, religion, and even history as the foundations of national identity, and to stress instead the unifying role of terrain. There was no necessary contradiction, for he could always argue that what mattered was the spiritual unity of a people and not the material conditions on which that spiritual unity rested, but that sort of inconsistency is what left him open to the charge that he lacked intellectual rigor. It was not intellectual rigor that he was after, but political leverage, and this was particularly difficult to attain in Switzerland, where the principles of national unity, administrative centralization, and involvement in European affairs that he proposed met with enormous resistance. To get out his message he had to rely on ephemeral and obscure publications, the most important being *Jeune Suisse*, a journal that was the voice of Young Switzerland from June 1835 to June 1836.[48]

He called on the Swiss to abandon their immoral policy of neutrality in international affairs and take up the cause of republicanism in Europe. Young Switzerland was there to lead the people with propaganda and public demonstrations. Privately, he confessed his hope that popular agitation would provoke the intervention of Austria or France and trigger a general European conflagration that would destroy Austria, the bulwark of European despotism.[49] For the time being his attention was on domestic politics, which revolved around the often bitter rivalry between conservatives and liberals. Conservatives wanted looser ties among the cantons, while liberals asked for a stronger central government; conservative sentiments prevailed in the more rural and isolated cantons, while liberal sentiments were strongest among members of the urban middle classes and workers. Mazzini aligned himself with the extreme liberals who formed the Radical Party. There he found the strongest anti-Catholic sentiments and the deepest commitment to popular revolution. The Radicals' rifle clubs and reading societies were putting books and guns in the hands of the people. The armed nation that was their ideal was also his; he would cite it in years to come as a splendid model of grassroots democracy.

The religious debate going on in Switzerland sharpened his thinking on the historical role of Catholicism, which he now saw from a decidedly Protestant perspective. It was time to introduce democracy in the governance of the Roman Catholic Church, he argued, so that the faithful could establish a direct relationship with God. The papacy was the enemy of liberty and individual conscience, and should be replaced by a general council of believers; God would speak to the faithful through this democratically elected council. The unholy alliance between throne and altar would perish as Austria was swept away by the triumph of *la patrie* and the papacy was replaced by the religion of humanity.[50] Politics and religion were now fully merged in Mazzini's mind. He was no longer Catholic or even Christian, except in a formal sense: "But I am a *believer*; no one believes more ardently or deeply than me; no one more than me is convinced that the spirit of religion must dominate the new Italy and the new Young Europe."[51]

Vehemence was his undoing. Never one to hesitate, he plunged into Swiss politics with an ardor that alarmed his hosts. Many resented the efforts of this foreigner to meddle in Swiss affairs, but Catholics were most outspoken against him, for they not only resented his attacks on the papacy, but also feared for the autonomy of their cantons in a centralized, Protestant-dominated Switzerland. Mazzini antagonized conservative opinion in a public affair that saw him and the French government on the same side in a diplomatic and legal battle to uphold the right of Jews to own property in Switzerland.[52] He was too radical even for most Radicals, who found him an embarrassing ally and disavowed his support.[53] The order to expel him was still in effect; he was able to avoid deportation only by moving quickly from place to place. After leaving Geneva at the end of February of 1834, he lived in Lausanne, Bern, and the German-speaking village of Grenchen at the foot of the Jura Mountains in the extreme north of the country, where he and the Ruffini brothers found refuge in a large bathing establishment run by a local family.[54]

The Girards treated their guests as family members, sharing meals with them, including them in their own festivities, and welcoming their help in domestic chores. The egalitarian ethos of the Girard household suggested to Mazzini that domestic labor should be abolished as a form of servitude similar to that of slaves and Jews. He found Swiss women refreshing, more spiritual and sensitive than the Italian women he knew, more attuned to the beauty of nature, freer with men in a comradely sort of way, and less inclined to develop romantic attachments. He may have been mistaken on that last point, or deliberately blind, for at least three Swiss women developed strong romantic attachments to him; but he treated the Girards' three daughters like the sisters he had left behind. He liked the frankness of the men, although he found their manners rough and thought that they drank too much—especially college professors who threw empty bottles out of their classroom windows and fell asleep under their desks. The Swiss were kind to animals, and that made animals friendly toward humans. He kept a cat, the pet he could not have as a child, and put it out reluctantly at night, more for the animal's convenience than for his own, he said.[55] He shrugged off petty annoyances with humor, as when he had to endure the company of a retired colonel who never tired of retelling the same stories, and of the colonel's daughter who insisted on playing the guitar for the guests, badly and for hours on end. He carried on a thick correspondence with his parents, even with his father, who gave him advice on how to succeed in the world. He kept on pretending to be their niece Emilia, a ruse that did not fool the Piedmontese police, but did deprive them of legal evidence of correspondence. That mattered, especially to Giacomo, who wanted to avoid legal challenges to his right to dispose of his property at will, which the government might have been able to contest with evidence of contacts with a condemned traitor. His son resented the tampering with letters, and seldom missed an opportunity to insult the king or the government, knowing that his jibes would be passed on to those in charge. But he also found the situation amusing and often joked about his epistolary sex change. Once, after quoting the proverb that man proposes and God disposes, he specified that in his case it was "woman who proposes because, as you know, I am a woman."[56]

In the calm of Grenchen Mazzini's thoughts turned to art, literature, and music, interests that he had neglected since leaving Genoa. He contributed articles to *L'Italiano*, a publication put out by Italian exiles in Paris, revisiting in his writings the old controversy between classicists and romanticists from a political perspective, crediting romanticism with breaking the tyranny of classicism but questioning it also as an expression of socially irresponsible individualism. Napoleon, Byron, and Rossini represented the triumph of individuality in the fields of politics, literature, and music respectively; precisely because they represented the highest achievement of individuality, they brought the era of individualism to a close. The future belonged to a new art and to new voices capable of giving artistic expression to the spirit of association that marked the new era.[57]

Perhaps his most noteworthy contribution to artistic theory came with the 1836 essay "The Philosophy of Music," which he probably wrote with the help of the Ruffini brothers. Its main argument was that music was in a state of transition, from a form of amusement meant to alleviate boredom to an art form capable of inspiring great and worthy deeds. The race was on to create a new style of musical expression, particularly between the Italian and German schools. Italians offered their talent for melody, Germans theirs for harmony. The new sound would be a synthesis; it had not been heard yet, except perhaps tentatively in the operas of Donizetti. The new music would express the emerging spirit of association by deploying massive means, both orchestral and choral. Individual bravura belonged to the past. The new music would be a *dramma musicale*, an integrated performance bringing together lyrics and music to form a perfect whole. Mazzini's essay was an original and prescient contribution to the social theory of music. As often pointed out, it anticipated Richard Wagner's better-known views on the social function of music and drama, in its bold assertion that art must involve and inspire the masses to serious social pursuits. Music, like art in general, should speak not to specialists, but to "those who feel the mission of art and understand the immense influence that it can exercise on society."[58]

For all its moments of gaiety, relaxation, and serious intellectual pursuits, the stay with the Girards was also marked by tension. Living in forced daily contact with others was always painful for Mazzini. In this case, confinement with the Ruffini brothers brought out latent incompatibilities. The three of them were closeted for hours, gnawed by private worries and doubts, desperately seeking privacy by escaping to their separate rooms.[59] Giovanni showed proclivities that Mazzini found hard to comprehend in one whom he had designated an apostle of the truth. Physical comforts mattered to Giovanni, who escaped from confinement, carried on with women, and fathered illegitimate children. Mazzini was not prudish in the abstract, but he could be harsh with those from whom he expected much, and Giovanni was politically lax, often failing to carry out tasks that were assigned to him. If Giovanni could not be trusted, who could be?

He was more indulgent toward Agostino, who, at twenty-three, was like a younger brother. Yet, even Agostino could be infuriating. He fell in love with a married woman, Anna Courvoisier, who reciprocated while also feeling attracted to Mazzini. Mazzini's obvious enjoyment of her company led Agostino to conclude that Mazzini was courting her surreptitiously, and that she loved Mazzini rather than him and responded to his own advances only because she saw in him a surrogate Mazzini, while the real one courted her yet held himself aloof. The situation could not have been easy on anyone, least of all on Anna, who felt guilty for her infidelity, mental or physical. The tension spoiled an otherwise idyllic visit to Jean Jacques Rousseau's cottage on an island in Lake Bienne, during which Anna could not take her eyes off Mazzini and her husband barely contained his anger. Her death in September 1836, possibly by suicide, left a trail of guilt and resentments. Agostino blamed himself, but also thought that Mazzini had manipulated Anna's feelings

for his own gratification.[60] They continued to live together with a
pretense of civility, but their friendship was over.

THE PRESSURE TO LEAVE SWITZERLAND

On May 28, 1836, two hundred federal policemen surrounded the
bathing establishment in Grenchen and carted Mazzini and Agostino
Ruffini off to jail. The arrest had mysterious and unexplained aspects.
It was triggered by a sudden visit by Harro-Harring, who arrived under
the impression that there was going to be a convocation of political
exiles. A circular to that effect had gone out with Mazzini's name on it,
but Mazzini denounced it as a forgery, blaming it on the French ambassador who wanted him expelled. There were rumors that members of
Young Germany and Young Switzerland also wanted to get rid of him.
Mazzini must have suspected some trickery, for he warned Harro-Harring to conceal his identity from the arresting gendarmes. It was to no
avail, for the impulsive Dane declared himself Mazzini's friend, thereby
giving away their identities.[61] Mazzini's popularity with the local population, and the canton's pride in its autonomy, saved them for the time
being: Mazzini, Agostino, and Harro-Harring were released within
twenty-four hours following popular demonstrations in their favor. But
it was now too dangerous for them to remain in Grenchen. From then
on they were constantly on the run, barely managing to keep one step
ahead of the federal police who were hot on their trail.

It was no secret that the French wanted Mazzini expelled from
Switzerland, where they had reason to believe that he was plotting the
assassination of Louis Philippe. They wanted him as far away as
possible, preferably in America. The prospect of eviction frightened
Mazzini. Switzerland suited him just fine; he was learning German so
he could speak all the major languages of the federation, and he could
think of no other place from which to carry on the struggle. He resolved
to fight the federal government's efforts to extradite him. One murky
scheme he devised involved investing in a Swiss iron mine that doubled
as a weapons factory, owned by his friend Rosales. Ever mindful of
property rights, the Swiss hesitated to expel people who owned property,
even if they were not citizens. He convinced his father to lend him 7,000
francs by holding out to him the prospect of a quick and substantial
return on the investment. What he actually did with all that money is
not clear, but instead of investing it in the mine he apparently used most
of it to pay off his and the Ruffinis' mounting debts, and to bankroll *Jeune
Suisse*. In that publication he described the heart-rending plight of
political exiles like himself, who were rejected everywhere, turned back
at every border, and forced to live like common criminals. They were not
criminals, he pleaded, but sons and daughters, husbands and wives,

fathers and mothers, who should be protected from the arbitrary actions of repressive governments and deserved to be treated fairly.[62]

The lingering hope of revolution that kept Mazzini in Switzerland declined in the latter part of 1836, when even the most obdurate had to recognize that Europe was settling into a period of political calm. It was then that Garibaldi in faraway South America gave up hope of a quick return and decided to start a new life for himself on that continent as a *guerrillero*. Beside bleak political prospects, Mazzini also faced personal disappointments. Giuditta was having an affair in Italy; he and the Ruffinis were becoming estranged; they were running out of money; they had few political friends left in Switzerland; Young Italy and Young Europe were in shambles; and he feared being kidnapped and spirited to France or Piedmont, where he faced the death penalty. No wonder that Angelo Usiglio found him agitated, irritable, and snappish when he visited him in August 1836.[63]

This was the hour of his Gethsemane, which Mazzini described as the "tempest of doubt." Doubt, in Mazzini's vocabulary, was a damning condition that left the sufferer without guidance or sense of direction. Certainty was for him a psychological need, which he projected on the human condition as a philosophical necessity. Man's search for the truth was constant, endless, and paradoxical. No one could be sure of possessing the truth, yet no one could live without believing in it: "if something obscures our vision or impedes our search, we are left without guide, we doubt, we are unhappy. Such is our state today!"[64] It was certainly his state, and he suffered. It had all the symptoms of what modern medicine calls a nervous breakdown, including severe depression, inability to make decisions, loss of will to act, and thoughts of suicide. Later on he reminisced that he thought that the whole world was collapsing around him, that he felt himself hovering at the edge of madness, and that his thoughts fixed on "the life to come, where true love reigns and where we will see again all our loved ones."[65]

That is how he portrayed his own crisis years after the event, when it served to portray his decision to leave the continent as the result of spiritual rebirth following an agonizing struggle. In November 1836, however, right at the time when he was supposedly in the grip of darkest depression, he wrote a feisty letter to Rosales in which, after describing all his personal and political difficulties with clinical precision, he explains his decision to withdraw temporarily from politics as a tactical move dictated by necessity:

> As I withdraw, I feel compelled to declare that I yield to necessity and nothing else, that I would go on if I had the means to do so; that as soon as I have repaid my debts, which I hope will be soon, I will devote the first available penny to conspiring once again, perhaps differently and on my own, but certainly to conspiring; in withdraw-

ing, I will tell the Italian people that they have an obligation to conspire, and that if they fail to do so they are guilty of treason, that they have failed in their hearts and minds, that they betray their country, the legacy of our martyrs, and their duty toward Italy and toward Humanity.[66]

This is not the language of someone suffering from a debilitating mental condition. In fact, there is virtually no contemporary evidence that Mazzini underwent a deep spiritual crisis near the end of his Swiss stay. He was certainly frustrated, despondent, and angry, but not at the edge of the abyss. The image of doubt, abandonment, suffering, and purification is familiar to everyone brought up in a Christian tradition. It is the garden of Gethsemane, the Last Supper, the crucifixion, and the resurrection rolled into the experience of Mazzini the Christ-like figure. Like Christ, he too experienced a resurrection, as he tells us, when he woke up one morning after the ordeal, miraculously recovered, with his mind at rest, certain that he knew what he had to do.[67] The trauma was over, he claimed; he was reborn, his faith in the eternal principles restored by suffering. It must have been also at about that time that certain delicate negotiations that he had been carrying on in secret since September with a representative of the French government reached a satisfactory conclusion. Thanks to the intercession of the British minister in Bern, who thought Mazzini could be instrumental in spreading Protestantism in Italy through his secret network, the French agreed to give him and his friends safe passage through France on their way to England. They would have preferred that he go to far away America, but Mazzini refused to cross the Atlantic. Still, it was better for them to have him in England than in neighboring Switzerland.[68]

As the year wound down, Mazzini prepared to leave for England. The little that was left of Young Italy he dismissed as corrupt, cowardly, and salvageable only by going back to first principles.[69] He entrusted Young Europe to Melegari, without much hope for its future. He did not expect it to accomplish much in the short run, but hoped that the idea of a European revolutionary movement would survive; the tragedy of the revolutionary movement was that it did not understand the weakness of the powerful, he said.[70] He settled some last-minute business, including the sale of weapons stockpiled at the Swiss mine. On December 31 he wrote loving letters to his parents and to Eleonora Ruffini. He looked forward to a new life for himself, Agostino, and Giovanni, who were going with him, and to less unhappiness in the future: "I do not expect much from life, and believe more in the power of resignation than in hope and desire. Let us love one another, now and always."[71] He spent New Year's Day in Grenchen with Agostino, Giovanni, and their few Swiss friends, and left the next day. It was a new year, a new life. People accused him of relying too much on the dagger; now he would put it away "until the next shock occurs."[72]

NOTES

Works frequently cited in the notes have been identified by the following abbreviations:

EN   *Edizione Nazionale. Scritti editi ed inediti di Giuseppe Mazzini* (1906–90), 106 vols.

RSR   *Rassegna Storica del Risorgimento*

SEI   *Scritti editi ed inediti di Giuseppe Mazzini* (1861–91), 18 vols.

1. EN, V, 377.
2. EN, IX, 120; *Appendice Epistolario*, EN, VI, 430.
3. Marguerite Mauerhofer, *Zeitschrift für Schweizerische Geschichte* (Zurich: Leeman, 1932), 47.
4. Carlo Cagnacci, *Giuseppe Mazzini e i fratelli Ruffini* (Porto Maurizio: Tipografia Berio, 1893), 16.
5. EN, V, 442.
6. Aldo Garosci, *Antonio Gallenga. Vita avventurosa di un emigrato dell'ottocento* (Turin: Centro Studi Piemontesi, 1979), I, 29–57.
7. Giuseppe Ricciardi, *Memorie autografe d'un ribelle* (Milan: Battezzati, 1973), 233, 237, 241–43, 258.
8. SEI, V, 419–24; IX, 117.
9. EN, V, 343, 347; IX, 45, 70, 86, 111–12, 121, 210–12.
10. Paul Harro-Harring, *Memorie sulla Giovine Italia e sugli ultimi avvenimenti di Savoia* (Milan: Società Editrice Dante Alighieri, 1913), 60.
11. EN, IX, 3–6, 30–31.
12. Cesar Vidal, *Mazzini et les tentatives révolutionnaires de la Jeune Italie dans les états sardes* (Paris: E. de Boccard, 1927), 156–59.
13. EN, II, 258; V, 93–94, 256, 295.
14. Giuseppe Silingardi, *Ricordi della vita di Emilio Usiglio* (Modena: G. T. Vincenzi e Nipoti, 1896), 51.
15. Mazzini's subsequent account of the Savoy expedition appears in his Autobiographical Notes, EN, LXXVII, 173–83.
16. Guido Ratti, "La Savoia e la Giovine Italia. Note e documenti sulla spedizione del 1834," in *Mazzini e i repubblicani italiani* (Turin: Istituto per la Storia del Risorgimento Italiano, Comitato di Torino, 1976), 70–86.
17. See Gerolamo Ramorino, *Précis des derniers événements de Savoie* (Paris: Dupont, 1834), 54–60, and Maria Luisa Rosati, *Carlo Alberto di Savoia e Francesco IV d'Austria d'Este* (Rome: Segati, 1907), 39, 95.
18. Contrary to legend, and to what Garibaldi himself stated in an early version of his memoirs, it is unlikely that he met Mazzini in Marseilles in 1833. Garibaldi's role in the events of 1834 is discussed in Gustavo Sacerdote, *La vita di Giuseppe Garibaldi* (Milan: Rizzoli, 1933), 88–95.
19. EN, LXXVII, 182–83.

20. EN, III, 353–55.

21. EN, IX, 309.

22. EN, IX, 246–47, 257.

23. EN, VI, 389.

24. EN, IX, 431.

25. EN, II, 256.

26. EN, VI, 9–10.

27. On Young Europe, see F. Gunther Eyck, "Mazzini's Young Europe," *Journal of Central European Affairs*, XVII (1958), 356–77, and Hans Gustav Keller, *Das 'Junge Europa', 1834–1836* (Zurich: Max Niehaus Verlag, 1938), 60–70.

28. For the Pact of Brotherhood and the charter of Young Europe, see EN, IV, 3–6, 9–21. Also, Franco Della Peruta, "Mazzini e la Giovine Europa," *Annali dell'Istituto Gian Giacomo Feltrinelli*, V (1962), 11–149.

29. EN, X, 258.

30. EN, X, 298.

31. EN, VI, 125.

32. EN, VI, 127.

33. EN, X, 141–48. Also, Livio Pivano, *Lamennais e Mazzini* (Turin: Associazione Mazziniana Italiana, 1958), 51–62.

34. EN, XI, 313–14.

35. EN, X, 323, 325–26.

36. EN, XCIV, 69. Also, *Appendice epistolare*, EN, I, 159.

37. EN, IV, 321–22.

38. EN, IV, 378.

39. EN, X, 267; IX, 289, 341.

40. EN, X, 141–48.

41. EN, X, 325–26.

42. EN, VII, 324.

43. EN, IX, 347; XI, 43–45. Also, Luigi Ambrosoli, *Giuseppe Mazzini. Una vita per l'unità d'Italia* (Manduria: Lacaita, 1993), 83.

44. EN, X, 66–68. Also, Edmondo Solmi, *Mazzini e Gioberti* (Milan: Albrighi-Segati, 1913), 137–59.

45. EN, X, 78.

46. EN, VI, 390.

47. EN, IX, 311.

48. For other Mazzinian publications, and for the secret network that distributed them in Italy and Switzerland, see Giuseppe Martinola, *Un editore luganese del Risorgimento: Giuseppe Ruggia* (Lugano: Fondazione Ticino Nostro, 1985), 159–60, 169–77.

49. EN, X, 97.

50. EN, X, 142–44.

51. *Appendice epistolare*, EN, I, 159.

52. EN, VI, 401–19.

53. Giovanni Ferretti, *Luigi Amedeo Melegari a Losanna* (Rome: Vittoriano, 1942), 49–50.

54. On Mazzini's instrumental interest in Swiss politics, see the comments by Marguerite Mauerhofer in *Zeitschrift für Schweizerische Geschichte*, 72–76.

55. EN, XI, 4, 6, 130, 251, 264–65, 288, 304, 317.

56. EN, XI, 95, 293–94.

57. EN, VIII, 81–104, 239–59.

58. For the text of the essay on music, see EN, VIII, 119–65. Also, Marion S. Miller, "Wagnerism, Wagnerians, and Italian Identity," in David C. Large and William Weber, eds., *Wagnerism in European Culture and Politics* (Ithaca, Cornell University Press, 1984), 168–69, and Lorenza Somogyi Bianchi, "La natura della musica nel peusiero di Mazzini." RSR, LXXXIII (July–September 1996), 295–322.

59. EN, XI, 157.

60. Cagnacci, *Giuseppe Mazzini e i fratelli Ruffini*, 36–43, 70–75, 140–43, 302–3.

61. EN, LXXVII, 237–39. Also, Alda Manghi, "Un'amicizia scandinava di G. Mazzini. Con un appendice di lettere mazziniane inedite," in *Studi in onore di Pietro Silva* (Florence: Le Monnier, 1957), 195–225.

62. EN, XIII, 113–28, 187–92; *Appendice*, EN, VII, Tome 1, 197.

63. Alessandro Cutolo, *Gaspare Rosales, vita romantica di un mazziniano* (Milan: Hoepli, 1938), 152.

64. EN, VII, 420. On his personal anguish, see EN, XI, 218; *Appendice*, EN, I, 254–55, 284.

65. EN, XII, 5.

66. *Appendice Epistolario*, EN, VI, 443.

67. EN, LXXVII, 248–59.

68. EN, XII, 113, 115.

69. *Appendice Epistolario*, EN, VI, 446.

70. EN, XII, 244, 338.

71. EN, XII, 263.

72. EN, XII, 268.

CHAPTER 5

Dark Before Dawn: England 1837–1848

England, the country that Mazzini would later call his real home, was virtually *terra incognita* to him. Being there because no continental country would have him and America was too far away, he had some strongly negative preconceptions. To him England was the land of shopkeepers, materialism, and monarchy. The accession to the throne of young Queen Victoria a few months after his arrival did not change his mind; a doddering old man had merely been replaced by an inexperienced young woman, and the British monarchy remained part of the conservative order. His sympathies went to the radical opposition, but he doubted that the tactic of working for reform through parliament could achieve results. As a Carbonaro in 1830 he had urged Daniel O'Connell to stir up revolt in Ireland, but even O'Connell expected redress from parliament. Sooner or later, he believed, England would experience a blood bath worse than that of 1793 in France.[1]

Mazzini and his three companions (Angelo Usiglio had joined them en route in France at Mazzini's request) traveled undisturbed by the police. The only unpleasant incident occurred at an inn, where they were harassed on account of their beards and clothes; the beards gave away their politics and their clothes their gentlemanly status, a combination that did not sit well with some plain folks. Mazzini fainted during the rough crossing of the Channel, but the final leg of the journey by riverboat up to the London docks lifted his spirits. The cold air was bracing and the scenery impressive. Steamers and sail ships crisscrossed the river in every direction, the banks bustled with activity, and

Daguerreotype of Mazzini, ca. 1846. From *Edizione Nazionale*, vol. XVI (Cooperativa Tipografico-Editrice Paolo Galeati of Imola, 1912–1924).

the shipyards, arsenal, and public buildings denoted power and affluence. As English passengers proudly pointed out the sights to the
visitors, Mazzini sensed the feeling of English pride. He was hurt when
he overheard somebody saying that the Italians did not fight as well as
the Poles, but he could not disagree. Shame on his own people, who were
sunk in lethargy. The spectacle in front of his eyes drew him out of his
reverie. There was trafficking everywhere, even inside the customs area,
where passengers were assailed by hawkers selling guides to the city at
exorbitant prices.[2]

The four came ashore on January 12, 1837. The weather was bad and
the surroundings unfamiliar. He knew a few Italians in England and
had some bookish knowledge of the language, but London was an
intimidating city. There were elegant shops, vast squares, and parks,
but the shops were too expensive, the squares barely visible in the fog,
and the parks impossible to enjoy in bad weather. The thick mud that
covered the streets made walking difficult. On foot, you ran into bellig-
erent drunks and aggressive panhandlers. The English did not seem to
like bearded foreigners any more than the French. They found a decent
hotel, but it was too expensive; so they moved in with Giambattista
Ruffini, a friend of Giuditta's, unrelated to Agostino and Giovanni, who
was already settled in cramped quarters at 24 Goodge Street, in a
run-down neighborhood around Tottenham Court Road. Usiglio wrote
to Rosales that Mazzini was his amiable self, but according to the
Ruffinis he also experienced moments of depression, when he flung "wild
and injurious insults" at his companions.[3] Mazzini was torn: he knew
he should be grateful for the freedom he found in England, but he did
not know what to do with it: "Here I have my individual freedom, but
what does it mean to me when I neither use it nor know how to use it.
My freedom here consists of being able to move about, but I would prefer
to be shut up somewhere."[4]

The only redeeming feature of Goodge Street was its proximity to the
British Museum. Mazzini took an immediate liking to that institution.
One of the first things he did in London was to ask for permission to
frequent the museum's unique library. In March he moved to better
quarters at 9 George Street, in a respectable section of the city between
Regent's and Hyde Parks. With rooms spread out on three floors of a
three-story building, Mazzini and his friends enjoyed the luxury of
having a dining room, a parlor, a separate room for a domestic, and
private bedrooms, except for Angelo and Giambattista who shared.[5]

Even with more room, the five still quarreled. Giambattista left,
pushed out by the Ruffinis who complained that he did nothing and ate
too much. The Ruffinis continued to complain about the food, the wine,
and the servants. Servants were a problem, perhaps because they did
not pay them enough, but also because no one knew how to deal with

them; the Ruffinis were too demanding, while Mazzini was too easygoing. One maid "would have crapped on [their] heads" had they not fired her, according to Agostino.[6] There was one violent quarrel between Agostino and Mazzini, ostensibly over household matters, but really over a great many things that were unspoken. Afterward, they retired to their respective rooms, Mazzini to weep, Agostino to brood: "Pippo lives in a world of make-believe, a slave to himself without knowing it. He is very good toward us, but irreconcilable differences of personality and certain fatal memories will always come between us. Political idealism has not made him a better person."[7]

At least for the time being, idealism had to yield to the pressing concerns of setting up a household, earning a living, and making connections. Usiglio took charge of domestic matters, shopped, and ran errands; Agostino and Giovanni sulked; Mazzini stayed up till all hours of the night, wrote, drank great quantities of coffee, chain-smoked cigars, and got up late. The resourceful Usiglio did not have a religious bone in his body, but in the emergency of the moment he remembered that he was Jewish, and that there were other Italian Jews in London. They came to the help of their coreligionist and his companions with offers of hospitality and employment. Their principal benefactors were the Rosellis, a Jewish banking family from Livorno, and the Nathans, merchants also from Livorno. Sara Nathan, eighteen years old at the time, became a lifelong friend of Mazzini and a most useful supporter, putting at his disposal her home and a good part of the family fortune that she inherited.[8] Maria was disconcerted. Broad-minded and tolerant though she was, she warned her son to be careful. She need not worry, he reassured her jokingly; he was perfectly safe dining with Jews: with Angelo at his side, if they wanted the blood of a Christian they would have to slay one of their own first.[9]

They lived precariously, but not in abject poverty, as Mazzini and legend would have it ("poor, poor, poor" is how he described his condition).[10] The penury was largely self-inflicted. His parents sent him 3,000 lire every three months, the less affluent Ruffinis sent an additional 2,000 and everything was remitted regularly by the Piedmontese consulate. In 1838 Maria established a spendthrift trust in the form of an annuity (*vitalizio*), to which she added regularly and substantially until her death. Five thousand lire every three months translated into an annual income of 800 British pounds; moreover, Usiglio was employed. The income should have been adequate at a time when a university professorship seldom paid more than 200 pounds a year. It was not adequate because Mazzini spent too much, not on himself, but on others. The beneficiaries of his largesse were other exiles who came to him for help, and the Ruffinis both in London and Genoa.

For the only time in his life Mazzini dabbled in business, perhaps to convince himself and his parents that he was turning over a new leaf, but also so he could ask for more money. Giacomo, who had already loosened his purse strings to finance the bogus mining venture in Switzerland, was ready, though not overjoyed, to do the same to help his son get established in England. It was thus that Mazzini became an importer of olive oil, salami, cheese, wine, truffles, pasta, antiques, laces, scarves, stuffed birds, and even an Egyptian mummy. His suppliers in Genoa were mostly his mother and relatives, and his customers were small London merchants, shopkeepers, and private families. The stuffed birds deal fell through because even his usually obliging mother balked at shipping such cargo. The mummy, intended for a museum, arrived too moth-eaten to be marketable. It caused quite a stir and frightened away one of his several hapless domestics, who swore that she saw the mummy wandering about the premises at night. Needless to say, he had underestimated the difficulties of doing business. Goods were delayed, damaged, or stolen in transit, customs procedures were complicated and time-consuming, and customers complained or did not pay their bills on time. It is said that one of his oil customers was Louis Napoleon, the future Napoleon III, then a political outcast like Mazzini. If true, that might explain their subsequent deadly enmity, for Mazzini was known for neglecting his clients and the prince for not paying his bills.[11]

Giacomo and Maria were baffled by their son's sudden interest in commerce, but did not discourage it. They hoped he would settle down, Maria even suggesting that he marry Giuditta, after the two women met in 1838.[12] Mazzini sometimes complained that he felt lonely, but showed no interest in domesticity. The point of his business ventures, he explained, was to attain the financial independence he needed, so he could devote his time to writing. That should have made it clear that he never intended to do anything but dabble in business. His father encouraged him to persevere in writing; he could succeed, he wrote his son, provided he was willing to write silly comedies to please the public and cultivate influential English people who could help him, not refugees at loose ends. He knew how to play the guitar, and that should help him in polite society.[13]

The correspondence between father and son shows that they were learning to discuss their differences without bitterness or rancor. Giacomo tried to shake his son's political beliefs with practical arguments, while the son tried to explain himself to his father. Giacomo thought that his son lived in a world of illusions, that the Italian people for whom he was ruining his life did not exist, that public opinion was turning away from revolution, and that he should come to terms with the world as it was. Why not give up on politics and pursue worldly success?

Nothing would make him happier than to retire knowing that his son was wealthy; he and his wife could then afford to have mass said every feast day in their own chapel; he "would be merry and content, and would bless my son, as I bless him now and embrace him always."[14]

Mazzini met his father partway, promising to keep to himself whatever he thought of British politics so he could live undisturbed in England, free to fight his battles elsewhere.[15] As for his father's advice on how to succeed, he did cultivate British acquaintances, but had no intention of writing to amuse the public. His ambition was to succeed as a cultural and political commentator, interpreting continental developments and being recognized by the British public as the voice of the new Italy. His decision to address a British audience was a fundamental one that set his course in England. Other exiles had gained acceptance in England at the cost of dropping out of the Italian movement; he had no intention of paying so high a price.

Despite his ambitions, his first paid contributions were not for the English press, but for the French journal *Le Monde*, whose editor was Lamennais. Mazzini published fifteen articles in *Le Monde* between March and June 1837, on British subjects such as penal and fiscal reform, the Irish question (he did not think the Irish had a good case for independence), the administration of Canada, the workings of parliament, and the prospects of the radical party. So, instead of making his debut as the voice of Italy in England as he had hoped, he appeared in print as the voice of England for the readers of a French journal. The *Le Monde* articles reflected his reservations about English society, but also his journalistic sense of what would please French readers. He described the English mind as rigidly compartmentalized, reluctant to cut across the artificial barriers it created among intellectual disciplines, uninterested in tracing problems to their root causes, and therefore incapable of broad conceptualizations and comprehensive solutions. With their mentality, the English people would neither score big victories nor suffer big defeats. Perhaps to be on the safe side, none of the articles was signed.[16]

His first English publication was an article on the state of Italian literature, which appeared in October 1837 in John Stuart Mill's *London and Westminster Review*. Lamenting England's lack of interest in things Italian, the article depicted the Italian literary scene as one of intellectual vitality and effervescence in spite of the wholesale political persecution of literary talent. It was unfortunate, he wrote, that the English were familiar only with the works of Alessandro Manzoni and Silvio Pellico, which conveyed too much Catholic resignation and passivity in the face of adversity. Giovanni Berchet and Gian Domenico Guerrazzi, on the other hand, deserved praise for their passion and virile patriotism. He acknowledged the talent of Giacomo Leopardi, but objected to that poet's pessimism, which he ascribed to the prevailing sense of political despair.[17] It was not the time to indulge in art for art's sake: "We cannot at the present day merely amuse ourselves with being *artists,* playing with sounds or forms, tickling only our senses, instead of pondering some germ of thought which may save us. We are scarcely disposed, living in the nineteenth century, to act like that people mentioned by Herodotus, who beguiled eighteen years of famine by playing with dice and tennis balls."[18] Although he was urged to write objectively by Mill and others, the articles and reviews that he wrote for the *British and Foreign Review*, *Tait's Magazine*, and *Monthly Chronicle* on French and Italian historical and literary topics were essentially "occasions" for the expression of his personal politics. As far as he was concerned, writers who repudiated principles and claimed objectivity were either in bad faith or under the influence of a strange hallucination. All the great writers that he admired, from Dante on to Lamennais, Mickiewicz, Byron, Hugo, George Sand, and Ugo Foscolo, filled their writings with political passion. For their commitment he could forgive many sins; there was no doubt in his mind that espousing the right political principles was more important than accepting the rules of conventional behavior.[19]

Foscolo was Mazzini's obsession, because more than any other modern writer he combined literary skill with political commitment. It was an interest of long standing, which intensified in London, where Foscolo spent the last years of his life. He had died there nearly penniless in 1828 and was still remembered when Mazzini arrived. He collected everything of his that he could find, including a trunk full of unpublished papers that he bought from the book dealer William Pickering with help from others. Foscolo occupied him for over ten years, from the latter part of his exile in Switzerland to 1846, when he published an edition of Foscolo's writings with the Florentine publisher Le Monnier. He never wrote the biography he had promised to his Tuscan friends who subsidized his labors. Instead, he brought together Dante and Foscolo by publishing a text of the Divine Comedy that had been partly annotated by Foscolo. Some of the annotations were actually Mazzini's, so it is hard to tell whether what Dante described as "the great citizen, the reformer, the poet of religion, the prophet of nationality, of Italy" is Foscolo's or Mazzini's; that particular Dante certainly resembles Mazzini.[20]

Mazzini was impatient with himself for writing for a public like the English, "all numbers and Bible." He complained that to communicate with such readers he had to fill two pages with facts for every ten lines of ideas; they simply showed no understanding for concepts such as "mission, humanity, continuous progress, socialism, and so on." It annoyed him that editors urged him to be clear, analytical, and practical, not idealistic and metaphysical like a German. The British, he commented, might excel as builders and manufacturers, but their "moral and intellectual faculties lag two hundred years behind the Continent."[21] He fretted, but struggled to adjust like any other immigrant, learning to curb his imagination and rhetoric. In the process of adjusting, he gained greater self-control and composure, and even learned to mimic the proverbial English aloofness and self-restraint. He forced himself to think calmly, to articulate his views rationally and deliberately, and not to challenge or show "true sentiments."[22]

In that effort Mazzini succeeded more than he realized. After years of living in England, others saw him as a perfect English gentleman, a person of routine habits and sparing gestures, strolling "always dressed in black, black necktie worn high without collar, black cylinder top hat and black gloves, gold chain and watch."[23] George Meredith, an admirer of Mazzini, modeled the character of the political agitator after him in his novel *Vittoria*, depicting him in an imaginative pose, staring out over the plains of Lombardy from high up in the Alps: "The passions were absolutely in harmony with the intelligence. He had the English manner; a remarkable simplicity contrasting with the demonstrative outcries and gesticulations of his friends when they joined him on the height."[24] It was a triumph of mimetic art. Of all the imaginative disguises attributed to Mazzini, by far the most accomplished was that of gentlemanly imperturbability.

In November of 1837, Mill's future wife, Harriet Taylor, introduced Mazzini to Thomas Carlyle and his wife Jane Welsh Carlyle. Thomas Carlyle was no democrat, but his home in Chelsea attracted talented men and women of all political persuasions. Mazzini became a frequent and regular visitor; from August of 1840, when he moved to 5 King's Road, he was a short walking distance from the Carlyles. In the Carlyles' drawing room he was a reserved and often silent observer, unless provoked by Carlyle, who relished drawing him out. Carlyle's obsession with the dominant personalities of history, his admiration for elites, and the paternalism of his social philosophy clashed with Mazzini's faith in the people. In January of 1840, the *Monthly Chronicle* published Mazzini's review of Carlyle's *History of the French Revolution*, in which he observed that "Mr. Carlyle does not recognize in a people, and *a fortiori* not in humanity, a collective life, a collective end: he recognizes, and is occupied with individuals only; at least we have a right to infer this from his work."[25] Although he was apprehensive that Carlyle might take offense, the review, critical but respectful in tone, actually improved their relationship.

There was no need for Mazzini to worry about Mrs. Carlyle's feelings; her liking for him was unmistakable. He loved her like a sister, he wrote to his mother, but thought that she perhaps loved him differently, with womanly intensity. Agostino, ever the clinical observer, was sure that Jane Carlyle loved Mazzini with womanly intensity: "Poor soul, I truly feel sorry for her. . . . I foresaw what would happen. . . . I know of no worse form of human egoism than that which makes a man show off all his seductive charm of manner, appearance, and disposition when dealing with a woman, and then protests and complains if someone calls it making love."[26] Mazzini explained the attraction impersonally; women were attracted to him, he said, because he defended their rights: "I have and continue to defend women against unfair charges and mistreatment by many men."[27]

Mazzini's support for women's causes is a matter of record, and English feminists of his and later generations considered him an inspirational figure. One suspects, however, that in some cases he cultivated women for the sake of the men to whom they were attached. Jane Carlyle is an example; others are Elizabeth Ashurst and her daughters Matilda Biggs and Caroline Stansfeld, whose husbands championed Mazzinian causes in parliament and the press. Susan Milner Gibson's husband Thomas was a member of parliament, and Clementia Taylor's husband Peter Alfred was an influential businessman and politician. These couples, along with others like William and Emily Shaen, and William and Catherine Macready, served him as channels to the British public and to the inner circles of political power.[28] When sentiment touched on politics, Mazzini displayed the kind of self-control that one doctor described as "sexual anesthesia."[29] A close collaborator described him as a disciple of the Greek philosopher Xenocrates, who was known for his asceticism: "I saw that portent more than once, but could not admire it because it was odd and beyond human power. Mazzini unmanned [*non più uomo*] was a frightening sight."[30]

These diagnoses were mistaken, however, for we know that Mazzini was not "unmanned" or indifferent to women. Like Parsifal, he may have repressed and sublimated his drives in pursuit of some higher goal, but a curious and often overlooked episode from this period of his life suggests that the sublimation was not automatic. The first reference to the woman he called Susan or Susanna appears in a letter to his mother dated September 28, 1837. The very next day, he told his mother, he would hold a newborn child at baptism. A week later he wrote again to say that his godson was named Procida Joseph Henry Tancioni. This was an amusing letter, describing the reluctance of the officiating clergyman to name someone Procida, and how Mazzini had assured him that it was a good Christian name. The story he related to his mother, which is accepted by biographers, describes the mother of the infant as a homeless young woman who had appeared on his doorstep one day, hungry and desperate. Moved to pity, he had convinced his landlady to take her in as a servant. Susan then married an Italian expatriate named Pio Tancioni, who worked as a restorer of antiquities in the British Museum. He wrote that the child was theirs.[31]

Yet, information provided by Mazzini raises questions about the accuracy of his account to his mother. He reported that Susan's father, stepmother, and several other guests attended the baptismal reception. Could Susan, with parents and friends at a baptismal feast in September, have been homeless the preceding January? When did she meet her husband? Nine months before the birth of the child she had thrown herself at Mazzini's mercy. Did Mazzini know Tancioni, who had left Italy in 1831 after being implicated in Carbonari conspiracies, and arrange the marriage? If so, whose child was it?

There were rumors that Mazzini was the father, but it is almost impossible to imagine him in the role of sexual predator, taking advantage of a helpless woman like Susan. Yet, he was in a precarious emotional state at the time of his arrival in England, and a lapse from his customary standard of behavior is perhaps not unthinkable. Other explanations are possible. Susan might have been carrying another man's child when Mazzini met her, perhaps Tancioni's. In that case, his looking after her would indeed have been an act of kindness, exceeded only by Tancioni's willingness to marry her if the child was not his. Whatever the case, Tancioni was in despair only a few months after the birth of the child.[32]

Suspicions of a sexual relationship between Mazzini and Susan were kindled by their closeness. They addressed one another as Susan and Joseph. In August of 1840 Mazzini and Giovanni Ruffini moved in with the Tancionis at the address on King's Road in Chelsea, after the all-male household at 9 George Street broke up. Mazzini and Susan lived under the same roof at various times both before and after Pio abandoned his family. When he left, Susan had two children (another son was born in 1844) and she depended heavily on Mazzini. The firstborn, baptized Procida but called Joseph, was always Mazzini's particular concern; he was still looking after him in the 1860s, when the young man was out of work.

Susan followed Mazzini to Europe in 1848 and was arrested in Genoa in 1849 on charges that she had cohabited with him; they lived again together in Switzerland where she joined him after her release. "Dear Susan," he wrote to her in July of 1849 from Geneva, "I had hoped to find you here. Come on, I will meet you at Lausanne and there we shall decide. But at all events, we shall live together for a time. Ever your, Joseph."[33] In Switzerland he paid her rent, provided her with a domestic, and introduced her as Madame. His Italian friends who knew of the relationship reserved judgment, but not the upper-class Englishwomen who idolized him and worked for his causes. Offended by such familiarity with a woman who was officially his housekeeper, they may have pressured Mazzini into distancing himself from her. When he returned to England in 1850, she remained in Europe for several years before returning to England in 1858. Mazzini was genuinely fond of the "poor proletarian" who was devoted to him, and resented the hostility of his English friends toward her, but he did keep Susan away from England.[34] She stayed in Europe reluctantly, finding it hard to raise her children abroad and wishing that they could have an English education. This obscure woman deserves a place on the roster of Mazzinian martyrs.

THE CHALLENGE FROM MODERATES

The difficulties of gaining acceptance in Britain paled in comparison with those Mazzini faced trying to maintain his credibility as a leader in Italy. An obstacle more serious than the problem of long-distance communication was the preference for moderate solutions shown by increasing numbers of reform-minded Italians after the disappointments of revolution. Government repression played a role, but there was also a genuine interest in risk-free reforms that might come in time from governments in power. The call for patience could be heard in Silvio Pellico's widely read and acclaimed account of his years spent in an Austrian jail, *My Prisons*, published in 1832. Mazzini found Pellico's book disappointing, but he was positively enraged by Ferdinando Dal Pozzo's *Of the Happiness That Italians May and Should Expect from Austrian Government* (1833). Dal Pozzo was a former Carbonaro, but he had been abroad since 1821, and time and a surfeit of exile politics had mellowed him. He is seldom remembered, but it is just possible that what he had to say was more representative of public opinion and popular expectations than Mazzini's insistent call for revolution.[35]

What Dal Pozzo had to say (and the title of the book was his message) alarmed Mazzini, who feared that Austria might consolidate its position by a policy of concessions and gradual reform, a fear that increased after many political exiles took up Austria's offer of political amnesty in 1838. Better that Austria should wield the whip than that it should endear itself with acts of false generosity. Equally worrisome was what was happening in Piedmont, where Charles Albert was beginning to promote economic and trade reforms, spend money on public works, and modernize the army and the administration. The new benevolent image of Charles Albert appealed even to Eleonora Ruffini, who began to explore the possibility of obtaining a royal pardon for her two sons abroad.

Governments were willing to experiment with reform because they felt less threatened by revolution than in the early 1830s, when repression was their immediate concern. Mazzini could not decide whether Austria or Charles Albert posed the worst threat; he suspected that they might be working in unison. When the rumor spread that Charles Albert was preparing for war against Austria, Mazzini railed at "incorrigible politicians who seek a liberator in one who has executed and dispersed those who tried to be liberators."[36] To his disappointment, diplomacy kept the peace or managed to isolate conflicts in trouble spots like Belgium, the Balkans, and the Near East. In the absence of dynastic conflicts, change would have to come from popular wars, but there was none in sight.[37] He looked for signs of international tensions, and fretted that he would be forgotten or that others would claim his mantle. He was upset to learn that an organization calling itself the Sons of Young Italy was active in southern Italy, capitalizing on his name but attacking religion and private property. That kind of materialistic atheism he could not condone. The founder of the Sons of Young Italy was Benedetto Musolino, a former member of Young Italy; he adopted the name for its prestige, but he also regarded Mazzini as a weak thinker indifferent to social problems.[38]

Another and more formidable challenge came from Nicola Fabrizi, whom Mazzini knew well. Fabrizi had been imprisoned in 1831, but had escaped to Marseilles, where he joined Young Italy; later he had taken part in Mazzini's Savoy expedition. From Switzerland he had gone to Spain to fight the Carlists and then moved on to Malta, where, with British acquiescence, he had set up a paramilitary organization called the Italic Legion. He was as much a conspirator as Mazzini and a better commander. He was willing to let Mazzini theorize and propagandize for the movement, but he wanted to be in charge when the time came to take to the field. That posed a problem for Mazzini, who insisted on unity of command and questioned Fabrizi's tactics.

Both Mazzini and Fabrizi were staunchly republican, and both believed in armed insurrection; but while Mazzini looked to the north, Fabrizi looked to the south, particularly to Sicily, where an uprising broke out in the summer of 1837. Although the Sicilian uprising did not aim at unifying the country, the very fact that it had occurred when no one else stirred seemed to vindicate Fabrizi's faith in the southern strategy. Mazzini was not convinced that the south was ready or that the time was right, but the Sicilian uprising, the presence of the Sons of Young Italy, and the evidence of other conspiratorial activities going on in the peninsula were food for thought. Could he afford to remain inactive? What could he do from where he was? On May 24, 1839, he wrote to Melegari that his strategy for the coming decade would be to organize abroad in order to intervene in Italy, banking on a new generation and on the prestige attached to the names of Young Europe and Young Italy.[39]

Young Europe was little more than a name, but it was a name capable of inspiring and uniting disparate elements in places as far away as Asia Minor, North Africa, and the New World. It was heard in South America, where Giuseppe Garibaldi and others of various nationalities were attracted by the ideal of international solidarity and came together to fight for causes that had nothing to do with their countries of origin. Mazzini counted more on the name of Young Italy to organize Italians abroad, and to bring them together regardless of social status. It was not a novel approach, because workers had been present in Young Italy from the beginning, but the effort to reach out to workers was now deliberate and explicit. The most promising places were Switzerland, Belgium, England, and the Americas, where Italian working-class immigration was just beginning.[40]

Mazzini, now thirty-four, aimed at a younger cohort with no memory of earlier failures. He would have liked Melegari to take charge of organizing Young Italy on the continent, but Melegari, recently married to a Swiss woman (who once had been in love with Mazzini), showed no interest in resuming a political relationship with him; Melegari's interests were now domestic and professional. Mazzini then turned to Giuseppe Lamberti in Paris, who agreed to take charge of the French section, to which Mazzini assigned the important role of competing with the socialists for the support of workers. The truth was that many of his old collaborators either had dropped out of politics or had reservations about rejoining his movement. Agostino and Giovanni Ruffini distanced themselves for personal reasons. Benza liked the quiet life, practiced law, and had supplanted Mazzini in the affections of the much older Eleonora Ruffini. Gallenga was in London, but, mellowed by the experience of exile, talked of serving any prince who would champion the cause of Italian independence. Only Mazzini remained "monomaniacally" tied to the past. That was Giacomo Mazzini's clinical description for his son's obsession with politics. Mazzini gave a religious twist to the diagnosis: "This fixation with Italy is a command from God."[41]

The announcement that Young Italy was to be reactivated was made in London on April 30, 1840. This second Young Italy, as it is sometimes called, was envisaged by Mazzini as a renewal rather than as a refounding. It still addressed the young, but the young were now defined as those who were no more than eighteen to twenty years old, too young to remember the disappointments that had sapped the vitality of the first Young Italy.[42] In practice, Mazzini had no choice but to call on older collaborators. Lamberti in Paris was again paired with the even older but respected Pietro Giannone, so old and befuddled now that some thought him mentally incapacitated. Federico Campanella, living in Marseilles, agreed to take on the difficult task of reviving the network in Italy. Two other older exiles, Felice Foresti in New York and Giambattista Cuneo in Montevideo, were to organize Italians in North and South America respectively.

The new Young Italy was to be flanked by a Union of Italian Workers (*Unione degli operai italiani*) and would publish a periodical for workers. Twelve issues of *Apostolato Popolare* came out from November 1840 to

September 1843, and achieved a respectable circulation of some two thousand copies distributed or sold in England, Europe, and the Americas. Perhaps Mazzini had seen enough of conflicts among workers of different nationalities to conclude that efforts at international organization were doomed to failure. Workers who spoke the same language were much more likely to help one another than workers of different nationalities. Cooperation was a worthy ideal, but without a national identity and a national organization of their own Italian workers would be doubly victimized by their masters and by workers of other nationalities.

Organizing workers separately was for Mazzini a prerequisite, if they were to develop organizational skills and become self-sufficient. At the same time, he did not want to sacrifice the goal of cooperation across class lines. Hence his insistence that as long as workers lacked the skills or resources to look after their own interests they had a right to expect help from the middle and upper classes, who had the means and the education. Educated Italians were morally obliged to help their less fortunate compatriots, until they could stand on their own. This paternalism flowed logically from labor tactics that were based on national identity and collaboration; it was present in Mazzini's social philosophy from the beginning, and was not a reaction to the later efforts of Karl Marx and others to organize workers internationally along class lines, as some historians claim. He told workers that "if the revolution is to succeed, it must be carried out *for you* and *with you*, while all the previous revolutions have been attempted *not for you* and *without you*."[43] But he did not advise them to carry out the revolution by themselves; to do so would have compromised the tactic of cooperation among classes that was at the heart of his strategy of revolution.

The principle of autonomous organization applied also to women, for whom Mazzini envisaged an important political role both within and outside his movement. In their case, however, he addressed himself primarily to women of the middle and upper classes, perhaps because he feared antagonizing male workers if he attempted to organize the women who were their competitors in the workforce. Although he did find support among women in Genoa and elsewhere in Italy, it was mostly English women from the middle and upper classes who rallied to him, probably because he offered them opportunities for philanthropic work that were socially acceptable; his paternalism and their "maternalism" matched. Mazzini believed that cooperation between men and women in the same organization would have to wait. At some point women would be able to stand on their own and deal with men on a basis of equality, even if others derided them "as they once derided the poor workers, though now they begin to take them seriously."[44] To stand on their own, however, they must develop skills and confidence by participating in single-gender activities and organizations where they would not be overshadowed by men. Separately organized, women could still be part of his revolutionary coalition, along with workers and all educated, progressive-minded people regardless of class affiliation.

To provide unity for Young Italy Mazzini stressed its collective character, referring to it in one instance as *la cosa nostra* (our thing). He reserved for himself the role of "moral head," assuring the chiefs of the various *congreghe* (sections) that they would have ample autonomy. In practice he exercised as much personal supervision as distance and the means of communications allowed.[45] He envisaged a long-term campaign of education and propaganda to train a new generation of leaders and to enlarge popular support for the revolution. That was Young Italy's tactic throughout its existence, but it was especially true of Young Italy in its second phase, when revolution seemed a distant prospect. The converts of the 1840s were of a different breed from those of the preceding decade. Generally ten to twenty years younger, they were a more ambitious and worldly lot. Many rose to high positions in public and private life. While first-generation Mazzinians like Melegari who went on to prominence were fairly rare, the second generation produced four prime ministers (Depretis, Cairoli, Crispi, and Zanardelli), countless other ministers of state, military men, businessmen, and prominent intellectuals.

There are no reliable membership figures for the new Young Italy, but the evidence suggests that Mazzini did not aim for the kind of following that Young Italy had in the early 1830s. In the 1840s he envisaged Young Italy more as a church of true believers and as a training ground for the elites of the future than as a broadly based organization. Federico Campanella did not understand that tactic and was upset by his friend's half-hearted commitment to large-scale recruiting in Italy, where he thought it should be most active. "Young Italy," he complained, "gives the appearance of being an association outside Italy to mislead and keep content those inside Italy."[46] Recruitment efforts in Italy were hampered by all sorts of obstacles. Government vigilance and fears of retaliation were obvious problems, but there was also competition from moderates, who found Mazzini too radical, and from radicals, who found him too moderate. Mazzini's drawing card was his growing reputation. As memory of past failures faded, Mazzini became something of a cult figure among young radicals, replacing Buonarroti who had died in 1838.[47]

The comparison with Buonarroti is apt, because even in his new phase Mazzini pursued the tactics of conspiracy and centralization, although with very different motives and aims. He had more than education and propaganda in mind when he relaunched Young Italy. As he told Benza in May 1840, "in starting all over I have a double intent: I want to do and I want to prevent others from doing; to do according to our beliefs if possible, and to prevent others from doing differently."[48] To remain politically inactive would have meant yielding to newcomers with whose programs Mazzini disagreed; these included both political moderates who welcomed amnesties, economic reforms, and political concessions, and republicans more radical than he was.[49]

The moderates were the more immediate threat. To them, a constitutional monarchy was better than a republic, a loose federation better than unity, diplomacy better than revolution. They appealed because they seemed so much more reasonable and practical than those who were moved by higher ideals worthy of Italy's historic mission. Yet, Mazzini argued that the moderates were the ones who lacked realism and lived in a dream world, because there were no monarchs of historic stature in Italy to carry out their plans, because Austria would never surrender its Italian possessions peaceably, and because the Roman Catholic Church would never espouse popular causes. The only realistic course was the one he proposed: A "new republicanism" based on a religious commitment to human solidarity. Only his religious republicanism brought together the two antagonistic principles of individual rights and community obligations.[50]

The theme of social religion was now intensified by personal experience and by reflection. The death of his sister Cichina in 1838 left him feeling more isolated and vulnerable. He thought of writing a novel entitled "Relics of an Unknown Man," to show how religious faith had rescued him from despair. It would have been his answer to the hero of his youth, Foscolo's Jacopo Ortis, who had surrendered to despair. There was an evident revival of interest in religion in the 1840s, which he followed with interest and took to mean that the world could not do without religion. The problem was that established religions no longer met the needs of individuals and of society. There was no true religion "except in the hearts of the righteous few."[51] He reread the Koran and modified its message: "God is God, and Humanity is his prophet."[52] God no longer spoke through prophets or popes, but through the apostles of the people. His close association with Polish political exiles like Charles Stolzman and Stanislas Worcell confirmed his belief in the redemptive power of suffering. The Slavic populations of Eastern Europe earned his respect because in persecution they drew political strength from religious faith. Their will to act came not from philosophy or social science, but from religion. Even the Catholic Church could still play a role in history, but only if it moved toward the people, became democratic, rejected papal authority, and vested supreme power in a popular council (*consiglio dell'umanità*) elected by the body of the faithful.[53] With such a system of government, Catholicism would achieve the balance between freedom and authority that eluded other religions.

Mazzini did not expect the Catholic Church to reform itself, and did not wait for the publication of Vincenzo Gioberti's famous treatise *The Moral and Civil Primacy of the Italians* (1843) to castigate the notion aired in that book that the papacy would support the movement for Italian independence. Gioberti and the Neo-Guelphs for whom he spoke held out the prospect of national independence without war or revolution, to be achieved with the cooperation of Austria and its Italian dependencies. The pope, shorn of temporal power, would serve as president of a confederation of Italian princes. Mazzini replied that Austria would never consent, that there were no Italian princes capable of carrying out such a design, and that the proposal was therefore wildly utopian and unrealistic. The man who was always accused of being a visionary thus turned the tables on his critics. Especially galling was Gioberti's appropriation of the idea of Italian world primacy, "the most beautiful theme that I know, which he fills with ultra-Roman Catholicism, praise for Charles Albert, and all possible stupidities."[54] If it ever came about, Gioberti's Italy would be a travesty of the revolutionary Italy of Mazzini's Third Rome.

The moderates weighed in again with the publication of another learned tome, Cesare Balbo's *On the Hopes of Italy* (1844). Balbo believed neither in Italian primacy nor in popular revolution. The argument of his book was that the solution to the Italian question could be achieved diplomatically by compensating Austria for the loss of its Italian possessions with territorial concessions in Eastern Europe at the expense of the Ottoman Empire, which, Balbo assumed, was on the verge of dissolution; the keys to the Italian question were in the Black Sea. The major beneficiary of Balbo's plan would be Piedmont, which, with its disciplined army, its trained bureaucracy, and its diplomacy, would dominate a federation of Italian states. Mazzini paid less attention to Balbo than to Gioberti, and at least credited Balbo with good intentions, perhaps because he expected nothing better from a Piedmontese nobleman. Balbo's proposals, he wrote, simply made him nauseous.[55]

To deal with these new currents, Young Italy had to be disciplined and united, expand, absorb other societies, find support among intellectuals and workers, and make itself visibly the sole representative of the Italian national movement. Its members must set an example of probity in their personal lives, refraining from gambling, drinking, or womanizing, and repaying their personal debts. That he did not forbid debts outright was no doubt due to the fact that he was in debt up to his ears, borrowing and pawning his personal possessions to raise money for Young Italy until he had no credit or possessions left, and faced going to debtors' prison. It was also a difficult time for his parents, who had lost money in some bad investments. Lamberti was his last resort, not because Lamberti had any money of his own, but because he was respected and could intercede for him with those who did have money to lend. Lamberti came through with 5,000 francs, leveraged from Tuscan friends who were well aware of what the money was to be used for. The experience of begging and scraping was not to Mazzini's liking: "Money is shit, if you will allow me to use the street term," he wrote to his mother in June of 1843.[56]

THE POLITICS ON REVOLUTION

There was competition in Italy, but in England he was acknowledged as the voice of liberal Italy. The Carlyle connection loosened somewhat as his circle of acquaintances expanded. In October of 1843 the *Foreign Review* featured a second article by Mazzini on Carlyle, which insisted on criticizing Carlyle's individualistic philosophy: "Mr. Carlyle comprehends only the individual; the true sense of the unity of the human race escapes him."[57] That same month Mazzini moved from Chelsea, where he was a neighbor of the Carlyles, to 47 Devonshire Street, near Queen Square; the physical distance from the Carlyles mirrored an emotional distance from them. The Tancionis followed him to a nearby location, so that Susan could continue to look after his needs and he after her and the children. Pio was still with them, and Mazzini had found a use for him as secretary of the workers' union, to replace the elderly Filippo Pistrucci, but the marriage was in trouble. The new location was more convenient because closer to the heart of London, where his renewed political activities often took him on business. From then on Mazzini lived alone; the image of solitude was appropriate to somebody who wanted to be seen as moving men by the power of the spirit.

In 1844 Mazzini met the Ashurst family and became a regular visitor at their home at Muswell Hill. The patriarch of the family was the solicitor William Henry Ashurst, a "free-thinking Christian" and political activist who campaigned for radical causes, including the emancipation of women. Some said he had no choice, for four of his five children were women, and they were educated, talented, and outspoken. One of his daughters dared to visit Mazzini unaccompanied, and then introduced him to the rest of the family, which welcomed him as a celebrity and a kindred spirit. He was *their* celebrity, for they monopolized him socially, flattered him, and made him the centerpiece of their drawing room. They called him their angel, or simply Mazz. Mazz took it all in good grace. "They kiss my hands," he wrote his mother, "embrace me if need be, bring me flowers; in other words, they are sisters to me, loving sisters."[58] Jane Carlyle was acerbic: "Mazzini is pretty well . . . having got up to the ears in a *good* twadly [sic] family of the name of Ashurst, who have plenty of money and help 'his things' and *toady* him till I think it has rather gone to his head." She wondered what else the women did for him, "while the men give *capital* towards his *Institutions* and adopt 'the new ideas' at his bidding."[59]

The most devoted of the four sisters was Emilie Ashurst, who later married Sidney Milner Hawkes, divorced, and then remarried to the Italian Carlo Venturi. Emilie Ashurst Hawkes Venturi made it her life's mission to spread the religion of Mazzini. She was his devoted disciple, but Mazzini seemed more attached to her older sister Caroline, who was married to James Stansfeld, a member of parliament and the owner of a beer brewery where Mazzini hatched some of his headier plots. Someone has clipped many passages from the surviving letters that Mazzini wrote to Caroline, but even with those excisions what remains is suggestive, for it shows Mazzini in the act of verbal lovemaking, as in this revealing passage: "My being merry yesterday night when I came in, gloomy when I saw you, calm and at ease again as soon as you came near me smiling, ought to have explained more of me to you than the hurried words we had together."[60]

At the other end of the social scale, Mazzini turned his attention to working-class immigrants. Soon after his arrival, he had begun to notice the presence of Italians who had little in common with the political expatriates he knew. The better off were hat makers, clock makers, tailors, and restaurant owners, who were more or less regularly employed, but there was also an itinerant population of fish and fruit peddlers, figurine makers, fair workers, acrobats, and organ-grinders, who worked the streets of London. They clustered around Hatton Garden and Saffron Hill, in the cheap rent section of Holborn, within striking distance of the City and the West End, where they plied their trades. Marginal in every respect, they were barely distinguishable from vagrants and other social undesirables. He worried for them, but also for the discredit that they cast on the good name of Italy.[61]

Mazzini prided himself on frequenting a cross section of society: dinner with the Carlyles one day and with his laundress the next. Without preaching or proselytizing, he helped the poor and illiterate Italians with their correspondence and with small legal matters, and interceded on their behalf with his influential friends; he even paid their medical bills. Like a good political boss, he won them over by making himself useful. In his own way, he was sensitive to their economic plight and mindful of their sense of dignity, never asking them to pay political dues out of fear that they would go away rather than admit their poverty: "If we ask our people for money, especially the workers, instead of helping them as we should, we risk losing them from shame or want."[62]

In the spring of 1840 a group of workers came to ask for Mazzini's help in setting up a school. Rather than accede immediately to their request, he urged them to start a fund for the school with their own

money. It was a clever condition, for when they did set up a fund, and
kept contributing to it for over a year, he knew that they were in earnest,
and he had the evidence to convince his English friends that these poor
workers were committed to improving themselves.[63] It took time, but on
November 10, 1841, the Free School for Workers opened with fifty-one
students, mostly children of figurine makers, woodworkers, organ-
grinders, and other street entertainers. Located at 5 Greville Street,
Hatton Garden, in the heart of the Italian section, the school was a hit
with the children, their families, the sponsors, and the press. Within six
months the enrollment reached two hundred, including seven girls.
Writing implements, books, and supplies were distributed gratis; lessons were held evenings and on Sunday afternoons, when the children
did not have to work. They came to school tired and dirty, and sometimes
they fell asleep, but Mazzini noted with satisfaction that "when expected
to learn, they try their best."[64]

The school was supervised by a board of directors consisting of
Mazzini and two other Italians, Filippo Pistrucci, a painter, engraver,
and improviser of verse whose son Scipione was one of Mazzini's most
devoted followers, and the Tuscan exile Luigi Bucalossi. Teaching was
in Italian, done by volunteers who were also political expatriates,
including prominent figures like Antonio Gallenga, Carlo Pepoli, and
Dante Gabriele Rossetti. Mazzini ran the school, raised funds, and did
his share of teaching; his favorite subjects were geography ("it teaches
Italian unity") and astronomy ("it proves that God exists"). He had
followed developments in teaching and pedagogy since his student days
in Genoa, when he had made contact with progressive Tuscan educators
like Enrico Mayer, Raffaello Lambruschini, and Pietro Thouar, who were
experimenting with new methods of popular education. Mazzini believed in the hands-on approach and in relating learning to everyday
life. To teach hands-on, he bought a "pneumatic machine" (probably an
air compressor) and an "electrical machine" (probably a battery), with
which he administered shocks to the students to teach them about the
power of electricity.[65] The school published a paper called *Il Pellegrino*
(The Pilgrim), which was distributed free of charge to students and their
families. The social highlight of the school year was the annual dinner
on the anniversary of the school's opening. It consisted of pasta, cheese,
and no more than one pint of beer per person, regardless of age. Mazzini
insisted that the teaching staff, himself included, wait on the students
and their families in a democratic reversal of roles.

Many suspected that school was a pretext for teaching the four R's
(reading, 'riting, 'rithmetic, and revolution), including Antonio Panizzi,
a well-connected expatriate who would later be appointed chief librarian
of the British Museum, and Carlyle, who called the school "a nest of
young conspirators" and cautioned his wife to stay away.[66] The *padroni*

who employed many of the students objected when the school sponsored a society for the protection of apprentices. Opposition also came from the Italian clergymen attached to the Piedmontese and Tuscan chapels, who put pressure on students and their families to boycott the school and who organized hostile demonstrations. Mazzini once rushed to the school to confront the demonstrators and turned a particularly unruly one over to a waiting bobby, warning him "never again to come busting our balls . . . where we command."[67] The incident made him appreciate the benefits of living under British law.

When public opinion supported the school, the opposition decided to change its tactics; instead of trying to shut it down, they decided to open one of their own. Mazzini showed his new understanding of public relations by welcoming their decision, and taking credit for Italian children having two schools instead of just one. Had his enemies succeeded in shutting down his school, he said, they would have shown the poor "that there is only one way for them to succeed: with the gun."[68] The Free School for Workers survived even after Mazzini distanced himself from it, but it lost much of its momentum. By 1861, when it was taken over by the Italian government, its enrollment was down to twelve. Italy was independent by then, and Mazzini felt that it was the responsibility of its government to educate the children of Italian workers abroad.[69]

Even more than the four R's, the school taught the ethic of class cooperation. Most of the children were temporary immigrants, and Mazzini counted on them to remember when they went back home that they owed their education to the efforts of middle-class Italians like himself. He believed that education had the power to change social attitudes. With similar schools elsewhere, he wrote, "who can predict the ties of love and reciprocal trust that will be formed between the two classes in Italy?"[70] Similar schools did open elsewhere, in Paris, Boston, and New York, but apparently with less success. In the United States instruction was in English rather than Italian, because Mazzini did not expect emigrants to North America to return to Italy in significant numbers. Instead, he hoped that their presence and good behavior would create sympathy for the cause of Italian independence among Americans, who would then support the movement financially and politically.[71]

It was not an idle prospect, for Mazzini was looking for new sources of financial support to resume conspiracy in Italy. He was broke, and rather than rely solely on affluent individuals as he had done in the 1830s, he relied on organized groups and broadly based fund-raising efforts: "The only power that counts in politics is the power of money; whoever succeeds in getting it will unify the country."[72] This was a major conceptual breakthrough for one who usually insisted on the power of the spirit, and it may explain why he wanted to reassure those who had money to give that republicans were not wild beasts out to slaughter the rich or deprive them of their possessions. On the contrary Mazzini argued, republicans wanted more opportunity for everyone, but especially for those who had the talent to enrich themselves. Everyone would benefit from the abolition of trade barriers that republicans proposed, from the reduction of wasteful royal expenditures, from government policies to stimulate private investments, and from tax reductions that would put more money in the hands of consumers.[73]

In 1842 he made contact with an American religious group, the Christian Alliance. Headed by the reverend Lyman Beecher, the Christian Alliance was a Protestant missionary organization that wanted "to promote religious freedom, and to diffuse useful and religious knowledge among the natives of Italy and other Papal Countries."[74] The Alliance promised to support Mazzinian schools, but it was of even greater interest to Mazzini that it wanted to deprive the Pope of temporal power and was willing to support revolution in Italy in pursuit of that objective. The plan was simple: He would help smuggle Bibles into Italy in return for dollars with which he would buy guns. This strange alliance between red republicans and Protestant fundamentalists never lived up to Mazzini's expectations, but it created considerable alarm. When the pope heard of it, he urged bishops and priests to seize all copies of the Bible "printed in the vulgar tongue."[75] Through his contacts in the Christian Alliance Mazzini met Margaret Fuller in London in 1846. An important figure among the Transcendentalists of New England, Fuller brought Mazzini to the attention of her influential friends. The relationship was of minor importance in Mazzini's life, but it was a development that increased his interest in the United States as a potential supporter of revolution in Europe.

South America figured differently in Mazzini's plans. Rio de Janeiro, Montevideo, Buenos Aires, and other cities of South America had large concentrations of Italians, who came mostly from Genoa and Piedmont. Drawn there by the revival of Genoese trade that began in the 1820s and by political persecution, the Italians of South America, unlike those of North America, stayed in touch with Italy and Italian politics, to the concern of the Austrian, Piedmontese, and Papal governments, which began political surveillance of Italian expatriates in the early 1830s. Seasoned political veterans gave Giuseppe Garibaldi a hero's welcome when he arrived in Rio at the end of 1835 as second in command of a vessel flying the French flag. They outfitted a small boat, ostensibly to fish, but in reality to prey on Piedmontese ships plying those waters, named it after Mazzini, and put Garibaldi in charge. Garibaldi requested letters of marque from Mazzini to give official republican sanction to his depredations, thereby acknowledging Mazzini's status as guide and mentor. The future liberator of Italy thus began as a privateer who was authorized to rob by an outlaw who claimed to speak for a nonexistent republic. The pickings were slim and Garibaldi was soon looking for more promising ventures. First he joined the losing side in the war between the Brazilian government and the breakaway republic of Rio Grande do Sul, whose effort at secession was put down after considerable fighting; then he fought on the winning side in the war for the independence of Uruguay from Argentina.

Win or lose, Garibaldi showed audacity and stamina, and seemed to be just what Mazzini was looking for: a fighter with lots of courage and few ideas. Mazzini would prescribe and Garibaldi would carry out. With that vision, Mazzini organized a press campaign to make Garibaldi's name familiar in Europe. His publicity blitz, carried out by means of letters, publications, petitions, and subscriptions, made Garibaldi a figure of legend before he had a chance to do anything significant in Europe. "Garibaldi is a man who will be useful to the country when it is time to act."[76] That was Mazzini's prophecy in October 1843.

The republican movement did lack a charismatic personality. Mazzini was influential for his ideas and his dedication, but he inspired better from a distance than from close up, and was ineffective in the field. He had his critics in the movement, like the Neapolitan firebrand Giuseppe Ricciardi, who thought that Mazzini placed too much faith in education, and the Roman Pietro Sterbini, who urged Mazzini to stop theorizing, lead his followers into the mountains, and descend on Rome at their head.[77] What Sterbini preached Fabrizi practiced, with little success. In August of 1843 a small band of Fabrizi's followers went into the mountains around Bologna, clashed with papal troops, and were quickly dispersed. Mazzini considered such isolated attempts foolhardy, but feared that if he opposed them openly he would lose the confidence and support of the few who were ready to act.[78]

His own plans were not necessarily more realistic. Living in close contact with political exiles of Hungarian, Polish, and Russian nationality gave him the idea, or the illusion, that through them he could orchestrate revolts in their lands. Thus, his plans encompassed half of Europe and aimed at nothing less than the collapse of the Austrian Empire. In August of 1842 Mazzini received a secret communication from an officer in the Austrian navy informing him of the existence of a secret Italian society called Esperia. It was active in the Austrian navy, whose official language before 1848 was Italian, because most of its personnel came from the Italian-speaking regions of Venetia and Istria. Mazzini's heart must have jumped when he saw the name of the officer who was writing to him, Attilio Bandiera, born in 1810 to a Venetian family considered to be particularly loyal to Austria. Mazzini knew the name well, for Attilio's father, now an admiral, was the officer who in 1831 had turned Italian patriots trying to flee Italy over to his government after promising them safe passage to France. Mazzini must have seen the hand of God in the son's rejection of the politics of the father.

Attilio and his younger brother Emilio were apparently determined to strike a blow for Italian independence against the government that they were sworn to serve. Mazzini was already in contact with Italian officers in the Austrian army who were similarly inclined; Hungarian, Polish, and Russian exiles promised to mobilize support for revolution among their respective peoples. Ever the optimist when it came to estimating the results of his own initiatives, Mazzini imagined a vast subversive sweep covering much of central Europe and striking at the very heart of Austrian power, its army and navy. He could not resist a little premature boasting. "Given time," he wrote to Lamberti in August of 1843, "the Italian insurrection will be accompanied by revolts that they do not even dream of, and we will have the initiative in Europe."[79] While the moderates talked idly of reforms and the hotheads wasted lives and money in trivial local uprisings, he would set Europe on fire from one end to the other.

Time was the problem, for a plot with so many ramifications could not be kept secret for long. Hence his desperate pleas for unity under his own direction, and his impatience with Fabrizi and others who had more military experience and questioned the practicality of insurrections staged by amateurs, or wanted reassurance that matters were indeed as he claimed. To obtain support, Mazzini vowed to cooperate with anyone willing to act, to set aside personal beliefs, and to postpone discussion of political matters until Italians were free to elect a constituent assembly that would decide the form of government. This was Mazzini the politician speaking, offering the type of compromise that he would later offer to moderates, but hoping this time to persuade radicals who shared his republican objectives to accept his leadership of the movement.[80]

There was also another Mazzini speaking, more truculent but every bit as real as the seemingly accommodating politician. We hear the truculent Mazzini telling his mother that he could not make a revolution with only the virtuous on his side, but that it was nevertheless the duty of virtuous people to seize control of revolutions once they were in progress.[81] The initiative could not come from the people at large, but the masses would follow the leaders and "massacre the *tedeschi* in groups or individually one at a time; spare the Swiss (mercenaries) if they surrender or run away, not for their sake but for what we must do in Switzerland."[82] If the mass refused to follow, it was still important to act simply for the sake of one's conscience: "Let us be frank: rights and duties do not come from this or that class, or from the people as a whole. They come from much higher, from God the creator and educator of the human race, from God who designed the universe, from God the only sovereign."[83] God was always there, ready to lift the burden of responsibility from Mazzini's shoulders.

Time was running out, most of all for the Bandiera brothers, who were surrounded by spies. One was Tito Vespasiano Micciarelli, a spy for the papal government, sent by Mazzini to the Bandieras as one who could be trusted. Another was Attilio Partesotti in Paris, recommended by Mazzini to Lamberti for membership in Young Italy, who conveyed to the Austrians information gathered from an unsuspecting Lamberti. Partesotti died suspiciously in 1844, perhaps poisoned, after he had done his dirty work for Austria. Then there was a mysterious Doctor Clemente Paolini, who worked for the Tuscan police. Lamberti suspected that Paolini was a spy, but Mazzini always defended him as a true patriot maligned by his accusers. Everyone was caught up in a treacherous underworld of agents and counteragents, but it was the Bandiera brothers who paid the price. Lured into Calabria with only nineteen companions on the false information that a revolt was making headway, they were captured by Neapolitan troops and executed by firing squad with seven of their companions on July 25, 1844.[84]

The capture of the Bandieras compromised the larger plan of which their insurrection was part. The element of surprise was lost, governments were on the alert, and Mazzini was on the defensive, accused of instigating the whole affair. That was not true, for he had aided rather than instigated, but the Bandieras were indeed part of a larger plan and there was fear that revelations would compromise others. That fear perhaps explains Mazzini's intemperate reaction to rumors that Attilio Bandiera had offered to reveal all he knew in return for his life. Furious, Mazzini railed privately against Attilio and Italians in general: "Italians are whores [*sono troie*]; I never had much faith in them, and now I have none at all; all they can do is make noise."[85] Echoing perhaps rumors of Attilio's homosexuality, he called him immoral. When his fury subsided, however, he realized that Attilio and his companions were genuine martyrs, and therefore useful to the cause in death as in life. That was the message of his pamphlet of 1845, *Recollections of the Bandiera Brothers and Their Martyred Companions*, in which he praised their courage and charged that they were the victims of treachery.[86]

That charge was based in part on his discovery that British authorities had secretly intercepted and read his mail in the months before the expedition. To document his suspicion, he devised a series of ingenious tests, like putting tiny grains of sand in the envelopes, whose disappearance would show that the letters had been tampered with, and lined up impartial witnesses to the results. After gathering sufficient evidence, he denounced the British government for violating the privacy of personal correspondence, passing information to Austrian officials, and aiding Austria in the plot to lure the Bandieras to their death. The government first denied the charges, then admitted to them, and revealed that the letters of Mazzini and others had been opened on orders from Home Secretary James Graham, at the request of the Foreign Office. Graham had used powers granted by law and was exonerated of wrongdoing by a parliamentary inquest, but the Whig opposition seized upon Mazzini's charges to embarrass Peel's conservative government.[87]

Mazzini, in his new role as victim of Britain's foreign policy of peaceful coexistence with Austria, gained support. Prominent intellectuals and political figures took his side against the government. Carlyle, Dickens, Macauley, Mill, and other prominent public figures spoke up for Mazzini. Even the normally anti-Mazzinian *Times* criticized the government. The mail scandal gave him the kind of favorable publicity no money could buy; he took credit for measures adopted to prevent a repetition of the abuse of power and protect the rights of political refugees. His name was known outside London circles; he was someone to reckon with: "In any other country they would call me a ball-breaker [*seccacoglioni*], but not here. The Saxon race is hard, obstinate, insistent; it is not bad for them to know that Italians can be worse ball-breakers than the Saxons."[88]

Despite his new fame, the Bandiera incident convinced him to change his tactics: "If I did like the Bandiera brothers I would not hurt myself as much as I would hurt the cause, which must be advanced by other means."[89] He was also broke, claiming in October 1845 that he had only three lire left in his pocket, but over the next three years he tried to raise money through what he called a National Fund for Action. The launching of the Fund for Action marked the beginning of an effort to create a "party of action" that would give republicans a political profile distinguishable from that of moderates on the one hand and leveling radicals on the other. The failure of still another attempt at guerrilla insurgency in the Apennines in October 1845 confirmed the need for responsible and patient leadership. It was time to plan ahead and think in the long term, not to improvise.[90]

SEIZING THE REVOLUTION

On June 16, 1846, the College of Cardinals elected a new pope, who took the name of Pius IX. What followed was one of those surprises of history that leave even the most seasoned observers baffled and perplexed. The election was the result of stalemate between rival factions, but Pius IX did not behave like the compromise candidate that he was. A man of good intentions but questionable political judgment, Pius IX made his pontifical debut with a series of measures and pronouncements that smacked of political liberalism. A political amnesty, the easing of press censorship, and a promise of representative government made the new pope the darling of liberals and lifted the political prospects of

Gioberti and the so-called Neo-Guelph party, which looked to the papacy for national leadership. Along with Charles Albert's growing reputation as a reforming monarch, the popularity of Pius IX boosted the appeal of moderate politicians, who sought change guided from above. While the democrats scared public opinion with their demonstrations and insurrections, the moderates charged that democratic intemperance against "throne, altar, and patriciate . . . hindered all efforts at improvement."[91]

Mazzini was skeptical that either Charles Albert or Pius IX would live up to the expectations of reformers. He compared Pius IX to an apprentice sorcerer who would be overcome by the forces he had aroused. He deplored that even the normally anti-papal British public was showing enthusiasm for his reforms.[92] But there was no denying that the enthusiasm for king and pope was real. Donning his politician's hat, he said he would accept the king and the pope if they were acceptable to the nation.

While the moderates held sway in Italy, Mazzini turned his attention to the European exiles in London who shared his democratic views. He formed a committee of exiles from Russia, Poland, and central Europe to step up the fight against the absolute monarchies. The European perspective dominates the long and diffuse but important essay "Thoughts upon Democracy in Europe," which the *People's Journal* began to publish in installments in August of 1846. Its basic argument was that the triumph of democracy was tied to the triumph of movements for national independence throughout the world:

> The democratic tendency of our times, the upward movement of the popular classes, who desire to have their share in political life, hitherto a life of privilege, is henceforth no Utopian dream, no doubtful anticipation: it is a fact, a great European fact, which occupies every mind, influences the proceedings of governments, defies all opposition. . . . No one, now-a-days, sees in the ever increasing voice of rising nations . . . of oppressed races claiming their place in the sunshine, nothing more than the vain imagination of a writer, or the cry of an agitator thrown out hap-hazard among the crowd.[93]

This message of liberation was to be carried by the People's International League, an educational initiative announced in London in April of 1847. Its significance was largely symbolic, because its membership consisted entirely of English stalwarts like the Ashursts, John Bowring, William James Linton, and James Stansfeld. Mazzini envisaged it as a rejuvenated Young Europe, and expected that it would help the democrats to regain the initiative.[94] There was little time for it to develop into something meaningful. That summer brought unmistakable signs of an impending confrontation between "the two principles of progress and

resistance, liberty and tyranny."[95] Popular demonstrations in Rome in
June suggested that the papal government might be losing control over
the process of reform. In September there were more popular protests.
Mazzini noted that in Lucca the demonstrators marched for the first
time behind the national tricolor. Painfully aware of his own lack of
preparation, he complained that Young Italy amounted to very little; it
had "tried for ten but achieved only two."[96] He encouraged his Polish
friends to infiltrate the papal army, where they would be welcomed on
account of their Catholicism and where they could be of service in the
future.

In September Mazzini wrote a letter to Pius IX, which someone may
have slipped into the pope's carriage. This showed that Mazzini had a
long arm, but the letter was really meant for public consumption.
Published in Paris, Florence, and Venice, it was distributed and discussed widely. In substance, it restated Mazzini's faith in Italy's mission,
in the principle of religion, in the immortality of the soul, in progress
and humanity. What was most striking about the letter was its tone,
which could be interpreted as either serious or ironical. As he had done
with Charles X and Charles Albert, Mazzini presumed to give advice,
this time to the pope on matters of faith and politics. Introducing himself
as a believer in God and as an enemy of materialism and communism,
Mazzini reassured Pius IX that he considered him to be a person of good
will, but added that Catholicism was a lost cause because it was the ally
of tyrants. The pope had it in his power to change that policy and save
the Church, but to do that he needed the strength that comes from faith.
He urged Pius IX to "Be a believer" and "Unify Italy, your country;" if
he refused, Italy would be unified without him, for such was the will of
God.[97]

On October 12 Mazzini left London for Paris, where he spent nearly
two months. He went there to get a better sense of what was happening
on the continent and to help Lamberti, who was in declining health and
unable to keep up with the work of Young Italy. Giovanni Ruffini saw
him after three years, and noted that he had changed little physically,
but that he looked wiser. He still had his prophetic mannerisms, spoke
emphatically, and shook his head to show disapproval, but seemed sober
and restrained. Mazzini practiced his diplomacy on Gioberti apparently
with success, for Gioberti left their meeting under the impression that
Mazzini favored gradual reform under Piedmontese and papal leadership. The likes of Lamennais and George Sand showed respect for him,
while others paid him the compliment of showing jealousy for the
attention he was getting. The police observed, but kept their distance.

The trip confirmed Mazzini's dislike for French socialism, which lured
Italian workers away from Young Italy. Writing to George Sand from
London, he told her how he "detested terror and the guillotine system-

atically applied."[98] If that left some room in his mind for terror on a less systematic basis, he did not elaborate. But his mind definitely turned to thoughts of action. With no organization to speak of, he gathered what little he had. He wrote to experienced officers who had fought in Spain and South America to get ready for action, and dispatched Giacomo Medici to Uruguay with instructions to bring back Garibaldi with one thousand volunteers. That could be the secret weapon that he needed. With it, he could perhaps steal a march on everyone else.[99]

When the revolution broke out in Paris in February of 1848, Mazzini regretted that Italy had once again lost the initiative to France. He was grateful that at least Palermo had risen first, in January, against the king of Naples. An uprising in Sicily against Naples was not the national initiative he was looking for, but at least it showed that there was a spark of life among Italians. The hour of reckoning had come, and he sensed the opportunity. As he had once told his mother, "the darkest hour of the night is the one just before the coming of dawn."[100] He would go to Italy to conspire and inspire, knowing that to prevail he would have to summon the moral courage of the high priest and the cunning of the politician.

NOTES

Works frequently cited in the notes have been identified by the following abbreviations:

EN   *Edizione Nazionale. Scritti editi ed inediti di Giuseppe Mazzini* (1906–90), 106 vols.

PGI   *Protocollo della Giovine Italia. Appendice agli scritti editi ed inediti* (1916–22), 6 vols.

RSR   *Rassegna Storica del Risorgimento*

SEI   *Scritti editi ed inediti di Giuseppe Mazzini* (1861–91), 18 vols.

1. EN, XII, 339; XX, 54. For Mazzini's negative perceptions of England before 1837, see EN, I, 184, 188; IX, 356, 386–87. On O'Donnell and the Irish movement, see EN, XVII, 124–27, and Alessandro Luzio, *Giuseppe Mazzini carbonaro* (Turin: Bocca, 1920), 55–56, 430.

2. EN, XII, 277–83.

3. See Usiglio's letter to Rosales in Luigi Ordono de Rosales, ed., *Lettere inedite di Giuseppe Mazzini ed alcune de' suoi compagni d'esiglio* (Turin: Bocca, 1898), 208–12; also, Carlo Cagnacci, *Giuseppe Mazzini e i fratelli Ruffini* (Porto Maurizio: Tipografia Berio, 1893), 169.

4. EN, XIV, 76–77.

5. EN, XII, 277–83.

6. EN, XII, 201.

7. Quoted in Cagnacci, *Giuseppe Mazzini e i fratelli Ruffini*, 163n; see also pages 155–58, 163–65, 178–79. The "fatal memories" were probably those of Anna Courvoisier.

8. On Sara Nathan see Giannetta Nathan Rosselli, "Una biografia di Sarina Nathan," *Il Pensiero Mazziniano*, XXXIV (September 1979), 52–53.

9. EN, XX, 5, 18; XIX, 367–69.

10. EN, XII, 283–84.

11. On the unlucky vicissitudes of Mazzini's business ventures, see EN, XV, 195–96, 296, 357, 427; XVIII, 11–12, 28–30, 106, 117–18, 127–28, 167, 192, 196, 203, 209–12, 216, 225, 235, 255, 296, 304; XXIII, 239; *Appendice epistolario*, EN, VIII, 591.

12. EN, XIV, 317.

13. EN, XIV, 20, 314–15, 331; *Appendice epistolario*, EN, VIII, 480, 486, 555–56, 585, 640.

14. *Appendice epistolario*, EN, VIII, 657–58, 697.

15. EN, XII, 354, 394.

16. EN, XVII, 36–39.

17. EN, VIII, 288–314.

18. EN, XXIX, 61.

19. EN, XXI, 39–65.

20. EN, VIII, 296. Also, EN, XXIX, 3–15, and Arturo Linaker, *La vita e i tempi di Enrico Mayer* (Florence: Barbera, 1882), II, 22–93.

21. EN, XIV, 82, 300, 332, 348; XIX, 105–6.

22. EN, XV, 12.

23. SEI, IX, lxviii.

24. George Meredith, *Vittoria* (New York: Charles Scribner's Sons, 1923), rev. ed., 9.

25. EN, XXI, 141.

26. Quoted in Cagnacci, *Giuseppe Mazzini e i fratelli Ruffini*, 255. Mazzini's comments on Jane Carlyle appear in EN, XIX, 32, 304–5.

27. EN, XIX, 331, 349.

28. Mazzini's circle of devoted and influential friends is well described in Emilia Morelli, *L'Inghilterra di Mazzini* (Rome: Istituto per la Storia del Risorgimento, 1965), 77–82.

29. Arturo Salucci, *Amori mazziniani* (Florence: Vallecchi, 1928), 150.

30. Giovanni La Cecilia, *Memoriale storico-politico dal 1820 al 1876* (Rome: Artero, 1876–78), III, 160.

31. EN, XIV, 106–7, 112–13.

32. EN, XIV, 189. There is no record of a child named Tancioni being born in London in the month of September 1837 or later, but it is possible that the child was registered under another surname. When Susan's surname is mentioned, it is always Tancioni; her maiden name is unknown.

33. EN, XL, 224.

34. EN, XLVII, 31–32.

35. EN, XV, 7. For Mazzini's comments on Pellico, see EN, IX, 283.

36. EN, XV, 27.

37. EN, XV, 366; XVIII, 171–72.

38. EN, XV, 267–68. Musolino's critical reflections on Mazzini are scattered throughout the two volumes of his posthumously published *Giuseppe Mazzini e i rivoluzionari italiani* (Cosenza: Luigi Pellegrini Editore, 1982).

39. EN, XVIII, 53–54.

40. EN, XIV, 229–30.

41. EN, XIX, 10.

42. EN, XX, 32, 150–51; PGI, I, 12.

43. EN, XXV, 14, 53–57.

44. EN, XXIII, 345, and XXV, 3–20.

45. EN, XIX, 48; PGI, I, ix–xli.

46. PGI, I, 62.

47. The evidence for renewed interest in Mazzini by the early 1840s comes from a variety of sources, including *Carte segrete e atti ufficiali della polizia austriaca in Italia dal 4 giugno 1814 al 22 marzo 1848* (Capolago: Tip. Elvetica, 1851–52), II, 378–80, 481; III, 59, 79, 92, 100, 102. Also, Ludmilla Assing, *Vita di Pietro Cironi* (Prato: Giachetti, 1865), 18; Nicola Niceforo, *Misteri di polizia* (Florence: Salani, 1890), 226–29; Giovanni Visconti-Venosta, *Ricordi di gioventù* (Milan: Cogliati, 1904), 40.

48. EN, XIX, 117.

49. EN, XIX, 47–48; XX, 9.

50. EN, XIX, 115; XXIII, 303.

51. EN, XXIII, 298.

52. EN, XIX, 358.

53. For Mazzini's thoughts on religion in these years, see EN, XV, 90–92, 391–92. Also, Mazzini's *Zibaldone pisano* (Pisa: Domus Mazziniana, 1955), 19–36, 77. The entries in the *Zibaldone* are not dated, but these pages seem to refer to the period 1842–45.

54. EN, XXIV, 160.

55. EN, XXVI, 193.

56. EN, XXIV, 146; XXIII, 224, 272–73, 320, 340–41. Also, PGI, I, 10–11.

57. EN, XXIX, 90.

58. EN, XXXII, 40.

59. *Jane Welsh Carlyle: Letters to Her Family, 1839–1863*, (Garden City: Doubleday, 1924), 300.

60. *Mazzini's Letters to an English Family*, 1861–1872 (London: John Lane, 1922), III, 153.

61. On the Italian population of London, see Lucio Sponza, *Italian Immigrants in Nineteenth-Century Britain: Realities and Images* (Leicester: Leicester University Press, 1988), 19–29.

62. PGI, II, 105.

63. EN, XIX, 25, 52–53, 57.

64. PGI, I, 146; also, 148, 174, 340.

65. EN, XXVIII, 22.

66. Quoted in Margaret C. W. Wicks, *The Italian Exiles in London, 1816–1848* (Freeport: Books for Libraries Press, 1968), 174.

67. EN, XXIII, 131.

68. EN, XXIII, 133.

69. *Appendice epistolario*, EN, VI, 129.

70. EN, XXV, 84.

71. EN, XXIV, 26.

72. EN, XXVIII, 157. Also, PGI, III, 248–50.

73. EN, XXIV, 57.

74. EN, XXIII, 269–71; XXXI, 85.

75. On the Christian Alliance, see Joseph Rossi, *The Image of America in Mazzini's Writings* (Madison: University of Wisconsin Press, 1954), 31–46.

76. EN, XXIV, 316; PGI, II, 114. Also, Giacomo Emilio Curatolo, *Il dissidio tra Mazzini e Garibaldi* (Milan: Mondadori, 1928), 52.

77. Giuseppe Ricciardi, *Memorie autografe d'un ribelle: ovvero, Prolegomeni del fuoruscito* (Milan: Battezzati, 1873), 5–6.

78. PGI, II, 114; EN, XXIV, 273–77.

79. PGI, II, 58. Also, EN, XXIII, 341; XXIV, 216, 393.

80. PGI, II, 140.

81. EN, XXIV, 73; PGI, II, 140.

82. PGI, II, 156. It is not clear how Switzerland figured in Mazzini's plans, but it is possible that he made a secret visit to Geneva in August 1844, although his correspondence from London shows no unusual breaks at that time.

83. EN, XXV, 228.

84. Riccardo Pierantoni, *Storia dei fratelli Bandiera e loro compagni in Calabria* (Milan: Cogliati, 1909), 77–97, 130–35, 144–53, 223–27, 246–53, 296–309. Also, Giovanni Pillinini, "Zone oscure nella vicenda dei fratelli Bandiera," RSR, LXXXIII (April–June 1996), 223–31.

85. Dominico Giuriati, ed., *Duecento lettere edite ad inedite di Giuseppe Mazzini* (Turin: L. Roux, 1887), 60–61. Also, EN, XXVII, 92, and PGI, III, 93.

86. EN, XXXI, 17–81.

87. J. T. Ward, *Sir James Graham* (New York: St. Martin's Press, 1967), 209–11.

88. EN, XXVIII, 50.

89. PGI, III, 227.

90. EN, XXVII, 152–53, 161–63; XXVIII, 99–100, 104–9, 188. Also, PGI, III, 319.

91. Giacomo Durando, *Della nazionalità italiana* (Paris: Franck, 1846), 383.

92. See "The Pope and the Italian Question" (published in *Lowe's Edinburgh Magazine*, November 1846 and January 1847), in EN, XXXIV, 249–91.

93. EN, XXXIV, 92–93.

94. EN, XXXVI, 3–30.

95. EN, XXXII, 236.

96. PGI, VI, 92; EN, XXXII, 256–60, 320–21.

97. EN, XXXII, 304, 318; XXXIII, 110; XXXVI, 229–30.

98. Fabio Luzzatto, *Giuseppe Mazzini e George Sand: la relazione e la corrispondenza* (Milan: Fratelli Bocca, 1947), 57, 69.

99. EN, XXXII, 30–32; XXXIII, 102–7.

100. EN, XIX, 211.

CHAPTER 6

What Has Not Been Must Be (1848–1853)

While Italians in Paris clamored for Mazzini's return, Lamberti wondered whether "a magic hand prepares the ground for him providentially, almost in spite of himself."[1] Why did he linger in London while the continent hurtled toward revolution? The answer was Mazzini's sense of timing and his priorities. What he called the "cause of liberty" did not need his help, he believed; its instruments were constitutions and parliaments, which he saw as potential obstacles to national unity: "If peace prevails, within a year we will have six constitutions and six parliaments, which will institute a federal system impossible to eradicate except by conquest."[2] He was waiting for the moment when unification became the issue, and that would not happen as long as moderate leaders controlled the national movement. Revolution and war, not parliamentary deliberations, were needed to create the Italian nation that had never been.

A customs union agreement signed by Piedmont, Tuscany, and the Papal States in October of 1847, as well as a constitution granted by Ferdinand II of Naples in January of 1848, intensified Mazzini's fears that moderate solutions would prevail. It worried him that such reforms were well received and that Charles Albert was becoming the darling of reformists. To Mazzini, Charles Albert was still the assassin of the companions of his youth. What he saw in his designs was not liberalism, but an unprincipled opportunism that played to both liberals and conservatives. Support for conservatism abroad and for moderate reform in Italy were different facets of the same "policy of the artichoke,"

Portrait of Mazzini as Triumvir of the Roman Republic (1849), by Emilie Ashurst Venturi. From *Edizione Nazionale*, vol. XXX (Cooperativa Tipografico-Editrice Paolo Galeati of Imola, 1912–1924).

whereby Piedmont sought to swallow Italy one leaf at a time. If Charles Albert was indeed *Re Tentenna* (King Waffle), as his critics charged, it was a purposeful waffling that Mazzini tried to match while waiting for the situation to clarify: "As long as peace prevails, the party of unity must proceed legally with the support of those who are well intentioned, theorizing peacefully to influence thinking youth, reach out to those who can influence the people and the soldiers, and leave the rest to circumstances."[3]

Popular demonstrations confirmed Mazzini's faith in the victory of the "upward movement . . . which seeks the formula for progress and for our national future from the very heart of the nation itself."[4] In June of 1847 there was a demonstration in Rome, led by one Angelo Brunetti, better known as Ciceruacchio, a wine merchant and *capopopolo* from the working-class section of Trastevere. *Capipopolo* like Ciceruacchio were new figures emerging out of the early political struggles of the Risorgimento, who promised to bridge the gap between the patriotic minorities and the masses. Usually local businessmen who provided jobs and made themselves popular by dispensing largesse in their neighborhoods, they would play key roles in organizing popular demonstrations. Mazzini had no connection with Ciceruacchio in 1847, and Ciceruacchio wanted little more than to encourage Pius IX to persevere with his reforms, but Mazzini and the pope misread Ciceruacchio's intentions similarly. It was said that Pius IX's comment on Ciceruacchio's demonstration was that no one should expect the pope to get along with Mazzini, and Mazzini was heartened by that report.[5]

In the Austrian-ruled regions of Lombardy and Venetia there was resentment of tax increases, government efforts to collect unpaid taxes, billeting of soldiers in private homes, discriminatory tariffs, and regulations that kept Italians out of high-level government positions. New Year's Day, 1848, saw the start of a boycott of tobacco and lottery tickets in Milan, which, like the Boston Tea Party that inspired it, was a political protest against lucrative imperial monopolies.[6] In Turin, there were demonstrations to pressure Charles Albert into granting a constitution, as Ferdinand II had done in Naples on January 29. Charles Albert obliged on March 4, but rather than calling it a constitution, which implied a diminution of royal authority, he named his document a statute *(statuto)*, which implied voluntary royal concession. Anti-Austrian demonstrations broke out in Venice and Milan when the news of Metternich's downfall reached those two cities. There was little bloodshed in Venice, where the insurgents raised the historic banner of the republic of Saint Mark, but it took five days of street fighting to force Austrian troops out of Milan.

As the Austrians were evacuating Milan on March 23, Charles Albert's council of ministers met in extraordinary session to declare war against Austria. The royal proclamation to the people of Lombardy and Venetia sounded almost Mazzinian:

> Peoples of Lombardy and Venetia, our arms, which were concentrat-
> ing on your frontier when you forestalled events by liberating your
> glorious Milan, are now coming to offer you in the latter phases of
> your fight the help which a brother expects from a brother, and a
> friend from a friend. We will support your just desires, confident as
> we are in the help of that God who is manifestly on our side; of the
> God who has given Pius IX to Italy; of God whose helpful hand has
> wonderfully enabled Italy to rely on her own strength (*in grado di
> fare da se*).[7]

The belief that Italians could liberate themselves was Mazzinian, but Charles Albert's motives were anything but Mazzinian. The foreign intervention that Charles Albert wanted to prevent was that of republican France, and the Italian initiative that he proposed was a Piedmontese war to take advantage of Austria's internal crisis and forestall republican initiatives. The ouster of Louis Philippe and the proclamation of the republic in France improved the prospects for revolution elsewhere in Europe, prompting Charles Albert to take the initiative and Mazzini to leave London on March 1 at Lamberti's urging. He arrived in Paris two days later, greeted effusively by the Italian exiles, who chose him over the more moderate Gioberti to preside over the newly founded Italian National Association. The association was overtaken by events, but the term "national" in its name revealed the intention to bring together the many strands and factions of political emigration. That was precisely the conciliatory image that Mazzini wanted to project at that moment to bolster his own scarce following. When nothing happened, he returned to London on March 10 to take care of personal business, and then rushed back to Paris two weeks later, after learning that Milan had risen.

That was the signal for which he had waited. Revolution in Italy increased his personal prestige, suddenly making him important enough to be received at the Hôtel de Ville by the head of the provisional revolutionary government of France. Alphonse Lamartine rashly promised him the help of republican France if Italy were attacked "on its soil or in its soul," a promise that Mazzini did not disdain although it came from resented France.[8] In fact, he counted on the support of France's republican government, confident that personal friends and radical republicans like Alexandre Ledru-Rollin, whom he trusted more than Lamartine and other moderates, would support a sister republic in Italy. The French card would be his to play in Italy against Charles Albert. His only other asset was his personal prestige, for he had no organization to speak of. Perhaps to give himself the semblance of one, he urged the about two hundred Italian exiles in Paris who were clamoring for "arms, money, and the republican flag" to return to their hometowns to fight for the republic.[9]

THE REVOLUTIONIST RETURNS

Mazzini crossed the snow-covered St. Gotthard Pass by sled on April 7, and returned to Italy after an absence of seventeen years. The border guards at Chiasso recognized him and recited passages from his writings; in Como cheering throngs surrounded his carriage. His arrival in Milan on April 8 was triumphal. A procession formed behind his carriage at the city gate and followed him to the Hotel Bella Venezia in the center of town. The crowd summoned him to the balcony of his room repeatedly. In the square below a band blared patriotic music. There were reunions with old friends and introductions to new ones. Federico Campanella was there for the old guard, Nino Bixio and Goffredo Mameli for the new. Maria Dal Verme, wife of Gaspare Rosales, offered him the hospitality of her palace, where he spent a few days. Then he returned to the hotel, where he was joined a few weeks later by his mother, with whom he shared a room. Curiously, the first members of his family to arrive were his sister Antonietta and her husband Checco Massuccone, who did not share his politics at all. His father did not come. He preferred the quiet of his country retreat and avoided visitors, especially those who came to pay their respects to the parents of the celebrity that was his son.

One of Mazzini's visitors was a personal emissary from Charles Albert, sent to test his intentions, who brought an invitation to run for a seat in the new parliament. Mazzini, acting like an independent potentate, did not accept the offer, but promised his cooperation if the king would declare his intention to unify the country with Rome as capital and break off relations with other sovereigns; *se no, no*![10] The technique of demanding more than could be granted was meant to embarrass Charles Albert, but it backfired when news leaked out that he was negotiating. Although nothing came of the royal overture, the very act of engaging in political conversations was interpreted as political opportunism. How could the man who personified republicanism and revolution contemplate a deal with Charles Albert?

In Milan, the capital of Lombardy, Mazzini was invited to participate in the deliberations of the provisional government. His meeting with Charles Albert's emissary, however, made him suspect in the eyes of the Lombards who feared Piedmontese territorial designs on their region. Prominent among them was the republican Carlo Cattaneo. An economist brought up in the Lombard school of empirical research, Cattaneo had little intellectual rapport with the mystical Mazzini. Although he felt Italian enough to want independence from Austria, he was too

Lombard to welcome annexation by monarchist, militarist, clerical Piedmont, which he regarded as the most backward state in Italy. Suspicious also of Mazzini's proclivity for conspiracy and for playing to the crowd, Cattaneo did not meet Mazzini until three weeks after the latter's arrival. In Cattaneo, Mazzini met a fellow republican who shared neither his religiosity nor his populism, a rival whom he respected and eventually came to love, but from whom he could expect no concessions on political matters that were dearest to him.

Before coming to Milan Mazzini had worried about competition from moderates, but in Milan he discovered that the republicans were also divided. There were republicans who counted on France and republicans who wanted domestic revolution, republicans who wanted a centralized state and republicans who wanted a decentralized federation of states, republicans eager to court popular support and republicans scornful or fearful of any initiative from the streets. Prominent among those who looked to France was the economist Giuseppe Ferrari, a radical critic of bourgeois society who had attained academic recognition in France and now made common cause with Cattaneo against Mazzini. Cattaneo and Ferrari did not see eye to eye on everything (Ferrari was far more egalitarian and "socialist" than Cattaneo), but both were philosophical positivists distrustful of Mazzini's religious republicanism. In the event, it was not their philosophical differences, but their differences over how to respond to the Piedmontese demand for the immediate fusion of Lombardy and Piedmont that made them clash with Mazzini.

Ferrari called a meeting of prominent republicans, who met in Mazzini's hotel room on April 30 to discuss the issue of how to respond to the Piedmontese request for the immediate union of Lombardy and Piedmont. Two positions were clear: on the one hand, the provisional government controlled by moderates favored immediate union to avoid popular disorders; on the other, republican separatists wanted to resist fusion with Piedmont to avoid a monarchist victory and domination by what they considered to be a militaristic and economically backward state. Mazzini chose an intermediate position that sought to preserve unity of action against Austria by delaying controversial political decisions: military help from Piedmont was to be welcomed as long as the Piedmontese agreed not to raise political issues for the duration of the war. Ferrari spoke in favor of French intervention to forestall annexation by Piedmont, while Mazzini spoke against it; it was one thing to welcome political help from French republicans, another to invite a French army into Italy. Cattaneo sided with Ferrari, declaring that if he had to make a choice he preferred the rule of Austria to that of Piedmont. Cattaneo and Ferrari were prepared to overthrow the provisional government to keep out the Piedmontese, while Mazzini feared Austria, France, and regionalism more than he feared Piedmont. The discussion degenerated into a personal confrontation when Mazzini called Cattaneo and Ferrari "municipalists," and an offended Cattaneo turned his back on Mazzini. "*Quest'uomo è un venduto!*" (This man has sold out!), said Cattaneo, referring to Mazzini. The confrontation broke up the meeting and left Mazzini temporarily isolated.[11]

In this instance, Mazzini's desire to play the role of political mediator damaged his reputation for republican virtue and revolutionary intransigence, which was an important source of his appeal. The politician compromised the prophet. It was a desire for political accommodation, not lack of realism, that undermined his credibility in the eyes of rigid republicans. In the paper *Italia del Popolo*, which Mazzini founded soon after arriving in Milan, he argued that "in times such as these absolute judgments are a serious error, intolerance a crime" and that Italians were being challenged "to relate heaven to earth, religion to politics."[12] Mazzini marched in the religious procession on the feast of Corpus Domini to show that he shared the people's religion although he no longer considered himself a Catholic. Subtle out of necessity, and realistic enough to see that what happened during the war would affect politics after the war, Mazzini understood that for the republicans to win the peace they had to be credible players in touch with public sentiment during the struggle.

When the question was put to a popular vote on June 8, a vast majority voted in favor of immediate union with Piedmont. The unionists prevailed with the support of the provisional government, the most influential families of Lombardy, and the Piedmontese army in Lombardy. True to his position that political decisions be postponed, Mazzini opposed holding the plebiscite while the war was still going on. That hardly helped him politically, for his willingness to accept Piedmontese military help aroused the ire of republicans and his opposition to the plebiscite alienated moderates. The crowds that less than two months before had cheered him now gathered under his windows to shout death, and street graffiti denounced him as a traitor.[13]

Such a rapid fall from grace was overshadowed by worse news from the front. The Piedmontese army had bogged down after reaching Milan on April 26, three days after Piedmont had declared war against Austria, giving the Austrian forces time to regroup in fortified positions south and east of the city, from which they harassed the Piedmontese and kept them off balance until they were ready to strike back. When they did, they sent the Piedmontese reeling back toward Milan, until an armistice was signed on August 5 by which the Piedmontese agreed to evacuate Lombardy. When news of the armistice reached Milan, angry demonstrators besieged Charles Albert and his generals in their quarters for several hours, until they were able to make their way out under guard. The emergency brought republicans together, with Cattaneo and

Mazzini jointly urging the provisional government to reject the armistice, entrust the defense of the city to a committee of public safety, institute a special war tribunal to deal with dissenters, prevent anyone from leaving the city, mobilize the national guard, and requisition food supplies in preparation for a long siege.[14]

With Austria the apparent victor in what Mazzini now called the "royal war," nothing prevented him from resuming his fight against monarchy in general and Charles Albert in particular. He did not sit on the committee of public safety, but he inspired it and praised its vigorous efforts to prolong the resistance. It was important for the republicans to mount a spirited defense to show that they were motivated by selfless patriotism. Even if they lost, a strong fight would be politically beneficial and would bolster their claim to the leadership of the national movement. He was conciliatory toward republicans like Cesare Correnti and Manfredo Fanti, who had sided with Piedmont, starting the trickle of defections that would become a mighty flow after 1848. Garibaldi was among those whom he courted. Recently returned from South America with a small force of sixty volunteers to offer his services to Pius IX, under the mistaken impression that the pope was leading a national crusade, Garibaldi was the secret weapon on which Mazzini counted to revive the fortunes of republicanism. By the time Garibaldi arrived in June, Pius IX had made it clear that he would not fight against Austria and would soon order the Papal army he had dispatched to the front to repatriate. Garibaldi then offered his services to Charles Albert, only to be turned down. Only then did he move on to Milan with his few followers, welcomed there by Mazzini and other republicans.

Yielding to the republicans, the Lombard provisional government bestowed on Garibaldi the rank of general. It was not until after the Piedmontese evacuated the city that the committee of public safety, at Mazzini's insistence, gave Garibaldi a command, with orders to leave for Bergamo at once and march on from there to relieve the town of Brescia that was being pressed hard by the Austrians. If he succeeded, he was to advance further east and link up with a remnant of the Papal army that had disobeyed the pope's orders to return home. If he failed, he was to retreat north to wage guerrilla warfare in the mountains, keeping the revolution alive while republicans mobilized popular resistance elsewhere. When Garibaldi left Milan on July 30 with a force of about twelve hundred men grudgingly put together by the provisional government, Mazzini remained in the city with some three hundred hard-line republicans under arms commanded by Giacomo Medici, perhaps to oust the provisional government. Medici, however, obeyed an order from the provisional government to join Garibaldi in the field, leaving Mazzini with no support in the city. He decided to join Medici's column as a simple soldier, as he had done with Ramorino in 1834, armed with a precision carbine that was a present from his English friends. In Bergamo he addressed a rally to call for volunteers: "What we sacrifice today will be rewarded tomorrow. Every man who joins the ranks of combatants now will increase the number of those who will defend our rights as citizens."[15]

The very next day, Garibaldi ordered the men out at four in the morning, not to relieve Brescia according to his original instructions, but to defend Milan, which had come under attack. Pursued by an Austrian force, he turned toward the mountains instead, with Mazzini in the ranks carrying the regimental flag and giving up his cloak to a young volunteer who suffered in the torrential rain. In the afternoon of August 5 his battalion took up positions for an enemy attack that never materialized, and then resumed the exhausting march. Mazzini described himself as "broken down by 22 miles of march on foot, but well enough for the rest."[16] He stayed with the battalion until August 9, when he crossed into Switzerland to organize reinforcements, he claimed, although his detractors ascribed the decision to less honorable motives, which later elicited a testimonial to his soldierly performance from Medici as commander of the battalion.

His detractors, including Garibaldi who held out three more weeks before crossing into Switzerland, later charged that Mazzini's desertion had a demoralizing effect.[17] When Garibaldi and Mazzini met in Lugano they had their first disagreement. As Garibaldi remembered it years later, Mazzini told him bluntly that they could fight better without him. Mazzini only remembered saying that they would fight on without him if he did not want to go back into Lombardy with reinforcements.[18] By then Mazzini headed an insurrection committee and was on good terms with Carlo Pisacane, a Neapolitan officer who impressed him as having more military expertise and political acumen than Garibaldi. Whatever was said, Garibaldi did not go back to Lombardy. Instead, he went to Nice to spend time with his family and recover from the "fevers," and then went to Genoa to raise his own volunteers.

Mazzini experienced life in Lugano as a letdown. He yearned for the excitement of action and missed the presence of a "gentle face . . . with whom to exchange a smile."[19] He called for Susan Tancioni, who hurried from London to look after him. The Swiss did not make his life easy. Pressured by Austria and Piedmont to get rid of political troublemakers, they ordered him out of the country, thus forcing him underground; he would not leave as long as revolution flickered in Italy. His attempts to stir up Lombardy failed, but republican hopes were kept alive in Venice, which still held out against the Austrians. Gioberti was prime minister in Piedmont, appointed at the insistence of democrats who wanted a national assembly to decide the future of Italy and demanded the resumption of war. In Tuscany, a democratic faction headed by Giuseppe

Montanelli and Domenico Guerrazzi also called for a national assembly to discuss national unity.

Rome held out the most exciting prospects. Pius IX's flirtation with liberalism had ended with his realization that as head of the Church he could not take sides in a war among Catholics. Pulling papal troops out of the war satisfied Austria, but worsened his political plight in Rome. In September of 1848 Pius IX appointed a new government under Pellegrino Rossi to deal with argumentative ministers and emboldened street demonstrators. It was the same Rossi whom Mazzini had met briefly in Geneva in 1831 on the way to France. He had been cool to Mazzini then and was downright hostile now. A reformer and a declared enemy of democrats, Rossi believed in government by experts, not by agitators. He understood that the pope had to strike a delicate balance between being an Italian patriot and the head of the Catholic Church; his plan was both to win a measure of national independence and to bolster papal authority by promoting a league of Italian states headed by the pope. Resistance to Rossi's plan came from the popular clubs controlled by Ciceruacchio. Their demonstrations were met by strong countermeasures, which escalated the conflict. Disdainful of threats, Rossi took no precautions for his own safety. He was assassinated as he dismounted from his carriage to attend the opening session of the Roman parliament on November 15.

Rome plunged into political chaos, the government resigned, and an armed crowd threatened to storm the Quirinal palace, where Pius IX sat protected by diplomatic representatives of the great powers. Although a monsignor was shot dead, the feared assault was averted when the pope promised more reforms. A week later, on November 24, Pius IX escaped to Naples disguised as a simple priest. The government he left behind had to decide how to deal with an absent head of state who had not renounced any of his prerogatives. After trying unsuccessfully to lure him back, the ministers vested the executive power in a committee of three. That measure did not satisfy the democrats, strong in the Marches and Romagna and attracted from all over Italy by the prospect of radical changes in Rome. They demanded a provisional government, universal suffrage, and elections to a constituent assembly that would decide the political future of the Papal States.

Mazzini's influence was felt indirectly as republicans who looked to him for leadership descended on Rome during the month of December. While the role of Mazzinian emissaries is often exaggerated, there is no doubt that the departure of Pius IX created opportunities for republicans who took their cues from Mazzini. Piero Cironi, Filippo De Boni, and Pietro Maestri were not blind followers, but they stirred up anticlerical feelings and organized a campaign to abolish the pope's temporal powers. De Boni in particular proved to be an effective organizer of the *circoli popolari* that formed a grassroots network in the provinces. Most organizers were not papal subjects, but Aurelio Saffi was; a respected lawyer from Forlì, Saffi became Mazzini's lifelong friend and collaborator. He made the legal case that Rome was a *de facto* republic, because in the pope's absence authority reverted automatically to the people, who were its original depositories.[20]

Not all who rushed to Rome were republicans, and not all republicans in Rome agreed with Mazzini, but Mazzinian ideas exerted a strong influence over those who worked to make Rome a republic.[21] Goffredo Mameli, republican and Mazzinian, mounted a press campaign against timid ministers who wanted to keep republicans out of Rome. The republican minority in Rome controlled the press and the streets. They prevailed because the other factions were weak and public opinion was confused. They appealed successfully to anticlerical sentiment, which was particularly strong in the northern provinces. Republicans who looked to Mazzini were in control by the end of December, long before Mazzini set foot on papal territory. He made no apologies for his followers who took over the Roman operation: *Il popolo è di chi lo fa!* (The populace belongs to those who make it!).[22]

News that his father had died on December 13 reached Mazzini while he was still in Switzerland. To his enemies' charge that he had neglected his filial obligation to visit his dying father, he replied that had his father lived just a little longer he would have had the satisfaction of seeing the triumph of the republican ideals that he had cherished in his youth.[23] He could not have gone to Genoa without risk, but risk did not deter him when Rome beckoned. After paying a sentimental visit to see the places and people who had sheltered him twelve years before, he left Switzerland on January 6, 1849, bound for Marseilles. There he learned that he and Garibaldi had been elected to the constituent assembly that was to decide the political future of Rome, part of an assemblage of noblemen, landowners, lawyers, doctors, and other notables who were perhaps not the best material for revolution, but who constituted the first popularly elected Roman assembly in modern times.

After leaving Marseilles on February 6, Mazzini stopped in Tuscany, where republicans were also at work. By the time he landed in Livorno in the afternoon of February 8, the Tuscan Grand Duke Leopold had abandoned Florence for the greater safety of nearby Siena and the Roman assembly had deposed the pope. The revolution, defeated in the north and in the south, was alive and well in central Italy. Mazzini, given the honor of announcing the grand duke's flight to a cheering crowd of livornesi, left immediately for Florence, where he received a more restrained welcome that same evening. The town belonged to Montanelli and Guerrazzi, who were democratic and republican but not overly fond of Mazzini. The political situation was confusing, for the grand duke had abandoned the capital but not the state and, like Pius in Rome, refused to abdicate. Montanelli wanted a republic, but Guerrazzi's priorities were hard to read, for his public professions of republicanism did not entirely hide his desire to reach an accommodation with the grand duke and an orderly transition to constitutional government.

Mazzini wanted a republican Tuscany to join with republican Rome, but did not press the case immediately because he knew he had little influence in Florence. To make himself better known there, he had sent ahead two trusted lieutenants, the actor Gustavo Modena and Scipione Pistrucci. There was also Giuditta Sidoli, who had settled in Florence and ran a salon that was frequented by liberals. Mazzini saw a great deal of her, but if their correspondence from this period reflects their true relationship, they were no longer lovers. Apart for thirteen years, they were friends who enjoyed each other's company and political allies who pursued similar agendas.[24]

On February 18 Mazzini *scese in piazza,* taking his case directly to the people at a large rally outside the Uffizi. With Modena at his side, he urged the crowd to call for a republic, a provisional government headed by Guerrazzi, and immediate union with Rome. It was a change of tactics on his part, and perhaps a political error, because by combining the two issues of republicanism and union with Rome he intensified widespread fears that Florence and other Tuscan cities would lose status and prerogatives. Some thought that the rally was an attempted coup on Mazzini's part, or certainly an effort to force Guerrazzi's hand. Guerrazzi confronted Mazzini that same evening, accusing him of harboring dictatorial designs and of furthering his own career at the expense of others, who paid with their lives for his foolhardiness. Guerrazzi apologized later, but did not change his politics. Any possibility that Rome and Tuscany might come together foundered on the clash between Guerrazzi and Mazzini.[25]

MAZZINI IN ROME

Florence was only a stop on the way to Rome, the city of Mazzini's dreams, on which he had never laid eyes. Approaching it by land, he first glimpsed its outline from the desolate countryside. It was the evening of March 5, and he dismounted from his carriage so that he could enter through the Porta del Popolo on foot, like a humble pilgrim: "Rome was the dream of my youth, the mother of all my ideas, the religion of my soul. I entered it on foot that evening in early March, trembling, almost in adoration."[26] It took faith and imagination to envisage the urban backwater that was Rome in 1849 as the cradle of a new civilization. A population of 160,000 lived within the perimeter of the ancient walls that had once sheltered a million people. Splendid palaces belonging to aristocrats and prelates coexisted with squalid tenements housing a marginal population that lived off the flow of tourists and pilgrims. Small-scale manufacturing establishments turned out religious vestments and articles of worship. The presence of approximately four thousand priests, monks, and nuns fueled charges that public revenues went to support an unproductive population. Papal largesse also benefited an unusually large indigent lay population, which the same critics accused of being idle as well. What was needed, argued the progressives, was less money for welfare and more for investments.[27]

Few visitors who came to Rome in 1849 were a boon to business. They were mostly people who came with an assortment of weapons and ideas to fight political battles. There were Garibaldi and his South American legionnaires, Polish exiles who had no other place to go, Lombards and Venetians who had deserted the Austrian army, and footloose adventurers. What they shared was a perception of themselves as fighters for liberty against the status quo. They were not universally welcome in Rome, where they were perceived as an economic burden and a political threat. The more that arrived, the harder it became to stop the flow. That was the view of a moderate politician like Terenzio Mamiani, and even of Pietro Sterbini, a former member of Young Italy; as Romans, they hoped for an accommodation with the pope that would retain liberal reforms and avoid the excesses of republicanism. On their side were the papal bureaucracy and army, which survived almost intact. It was not only political opposition that Mazzini had to confront in Rome, but also custom, caution, and inertia.

Being in Rome increased his sense of destiny, Mazzini told a cheering crowd gathered in front of the modest hotel where he took up lodgings. Public eloquence was not his strong suit, but, if the official record is correct, he excelled when he appeared before the Roman assembly the day after his arrival. All eyes were focused on him when he entered the hall at the conclusion of the day's business; the members stood and greeted him with shouts of *viva Mazzini*. From the place reserved for him on the right of the presiding officer he thanked the people of the city. Perhaps he meant no disrespect, but it was not the last time that he would go over the head of the assembly and appeal directly to the people. When he addressed the members, his tone was censorious. Moral mediocrity was not to be tolerated in such a place, he told the representatives, for eternal life and a world mission were entrusted to Rome by God: "After the Rome of the emperors, after the Rome of the popes, comes the Rome of the people."[28] The assembly could change the course of history by demonstrating that ideas had the power to change the world; they must not be hampered by legal scruples "because those who lead a revolution are responsible only to the people, to God, and to their own consciences. Revolutionary legality consists of interrogating, divining, and then applying the will of the people."[29]

These were the words not of a mere representative, but of a missionary eager to seize the historical moment. Elected with 8,982 votes, he was not the most popular figure; he did not belong either to the committee that conducted daily business, or to the executive triumvirate. What he did wield in Rome more than anywhere else was the moral power that came to him from years of championing the city's historical role. That prophetic aura and the concentration of zealous republicans in the city were the basis of his influence.

The assembly balked a few days later, when Mazzini asked it to dissolve and delegate its powers to a temporary dictator, as the ancient Romans had done in times of emergency. But the members were not convinced that there was an emergency; according to an eyewitness, on this occasion Mazzini showed that he "lacked the difficult art of persuading a representative body and bending it to his will."[30] The request was motivated by the imminent resumption of war in the north, where democrats pressured the Piedmontese government into denouncing the armistice with Austria. Resuming the fighting was a foolhardy decision, but Mazzini did not want Piedmont to fight alone. Whether the Piedmontese won or lost, it was important to have a republican army in the field to show that republicans were patriots who put national independence first. The assembly approved his request for a special levy of five million lire to send a force of ten thousand soldiers to the north, and obliged him further by setting up a war commission from outside its own ranks to recruit, train, and equip the forces of the republic.

Republican troops were already on their way when news arrived on March 29 that the Austrian army had won a decisive victory at the battle of Novara six days before. Faced by the prospect of an Austrian offensive against Rome, the assembly acceded in part to Mazzini's earlier request for greater power by appointing him to the triumvirate, where he was joined by Carlo Armellini and Aurelio Saffi, both carryovers from the previous triumvirate, where they had distinguished themselves more for their honesty and good intentions than for brilliance or revolutionary zeal. Dictator in fact if not in name, Mazzini now faced the challenge of his life. Recognized only by the United States of America, the Roman Republic was diplomatically isolated. Its treasury was nearly empty, its currency worthless, and its credit nonexistent. It also faced turmoil in the provinces, where the misbehavior of a few republican zealots spread fear and resentment.

Mazzini hoped to win public support at home and abroad by behaving responsibly, showing concern for law and order, guaranteeing property rights, practicing sound administration, and basing public appointments and promotions on merit. What radical measures were proposed or adopted were justified on grounds of public utility. Property was to be confiscated from religious orders that served no useful social purpose, the unemployed were to be put to work to construct defensive earthworks, and peasants were to be given land to make it more productive.[31] Although some religious institutions were shut down and some land was given to peasants, most of these proposals remained largely on paper due to lack of time and other more pressing concerns. There was not enough money to enact ambitious projects, and Mazzini did not make matters any easier when he told the assembly that he did not consider it his business to raise money. The government tried to meet the emergency by raising taxes, issuing large amounts of paper money, and debasing the coinage, which triggered inflation.

There was a dramatic turn in the international situation when the French national assembly declared that France would intervene militarily if Austria took advantage of Piedmont's defeat to expand its sphere of influence in Italy. French national interest would be protected by containing Austrian influence now that Piedmont was less effective as a buffer state. Mazzini welcomed that declaration because at that moment he feared Austria more than France and because he relied on the goodwill of radicals in the French assembly, whom he trusted far more than the government. Mazzini's endorsement, however, made it easier for Louis Napoleon, recently elected president of the republic, to gain the assembly's support for a French expedition to Rome. Radicals in the assembly saw no reason to object if Mazzini himself was ready to accept a French presence. Louis Napoleon encouraged Catholics to think that the real purpose of the expedition was to evict outside agitators and restore the pope to his rightful position.

Mazzini may have been duped if not by Louis Napoleon, then by his trust in French radicals, whose influence he overestimated. Pius IX showed better judgment when he insisted that the French be part of an international force, which included troops from Austria, Spain, and the Kingdom of the Two Sicilies, all involved in separate military operations. Mazzini was criticized for ostensibly allowing a French force of twelve thousand to land unopposed on April 25 in Civitavecchia, forty miles northwest of Rome. The failure to defend Civitavecchia may not have been inadvertent, for while the French paused in the port city Mazzini reassured the Roman assembly that they came with peaceful intentions, and when they began to march on Rome he expressed the hope that his friends in Paris would compel a withdrawal by rising against their own government.

Disappointment and fury took hold when he realized the extent of his miscalculation. Then he called for all-out resistance and for the spilling of blood to show the world that Romans were ready to die for their freedom. The disappointment was particularly severe because the start of military operations inevitably reduced his own influence and increased that of the military. Garibaldi proved to be the principal beneficiary, for the simple reason that he was in command of the sector of the city's defenses facing the French line of march. As the French approached unprotected in the morning hours of April 30, expecting perhaps to be welcomed as liberators by the bulk of the populace, as informers had assured they would be, they were stopped in their tracks by riflemen posted along the walls. From his command post at the San Pancrazio gate below the Janiculum hill, Garibaldi took advantage of the surprise and confusion of the French at this unexpected resistance by ordering flank charges that pinned down the enemy. Thus began six hours of fighting, at the end of which the French casualties amounted to 250 dead, 400 wounded, and 365 prisoners. Garibaldi, who had fought alongside his men, was the hero of the day.[32]

"Our honor is safe. God and our guns will do the rest," announced Mazzini, proud that republicans had given the lie to General Nicolas Charles Victor Oudinot's comment that "les Italiens ne se battent pas."[33] It was comforting, and politically useful, that the shame of Novara had been redeemed by republican fighters. The joy of victory was unfortunately clouded by an open disagreement with Garibaldi, who, thinking like a soldier, urged pursuit of the retreating enemy, while Mazzini, thinking like a diplomat, held him back, playing for time, fearing that a more humiliating defeat would make it impossible for the French to negotiate a settlement. Ferdinand De Lesseps, who later masterminded the building of the Suez canal, went to Rome as an envoy to negotiate with Mazzini; Oudinot kept a low profile while waiting for reinforcements. Turning on all his personal charm, winning De Lesseps's trust and admiration, returning prisoners with full honors, guaranteeing the safety of French citizens, and even welcoming French officers curious to see the sights of the city, Mazzini showed his conciliatory side. On May 17, he and De Lesseps agreed to a suspension of hostilities.

It is difficult to say whether Mazzini really believed that the republic could be saved by negotiations or whether he was only playing for time in the hope that a victory by radicals in the French national elections of May 13 would bring about a change of government in Paris. He may have entertained both hopes simultaneously, but, to his chagrin, the French elections produced a Catholic, politically conservative majority. That was not yet known in Rome on May 17, when Mazzini and De Lesseps signed their agreement, which became meaningless the moment Louis Napoleon knew that he could count on a conservative assembly. Mazzini still hoped for an insurrection in Paris. When nothing happened, he realized that the republic would have to either surrender or fight not for its survival, which was unlikely, but for the honor of the defenders and the future of republicanism.[34]

It was an unequal struggle. Against the overwhelming resources of the powers bent on restoring Rome to the pope, the republicans could muster a ragtag army of fourteen thousand, many carryovers from the old papal army and the others mostly volunteers from abroad. Election campaigns, popular clubs, processions, public festivals, and *capipopolo* like Ciceruacchio were popular and may have had a lasting impact, but there was not enough time to mobilize the people.[35] Mazzini made himself liked by living frugally, working hard, negotiating, and generally giving the impression that he had done his best to avoid violence. In the Quirinal palace, where he had moved, he occupied a small apartment, protected by only one bodyguard, receiving his many visitors from all walks of life in an atmosphere of informality that contrasted favorably with the stiff etiquette of the papal court. Even if most Romans were not behind the republic, his popularity was an asset for the republic.

Garibaldi's popularity was both an asset and a liability for Mazzini, for while Garibaldi was a magnet for volunteers who came to Rome to serve under him, and even cautious Romans appreciated his tactic of keeping the fighting away from the city by seeking and pursuing the enemy rather than waiting for it to approach, he was difficult and headstrong. After sending the French back to Civitavecchia, he was assigned to be part of a larger force sent out to meet a Neapolitan army approaching from the south, which he routed on May 19, not without friction with his superior officer General Pietro Roselli, a Roman who was favored because his presence gave the impression that Romans were active in their own defense. Garibaldi would have liked to pursue the Neapolitans, but was recalled back to Rome. Mazzini would not have minded bringing the war to Neapolitan territory, but gave in to his military commanders, who wanted to concentrate their forces around the city in anticipation of a renewed French attack. It is interesting to note that Mazzini erred on the side of caution when he had the responsibility of government, but that he regularly criticized those in government who did the same, most notably the Piedmontese, when he was in the opposition.

Garibaldi returned to Rome on May 31, covered with glory and dust, still suffering from a wound he had received on April 30. On the day he arrived Mazzini and De Lesseps signed a second agreement, which seemed to resolve the crisis. It was a "treaty of peace and alliance" that allowed the French expeditionary force to approach peacefully and encamp outside the walls of the city.[36] Since it said nothing about restoring the pope, it could be assumed that the issue would be the subject of further negotiation. The agreement, however, was worthless, because the French government, unknown to De Lesseps, had already decided to recall its envoy and a furious Oudinot denounced the provision that prevented his troops from entering the city. He could afford to show his anger, for his force had grown to twenty thousand troops, another ten thousand were on the way, and he had the equipment he needed to mount a regular siege of the city. The next day he served notice that military operations against "the place" would resume on June 4.

The attack on the outer defenses of "the place" began instead in the early morning hours of June 3, surprising the defenders and enabling the attackers to seize and secure dominant positions. Garibaldi was again in command of the threatened section of the perimeter, but he was not on or even near the scene. Still suffering from the effects of his wound, feverish and bedridden, he was recovering in another part of the city. By the time he arrived and gathered reinforcements, the French were in control of the strategically important high ground around Villa Pamphili, which controlled access to the San Pancrazio gate. If the French penetrated the walls, they would dominate the city from the adjacent heights of the Janiculum, and Rome's only options would be to surrender or to face systematic pounding from French artillery. In the days and weeks that followed, hundreds lost their lives in futile frontal attacks against the well-entrenched French troops. They are commemorated among the hundreds of marble busts that line the pleasant paths of the Janiculum today, dominated by the gigantic equestrian statues of Garibaldi and his South American wife Anita, who insisted on being at his side. Goffredo Mameli suffered a mortal wound in the fighting.

With all hope of saving the republic gone, Mazzini shifted from diplomacy to belligerence without ever losing sight of the political implications of his words and actions. In a series of articles published in *The Spectator* in London between December of 1848 and March of 1849 he had claimed that the initial victories and acts of heroism performed in the fight for national liberation were due to republicans, and that monarchists were responsible for the defeats and all the acts of treachery. Moderates, he charged, had forfeited their claim to leadership by supporting traitors like Charles Albert and Pius IX. They had squandered their chances of victory because they lacked the motivating principle, which was indispensable for success in revolution and without which they could not inspire acts of self-sacrifice and heroism.[37] Only republicans could accomplish that feat. With diplomacy defeated, it was clearly Mazzini's intention to conduct the resistance in such a manner as to legitimize republican claims to the leadership of the national movement.

On June 22, with French troops poised for the final attack, Mazzini called on all able-bodied males of military age to rush to the front lines, and on women and children to look after the ill and wounded. By invoking the example of the *levée en masse*, Mazzini showed how much he still owed to the example and the mythology of the French revolution.

Other measures called on civilians to donate their weapons to the state and on republican orators to take to the streets, "for when the *patria* faces the supreme test, ardent faith is needed to arouse the people."[38] The time had come to fight papal authority in all its forms. The republic had issued all its edicts in the name of God and the people, implicitly claiming that it spoke for both, but in the early days it had avoided interfering in religious matters. Among the emergency measures adopted during the last days of the republic, several aimed at severing the ties of discipline that bound the clergy to the pope. Members of the secular clergy were paid by the state and members of all religious orders were given the option of renouncing their vows.

These measures made it clear that Mazzini intended to modify the internal structure of the Church. That was the impression of Jessie White Mario, whose descriptions show Mazzini in the dual role of prophet and politician: "Mazzini not only wished to prove to the world that his government would do nothing to offend the susceptibilities of Catholics in Rome or abroad, but, in his profound wisdom, recognized the fact that the spiritual power of the Roman hierarchy can be extinguished only when men shall have ceased to accept any intermediary between their own consciences and the Invisible—between 'God and the People,' as he would have said."[39] Mario did not explain how Mazzini could at the same time reassure Catholics and extinguish the spiritual power of the Roman hierarchy. It was the logic of his position that the Rome of the Popes could not coexist with Rome of the People. It was never the official policy of the Roman republic to challenge the pope's spiritual role or his prerogatives as head of the Roman Catholic Church; unlike the republic, however, Mazzini intended to challenge the Church not only on political but also on sacramental and theological grounds.

On June 30 Garibaldi advised the assembly that further resistance would be futile. Sweaty from fighting in the heat, with his saber so bent out of shape that it stuck out of its scabbard, he explained that earthworks were crumbling under steady pounding, casualties were heavy, survivors exhausted, and supplies nearly depleted. He proposed not surrender, but carrying the war to the countryside and to the mountains: "Rome will be wherever we go."[40] Mazzini liked the idea of fighting in open country, but he also wanted to defend the city: "To the walls, to the walls! . . . You are the custodians of the walls. Let those rush to them who care about the honor of Rome."[41] While Romans manned the walls, others would fight in the countryside, but not necessarily under Garibaldi; it was Carlo Pisacane that he seemed to have in mind for the arduous challenge of taking the fight to the people.[42]

To the assembly meeting in closed session he presented the somewhat different proposal that its members should march out of the city with the army to confront the Austrians approaching from the north. That suggestion aroused no enthusiasm at all: "My proposal was followed by deep silence. . . . To me, continuing the war to extinction had appeared from the beginning such an elementary view for a republican party in power, that I had not prepared the ground in the assembly for it: a capital error."[43] When the assembly refused his advice, he stalked out of the hall in a fury rather than accept the assembly's mandate to surrender the city, just as he had escaped through a window rather than give in to his father as an adolescent. He considered the possibility of assuming the dictatorship, but only briefly because he had no support. He tendered his resignation as triumvir, an action that he chose to forget in later years, when he claimed to speak for the defunct republic.[44]

Mazzini was not with Garibaldi when the latter left the city on July 2 at the head of four thousand men, to begin the march to the north that became part of the national epic. He remained in Rome, again in defiance of the assembly, which, perhaps in retaliation for his earlier urgings that it join the army, designated him to be its representative on the march. While Garibaldi played his game of cat and mouse with Austrians and Spaniards for the next four weeks, only to meet with defeat and personal tragedy when his pregnant wife Anita died in his arms, Mazzini remained in Rome to bolster his and the republic's image. For a whole week, while French troops occupied the city, he lived as a private citizen, unprotected, strolling the streets with cane in hand, sitting in cafés, deliberately conspicuous and defiant, to make the point that he had nothing to fear and that the people were on his side. The French did not exclude him from their policy of letting the defeated defenders leave at their own discretion.[45]

On July 3 the assembly met one final time to ratify the republican constitution. Mazzini wanted the constitution ratified, but could not resist the temptation to berate the assembly one more time. An inconclusive discussion developed after he asked for a resolution that it could reconvene anywhere at any time at the request of no more than fifteen of its members. It is not clear whether his motion passed, because the meeting was chaotic and no one kept the minutes, but Mazzini acted as if the proposal had been approved. On that assumption, later on he claimed the right to act and be treated like a head of state and considered asking for diplomatic recognition as head of a government in exile. But he must have been miffed, for he was absent at the inaugural ceremony that members of the assembly held on the ancient capitol that afternoon. While the constitution was being announced to the public, French soldiers stared on in amazement from the steps of the nearby church of Ara Coeli.

At that time he may have already reverted to the role of conspirator, as dozens of secret groups were spawned or rejuvenated in the last days of the republic. A faction calling itself Reformed Carbonari met on the evening of July 3, vowing to "engage in permanent conspiracy and wage a relentless secret struggle against the political power of the pope and against foreign domination." It was probably no coincidence that a few days later "certain representatives of the people authorized a triumvirate consisting of Giuseppe Mazzini, Aurelio Saffi, and Mattia Montecchi to establish a National Association for the purpose of bringing together all those men of courage who are prepared to resume the struggle."[46] Mazzini designated Cesare Mazzoni and Giuseppe Petroni as his own lieutenants in Rome to carry on in his absence. Mazzinians and Carbonari managed to work together in Rome for several years, without ever resolving their fundamental differences of tactics and goals.

THE AFTERMATH OF REVOLUTION

On July 13 Mazzini left for Civitavecchia, where the American consul issued him a passport in the name of George Moore. With no money of his own, he took 1,000 francs from "the fund" to cover his expenses. On July 16 he sailed for Marseilles, with Switzerland as his second destination. The ship's Corsican captain, to whom he revealed his true identity, asked no questions. There was a tense moment when he was recognized by some Romans who got off in Livorno. They pretended not to see him, as they were more interested in reaching Gaeta to implore the pope's return to Rome (direct service from Rome to Gaeta had been halted). In Genoa he dared not step ashore to visit his mother. No one bothered him in Marseilles, from where he proceeded immediately to Geneva. The exiles who had preceded him there were already at each others' throats, full of bitterness and recriminations. Gallenga was among them, lamenting that casualties had not been higher and noticing that Mazzini seemed to be in good health: "True, a few thousand desperate adventurers have performed marvels in Rome, but not all of them are dead, and their chief, Mazzini, is here in Geneva, where he dines every day at the *Balance* with good appetite."[47]

Mazzini's mental state left much to be desired: "I can neither sleep nor stay awake as I would like; I cannot think or act. . . . Sensations are more like a memory than a reality; action, even the possibility of action, recedes to a distant future."[48] The future that he saw was a wasteland, its only landmark the grave that awaited his wasting body, he said. Poor vision, toothaches, neuralgia, and "spleen" were his constant companions. To satisfy his craving for action, he organized small groups of volunteers for hopeless missions into Lombardy, urging them to live off the enemy and the countryside. Not everything was bleak, however. When he learned that Charles Albert was dead (he had resigned the throne and gone into exile after the defeat of Novara), his only comment was that finally he could do no more harm. It also helped some to think that the French would sink deeper into the Italian quagmire now that they had an army of occupation in Rome. Louis Napoleon, soon to be Emperor Napoleon III, replaced Charles Albert as the personification of political evil in Mazzini's mind.[49]

"We must prove to Europe that Italians are practical, that we can be concrete, that we can turn our aspirations into reality, and that we pay attention to detail, even when it seems unimportant."[50] Thus he dedicated himself once again to the struggle, with his eyes on Europe and his impatience for action sharpened by the heady experience of power. His language mimicked the action that he craved. "Injure [ferite] the greedy in their interests" he wrote, urging Romans to boycott French products.[51] The word ferite was a command to inflict physical harm. He asked pointedly who authorized others to defend him from charges that he encouraged political assassinations; he was capable of defending himself, he asserted, if he wanted to.[52] He seemed to agree with Gallenga that there had not been enough martyrs, but he also blamed his rivals. If the revolution had failed, it was not only because of Austria and France, but also because moderates and royalists had nullified his efforts to unleash the people. "The people are our true strength," he wrote to his mother in December of 1849, "and I know that the people only need good leaders and education. If I were in Genoa I would do there what I did with the people in Rome."[53]

Mundane concerns intruded. It was annoying to have to share his toothpicks with his companions in exile. When his mother heard of his predicament she sent him more than toothpicks. Now that she controlled the purse strings she fully funded the trust that would provide for him after her death.[54] Susan also came to his rescue. She left London with her two children to join him so that they "could live for a time together." The Swiss wanted him out of the country, and a woman with two children made it more difficult for him to elude their searches. So he sent Susan to live near his mother in Genoa, where the police questioned her marital status and arrested her for cohabiting with the notorious Mazzini. They released her, but a furious Mazzini summoned her back to Switzerland in December to share with him a two-bedroom suite.[55] That same month the Piedmontese ministry of the interior sent an agent provocateur to kidnap Mazzini and spirit him away to face justice in Piedmont. That plot failed, but when a similar one by the Austrians brought about the capture and imprisonment of the Hungarian patriot Louis Kossuth, it created a fear that governments were out to apprehend revolutionists and bring them to justice.[56]

The following seven months were spent mostly in Lausanne with Saffi, Montecchi, Quadrio, and Pisacane as Mazzini's daily companions, raising funds, organizing small-scale raids into Lombardy, buying a printing press, setting up a publishing house, publishing a newspaper, and nursing the fledgling Italian National Association, which counted no more than twenty members in Switzerland but was making substantial headway in Rome. The association was supposed to bring in money by selling shares of stock at 100 francs each. The proceeds helped pay for publishing and distributing the paper *L'Italia del Popolo*. With a circulation estimated at 2,500–3,000 copies, smuggled into Italy at considerable cost, the paper may have struck fear in the hearts of governments, as Mazzini claimed, but its short life span, from September 1849 to February 1851, attests to an uphill struggle to stay alive.[57]

An article that Mazzini wrote for the paper was particularly noteworthy. Entitled "The Holy Alliance of the People," it was both a postmortem on revolution and a program for the future.[58] It cast recent events in broad historical perspective to show that the victory of reaction was only temporary. The lesson of 1848 was that democratic movements must be better organized and coordinated both nationally and internationally: "What we have today are instincts, aspirations, longings for an alliance, but not an alliance; we have democrats by the millions, and democratic schools, sects, and conventicles, but no democracy." By virtue of their size, cultural homogeneity, and resources, nations were the natural intermediaries between individuals and humanity, because individuals were too small and humanity too large, and they would be the vehicles for change. As to the forms of democracy, electoral majorities based on universal suffrage were not essential. Rather, faith in progress was necessary, because it predisposed the mind to accept change. Progress transforms the closed family that cares only for its members into an institution open to larger ideals; progress makes property accessible to all; progress transforms formal worship into true religiosity. Finally, "the People's Europe" would be united some day to avoid the extremes of "anarchy of absolute (national) independence and the regimentation of conquest [*concentramento della conquista*]." Before this scenario could unfold, however, the democratic movement must gain political control of the state through revolution, give itself an international organization based on councils of the different nationalities, and be governed by an international council of national representatives "venerable for their learning and character, for their intellect and their love, for the sacrifices endured in Europe and America." Such a council would also serve as an embryonic government, levy a "tax for democracy," provide low-interest loans to small businesses, support public education, and "extend fraternal help to all those populations who demand recognition of their rights." The article ended with a call to action: "Publicly or secretely according to place, let us regroup, understand one another, and prepare. The day when, like the first Christians, we will be able to say we are one in the name of God and the People, the new pagans will be powerless; we will defeat the old order; God will guide us toward the future."

Expecting an early resumption of the revolutionary struggle, Mazzini stressed the need for organization and international unity. Hence his efforts to reach out to other leaders in Central and Eastern Europe, and to American republicans and abolitionists, whom he looked upon as allies in the movement for international democracy. All that was consistent with his moral stance, but, typically, he did not stand only on principle. In the spirit of political realism, he reassessed Machiavelli, whom he had previously condemned. The flaw was not in Machiavelli, whose analytical intelligence had performed a useful service by exposing the failings of a decaying society, but in his modern-day followers, who persisted in being analytical at a time when a new age called for faith rather than critical intelligence. He had the moderate Gioberti in mind, but that did not prevent him from carrying on a dialogue with other moderates to broaden the base of the democratic movement. He stretched himself to study English economic theory so that he could better understand the practical issues of the day.

Mazzini excluded cooperation with socialists (the new pagans), who attacked private property and questioned the national ideal. Karl Marx was not a familiar name when Mazzini wrote his article for *L'Italia del Popolo*, but he was well acquainted with Louis Blanc and French "systematic socialists" like Etienne Cabet, Charles Fourier, and Pierre Proudhon, whom he blamed for frightening the French bourgeoisie into the embrace of Louis Napoleon.[59] Enemies cropped up both on the left and on the right. In Piedmont, which he called the "Siberia of Italy," perhaps in ironic reference to the presence there of thousands of political exiles, he was attacked both by the government and by political exiles.[60] Massimo d'Azeglio, prime minister from 1849 to 1852, was a patriot who nursed a visceral dislike for Mazzini. Aristocratic by birth and temperament, and loyal to the House of Savoy, he thought Mazzini foolish, dangerous, and cowardly.[61] More upsetting were the attacks that came from erstwhile collaborators like Felice Orsini, who had been at his side in Rome. Orsini was a temperamental radical who criticized Mazzini for negotiating with the French and for restraining militant republicans like himself. "All of which shows," concluded Orsini, "that Mazzini has great intelligence but little political common sense."[62] Others accused him of venal failings, calling him a lax administrator and blaming him for the disappearance of works of art and the squandering of public funds in Rome.[63]

Mazzini responded to such polemics with silence, but he could not ignore the alarming signs of competition. The French in Rome were in a good position to influence developments in the rest of peninsula, especially in Naples, where French agents promoted the candidacy to the throne of Louis Napoleon's cousin Lucien Murat, the son of Joachim Murat, who had ruled in Naples under Napoleon. Murat's name appealed to Neapolitan liberals, who expected to fare better under a French monarchy than under the reigning Bourbon dynasty.[64] There was never a Muratist party, but Mazzini feared Murat's candidacy because it attracted liberals and was an obvious stalking horse for French dominance. It was all the more alarming that the Muratist intrigue in Naples coincided with a new effort by Louis Napoleon to consolidate his personal rule. Mazzini spent almost the entire month of May 1850 in Paris, expecting a democratic uprising in response to government proposals to restrict universal suffrage. He did what he could to encourage the opposition and made contact with other European radicals to try to form a common democratic front against Louis Napoleon, all the time hiding from the police, who knew of his presence but were unable or perhaps reluctant to capture him. The bill, part of what one member of the opposition called "the internal Roman expedition," passed without any uprising.[65] There was nothing left for Mazzini to do but leave. The passage of the bill put an end to Mazzini's hopes that Paris might once again give the signal for revolution.

By May 27, 1850, he was back in London, feeling dispirited and ill. Two stressful years on the continent had taken their toll; he was overweight and suffering from headaches, backaches, digestive problems, and general malaise. Jane Carlyle noticed that her friend's beard and hair had turned gray since she had last seen him. He was forty-five years old, weighed down by a series of failures, and facing an uncertain future. The Roman experience had enhanced his public stature, but in private he questioned his own performance. When Emilie Ashurst tried to cheer him up by ascribing to him the attributes of greatness, his stilted English made the point that what he lacked was the vital ingredient of capacity for success: "In the *actual* time, the great man is the succeeding man. So many elements are at work, that there *must* be some vital deficiency in a man who cannot organize them so as to conquer."[66]

Dispensing bracing advice to others may have helped him heal himself. When Saffi complained that he was exhausted, Mazzini told him to eat properly, work hard, smoke many cigars, drink lots of strong coffee, and not to pity himself: "I admit no nervous illness among exiles; take walks, nourish yourself, do something concrete, don't think too much about your health, and you will get well."[67] There was always something to do. To begin with, now that Piedmont was a constitutional monarchy and therefore more likely to appeal to the British, he would have to convince the public and the government in Britain that Piedmont was still an unreliable ally and that republicans could still be counted on to oppose Austrian and French designs in Italy.[68] To that end, he launched the Friends of Italy Society. Based on the Ashurst clan at Muswell Hill and the European exiles drawn to that part of the city, the Friends of Italy did double duty as a propaganda organization and as a political lobby. Through that organization Mazzini pursued his own foreign policy, just as if he were still a head of government.

Undercover activities were more difficult now that telegraphy and photography permitted easier recognition and tracking of suspects. Mazzini countered with redoubled efforts at secrecy—more elaborate codes, inventive disguises, and sophisticated forgeries—and by cultivating his own secret sources of information. It was a game of psychological warfare at which he excelled, but what was needed to sustain the image of power was *fatti e non parole* (deeds, not words). The ordinary men and women who fought on the walls of Rome showed that the people could be counted on to fight, but the initiative still had to come from the few who dedicated their lives to interpreting the popular will. How, he asked, can we attribute to an enslaved population "that power which rightly belongs only to a free people?"[69]

For the Italian National Committee based in London, consisting of himself, Montecchi, and Saffi, he claimed the right to speak for the Roman republic, never defunct in his own mind, and for the national movement in general regardless of political orientation. The disappointing yield of a "national loan" intended to raise 10,000,000 lire by selling shares of 25 and 100 lire confirmed Mazzini's fear that the sense of *italianità* was poorly developed. As always when faced with disappointment in Italy, he turned to Europe, launching the London-based European Democratic Committee to coordinate activities on behalf of oppressed nationalities. The European democratic movement was like a rope, he argued; it did not matter whether one pulled from the left or the right, as long as someone pulled. Consisting originally of Mazzini for Italy, Alexander Ledru-Rollin for France, Albert Darasz for Poland, and Arnold Ruge for Germany, the committee was later expanded to include Demetriu Bratianu and Nicolai Golesco for Romania. The Democratic Committee served mainly as a cover for conspiratorial projects against Austria and as a sounding board for Mazzini's views on the issue of nationalities. As a publicity device, it confirmed Mazzini's image as one of the "great men of exile," which was a noteworthy achievement considering that Italian exiles were a minority in the movement.[70]

Publicly he exuded confidence that revolution was only a step away; privately he was doubtful, confiding that only mistakes by the great powers were likely to give revolution a second chance. He hoped secretely that governments would rather risk war and revolution than sustain the cost of maintaining large standing armies.[71] Keeping the specter of revolution alive might help to push governments into the abyss of war and revolution. The problem was that the finances of the revolution, not to mention his own, were in much worse shape than those of governments. He lived modestly, as always, in rented lodgings on Radnor Street in Chelsea, sharing them with Saffi, several songbirds, and a dog. With Susan still in Switzerland at his insistence, probably to avoid offending his disapproving English friends with her presence, the landlady cooked and provided for all. He put up with the indifferent cooking and the lack of privacy, but fretted at not being able to help the many exiles, and some who only claimed to be exiles, who came to him for help. An unexpected inheritance of 3,000 francs from an aunt provided a brief respite. His mother sent him whatever he asked for, worrying all the while that there would not be enough left over when she died to provide for him for the rest of his life.

Prominence brought on attacks and rumors meant to discredit his person and his work. Some rumors were scurrilous, depicting him as an oriental potentate living a sybaritic life surrounded by adoring concubines, or as the head of a religious cult served hand and foot by a coterie of female acolytes.[72] Others were more imaginative. A novel that claimed to be based on fact presented him as an incorruptible fanatic, all the more dangerous because he lived only to subvert society. Written by his old nemesis Antonio Bresciani, *The Jew of Verona* was first published in installments by the Jesuit journal *Civiltà Cattolica* in 1851, before appearing in book form in 1852. This compendium of conservative stereotypes cleverly combined fact and fiction to create the impression that Mazzini was the head of an international subversive conspiracy that brought together Jews and political subversives. It anticipated themes of antisemitic propaganda that would come together more than fifty years later in the notorious Protocols of the Elders of Zion.[73] The French weighed in with a full-scale attack that sought to expose his inconsistencies and described his mind as being "fertile in words and sterile in ideas."[74]

Mazzini's name often came up in Turin, the Piedmontese capital, where thousands of political refugees congregated after 1848, attracted by government subsidies for expatriates from other Italian states, by prospects of employment for the educated, by the political life made possible by the constitution, and by the reputation of King Victor Emmanuel II. Thirty-one years old when he succeeded to his father Charles Albert in 1849, ambitious, shrewd, and likable, Victor Emmanuel was still a political cipher, but publicists were already at work to create the image of the honorable, courageous, and trustworthy monarch (*il Re Galantuomo*) familiar to later generations. Cautiously so as not to incur the wrath of Austria, he was also being built up as a sensible ruler who would advance the cause of Italian independence without the risk of revolution.

Although Mazzini continued to believe that Piedmont would fight only for territorial gain, he kept his thoughts about Victor Emmanuel to himself for the time being and refrained from conspiring against him as he had against his father. He wished to attract the refugees in Piedmont, and attacking the king and government that protected them would have been a political mistake. Instead, he competed with the government by showing solicitousness toward the exiles wherever they happened to be. The Italian Emigration Society of Turin, founded in 1851, had Mazzinian officials in the early 1850s. Agostino Depretis, who belonged to the democratic minority in the Piedmontese, parliament worked closely with Mazzini in helping to organize Mazzinian societies that crossed class lines.[75]

The problem of the early 1850s was the same as that of 1848: how to maintain the unity of the national movement without surrendering to monarchists or, for that matter, to republicans who did not share Mazzini's vision of the future. His answer was also the same: postponing political decisions until Italy was liberated, and then submitting them to a freely elected national assembly. He wished to appear conciliatory both toward monarchists who worked for independence and republicans who did not agree with him. Of the latter there were now more than ever, for the republican movement had emerged from the events of 1848–49 richer in experience and more complex. There were republicans who leaned toward Piedmont (Enrico Cosenz, Giacomo Medici, Antonio Mordini), republicans who favored a federal solution (Carlo Cattaneo, Alberto Mario), republicans who leaned toward socialism (Giuseppe Ferrari, Benedetto Musolino, Carlo Pisacane), and republicans who were simply too independent, volatile, or doctrinaire to work well with Mazzini (Filippo De Boni, Giuseppe Mazzoni, Vincenzo Brusco Onnis, and Giuseppe Sirtori). Even in the Mazzinian stronghold of Genoa, a war committee made up of Cosenz, Medici, and Pisacane openly criticized Mazzini's abiding faith in the tactics of insurrection.

The publication in 1851 of Ferrari's *La federazione repubblicana*, Giuseppe Montanelli's *Introduzione ad alcuni appunti storici sulla rivoluzione in Italia*, and Pisacane's *La guerra combattuta in Italia negli anni 1848–1849* was a sign of republican diversity and marked the beginning of an Italian school of theoretical socialism. Cattaneo, Ferrari, Montanelli, and Daniele Manin were ready to challenge Mazzini's leadership. Manin was an important new figure who had emerged from the Venetian uprising. An independent-minded lawyer trained to think in practical terms, Manin did not approve of conspiracies and did not share Mazzini's faith in the educational value of action. Manin looked not for martyrs, but for the least arduous path toward Italian independence. Soon, he would decide that national independence was worth the sacrifice of his republican ideals.

In spite of Mazzini's efforts to keep the movement united, some dissidents bolted from him, charging that he spoke like a democrat but acted like a dictator. There was indeed something authoritarian about him, an intolerance of contradiction that was noticed even by those like Alexander Herzen and Carl Schurz who admired him. Sirtori, a republican even more mystical than Mazzini, resigned from the National Association after charging that Mazzini wanted to impose his republican views on the organization. Mazzini replied that the unity of the movement was his sole concern, but the simultaneous reiteration of his own intransigent republicanism was not reassuring. In July of 1851, Lamennais, Manin, Montanelli, and Giorgio Pallavicino formed what they called a Latin Committee. It consisted of French, Spanish, and Italian republicans in Paris, and its main purpose was to offer an alternative to Mazzini's leadership of the national movement. Cattaneo charged that Mazzini's small-scale conspiracies did more harm than good and suggested that they alienated wealthy Italians who might otherwise support the republican movement. Mazzini countered that he was willing to let others take the lead provided they were willing to do more than talk, but such criticisms coming from Italians living in Paris only confirmed his fears that France was a breeding ground for defectors.[76]

It was not France but Piedmont that beckoned, especially after Camillo Cavour succeeded d'Azeglio as prime minister in November of 1852. Cavour shared d'Azeglio's anti-Mazzinian sentiments, and knew how to advance his own agenda by playing on the fears that Mazzini aroused in sober-minded people. He courted dissidents, stood up to royal demands when they threatened the prerogatives of parliament, attacked clerical privileges, used the power of government to encourage economic development, and maneuvered skillfully in parliament to form political majorities behind his program. Moderates came to regard Cavour as their natural champion and to consider Mazzini a divisive presence that would alienate "the only orderly elements capable of fighting the foreigner." Probably more than by any other single development, Mazzini's appeal was undermined by Cavour's presence at the head of Piedmont's government.[77]

Mazzini, however, continued to see Louis Napoleon as his chief enemy. "Antagonism toward the French grows in my heart day by day," Mazzini wrote to Saffi in June of 1850, shortly after returning from Paris. Later that year he addressed an open letter to Louis Napoleon that was filled with embarrassing references to the French president's past as a conspirator.[78] What made Louis Napoleon particularly dangerous was the combination of expansionist designs and friendly facade as the protector of oppressed nationalities: "I dislike him because I like clear-cut positions."[79] Mazzini's personal animosity, which had spelled trouble for Charles Albert, did so again for Louis Napoleon. Rumors that Mazzini

was planning his assassination circulated in 1850 and intensified after
Mazzini paid a secret visit to Paris in 1851. After the bloody coup of
December 1851 that enabled Louis Napoleon to serve on as president
(he assumed the title of emperor a year later), Mazzini may have hired
a mysterious figure whom he called the Avenger to inflict retribution,
but the Avenger absconded with the money and the police broke up the
plot.[80]

A stream of French political refugees that included Armand Barbes,
Louis Blanc, Alexandre Ledru-Rollin, Victor Hugo, Démosthène Ollivier,
and Jules Leroux swelled the ranks of exiles that gathered mostly in
London to write, plot, and quarrel. "What sufferings, what privations,
what tears . . . ," commented Herzen, "and what triviality, what narrow-
ness, what poverty of intellectual powers, of resources, of understanding, of obstinacy in quarreling, what pettiness in wounded
vanity!"[81] The German exile Carl Schurz, who visited Mazzini in 1852,
reported that the favorite topic of conversation among exiles was "to
whom should belong the leadership in the coming revolution."[82]
Mazzini's answer was that the initiative belonged to Italy, but that the
revolution was universal. If materialism was the root of all evil, if the
dissolving power of rationalism caused spiritual malaise, if the modern
obsession with personal rights was responsible for the loss of community, then the remedy was in the formula that had been his since the
1830s: God and the People.[83]

From that position Mazzini launched a full-scale attack on socialism.
While in the past he had sometimes referred to himself as a socialist,
his tone changed after events in France showed that fear of socialism
could push peasants and the middle classes into the arms of Louis
Napoleon. Careful not to condemn French social thought in its entirety,
and to exclude from criticism reformers like Ledru-Rollin who believed
in the principle of voluntary association, he attacked those socialists
whom he found to be most infected by the spirit of materialism. Louis
Blanc was a special target for his principle that individuals should
receive according to need. Need, argued Mazzini, was not a fixed entity
that could serve as a basis for economic compensation. It was work done
(*opere*) that deserved compensation, because work entailed both material production and spiritual fulfillment.[84]

A highly polemical essay of March 1851 entitled "The Duty of Democracy" summed up Mazzini's case against French socialism and outlined
his social program. The free association of individuals, the breakup of
banking and other monopolies, government loans to help small businesses, a progressive income tax, tax credits for the poor, and free
education for all were the key features of his program. There was no
need for socialism, he argued, because republicanism and democracy
addressed the most urgent issues, which were feeding the hungry, giving

work to the unemployed, and educating the masses. These goals could be achieved by political means and by universal suffrage. As for what the socialists proposed, he did not mince words: "I accuse the socialists, particularly the leaders, of falsifying, mangling, and cheapening [our] great idea with the absolutism of their systems, of transgressing against individual liberty, the sovereignty of the people, and our law of progress."[85]

This was an open and deliberate declaration of war that cost Mazzini dearly. Even close friends like Ledru-Rollin and George Sand were put off by his bitterness and rancor, offended also by his animus against everything French. That animus manifested itself even in petty matters, like his insistence that Italians made better chocolate than the French, to prove which point he asked his mother for samples of Italian chocolate to give to his friends in London.[86] Italians were also put off by his phobia of France, including Ferrari, who was indeed influenced by French socialism, and Pisacane, who stressed that the masses had to be offered material incentives if they were to fight for national liberation. Against such materialistic notions, Mazzini proposed a more encompassing version of God and the People that underscored his ecumenical outlook: God is God, and Humanity is his Prophet. This he called the Italian social formula. Spelled out in more detail, the formula relied on liberty and association, which meant free people pursuing material improvements by means of voluntary associations. Let the French have their sectarian, materialistic socialism; the Italian road to socialism would be based on voluntary association and individual liberty.[87] Otherwise, he cautioned a group of Genoese workers who had made him an honorary member of their association, "a hideous class dualism will emerge, as is already evident in Lombardy and elsewhere, which we [must] try to eliminate by sharing sacrifice."[88]

There were not many movements or initiatives that combined spirituality and worldliness, concern for material and spiritual welfare, individualism and group solidarity, patriotism and social justice. His name was now popular among British workers, who saw him as a figure in the radical tradition of Joseph Priestly and Thomas Paine, but in Italy he had to rely on others to do his work. In Piedmont, Depretis proposed a pact of brotherhood among worker societies; he had other followers in Genoa and other towns in Liguria, but most worker societies developed under the control of moderates, who wanted to keep workers away from politics. An organization of workers in Austrian-dominated Lombardy that combined social and patriotic objectives caught his attention. Its organizer was a priest, Enrico Tazzoli, who devoted his life to teaching, charity, and work among peasants—the kind of patriotic, progressive clergyman that Mazzini looked for but seldom found. Heading a network of societies in Lombardy and Venetia, Tazzoli became implicated in activities that were as much political as social, and therefore suspect to the government. His arrest and that of many of his collaborators in January of 1852, the trials and severe punishments that followed, which included public whippings, were shocks that reverberated throughout the Mazzinian organization in Lombardy and Venetia, prompting many Mazzinians to question the wisdom of agitation and conspiracy at a time when calm prevailed everywhere in Europe.[89]

There were now clear divisions among monarchists, republicans, and socialists that threatened to divide the national movement. Antonio Gallenga warned Mazzini that he could not keep them all tied to his cart and that he should work with the half million Italians from the middle and upper classes who had shown their commitment to the national cause; Gallenga, however, also recognized that such a choice meant yielding to the moderates and to the Piedmontese leadership, which was precisely what Mazzini was not willing to do.[90] From the many discords emerged an important element that distanced itself from Mazzini without breaking with him and sought to mediate differences, particularly between republicans and monarchists, moderates and democrats. On this swing group of pragmatic democrats, which included prominent figures like Agostino Bertani, Nino Bixio, Enrico Cosenz, Giacomo Medici, and Antonio Mordini, Mazzini relied increasingly in the years of his declining influence that were still to come.

THE URGE TO ACT

The death of Maria Mazzini on August 9, 1852, was a shock to Mazzini, who had not seen her since 1848. She died following a stroke suffered while reading to a friend his latest letter. Her last words were "my son, my son."[91] Her funeral was a public event and a tribute to him, for it was their close relationship that made her revered. The loss of the one person in Italy on whom he could rely unconditionally made him even more dependent on his English friends, who offered him the same kind of unconditional loyalty. For several days he would see no one; then he wrote a few brief lines to the woman who was now his closest friend, Caroline Stansfeld, to say that he was strong.[92] Caroline's sister Emilie went to Genoa to arrange permanent burial. She chose the grave site and the inscription, which summed up Maria's life as she herself might have described it: "Maria Mazzini, Mother of the Exile Giuseppe Mazzini."[93]

The months preceding Maria's death had seen the start of a new round of conspiracies, by which Mazzini hoped to trigger upheavals similar to those of 1848. Funding these activities was one reason why he went through his inheritance at breakneck speed, to the dismay of his old friend Filippo Bettini, who was his mother's executor. Rome was the center of the organization, but his hopes centered on Lombardy, from where he thought he could strike directly at Austria. The individual cells of the Lombard network reported directly to him in London, from where he directed the conspiracy through secret emissaries. This created problems: individual cells did not communicate directly, Mantua competed with Milan, lines of command broke down, and workers and middle-class conspirators regarded one another with mutual suspicion. Mazzini insisted that these problems were really opportunities. He counted especially on workers to shake the middle classes out of their torpor and show them how to fight.[94] Insisting that Austrian rule was unpopular, but fearing also that the program of peaceful reforms initiated after 1849 would win support for Austria, he did everything to fan popular hatred of the *tedeschi* who humiliated Italian men and women by whipping them in public, invading their homes, barring qualified Italians from high offices, and claiming the best seats in theaters, parks, and cafés.

Mazzini counted on Hungarian troops stationed in Lombardy to support a popular uprising, spreading among them leaflets that accused the imperial government of using Hungarian troops to oppress Italians and Italian troops to oppress Hungarians. Louis Kossuth, he claimed, supported his plans for insurrection in Lombardy, which would be the signal for insurrection in Hungary and elsewhere.[95] He reached out to Italians in the Ottoman Empire and to sympathetic Americans. The shiploads of American dollars that Mazzini expected when Kossuth toured the United States in 1852 did not materialize, but after Franklin Pierce was elected president that same year, apparently with the help of the German-American vote and with the backing of the republican movement of Young America, American diplomats and warships received instructions to cooperate with republicans in Europe. It seemed to Mazzini that he was finally realizing his dream of an Italian initiative in world revolution.[96]

Many local insurrections breaking out simultaneously would produce a general European conflagration that would topple both the Austrian and French emperors. This would be "war, not conspiracies," he told the doubters who questioned the plan. Prepare for action, he told his contacts in Genoa; after what had happened in 1848 and 1849, he did not want to "feel ashamed of being Italian."[97] Before anything happened, the headquarters of the conspiracy in Rome fell to massive arrests by the papal police. That left the Lombard network still functional, in spite of the damage done by the arrest of Tazzoli and his collaborators. In Milan there were sporadic attacks on Austrian soldiers and public officials in the summer of 1852. The city was beginning to experience the problems of industrialization. Artisans and craftsmen in traditional occupations felt threatened by the rise of new industries, there was unemployment among textile workers, and labor unions were just beginning to form under liberalized laws that permitted workers to organize. Road workers, masons, shoemakers, printers, and goldsmiths were in the forefront of worker agitation. That August Mazzini received an appeal for help from a recently formed association of republican workers. An emissary from London assured them that they were not alone, that if they rose up in arms other cities would respond, and that theirs would be the spark that set off the revolution.[98]

On January 2, 1853, Mazzini left London to direct the conspiracies from Lugano. Things started to go wrong almost immediately. His plans may have been secret, but his presence was not, even though he had shaved his mustache and wore attire different from his usual. A premonition of failure came to him when he lost a ring that was a gift from his mother. "I shall be accursed," he wrote to Caroline Stansfeld a few days after his arrival in Lugano on January 8, "that is not much, [but] the cause will be lost, ruined, and subjected for ever to foreign initiative. This is something to be thought of seriously. I have never felt my own moral responsibility so highly involved." He did not get in touch with Bertani, Medici, and Mordini right away, perhaps because he knew that his regular collaborators did not approve of what he was doing. Depretis sent him some money raised in Piedmont, but he was the exception among what Mazzini now called the educated who liked talk more than action. Enthusiasm for action was to be found only among workers, some two hundred of whom were ready to take to the streets. If they did not act quickly, the police would soon put an end to the plot. It was a Mazzini full of foreboding who wrote on the eve of the insurrection that he could rely only on God and on himself: "all my plan is there."[99]

He also seems to have believed however, that success was possible if Milan moved and Genoa and Rome responded, and that success would not be confined to Italy. His messianic cast of mind stood fully revealed in this clash of foreboding and expectations; on the one hand he was prepared to bear witness to his faith even if it meant defeat and martyrdom, and on the other he was trusting in the power of will and conviction to inflame others and carry the day. It was his first encounter with militant workers so unlike the docile itinerants that he knew in London. Although he was always the first to warn about the dangers of class actions, he could not resist the temptation to play the social card. Hence his avoidance of contacts with collaborators who did not share his social views and his reassurances to workers that they could count on the support of his underground network, whose power was magnified in the popular imagination by the fear it inspired in governments and among the well-to-do. A group of Milanese notables met in the salon of the liberal Countess Clara Maffei to decide how to respond to Mazzini's intrigues with workers. Citing certain Austrian retaliation and the need to avoid useless bloodshed, many of them who until then had seen him as an inspirational figure decided "not to follow Giuseppe Mazzini, never to follow him again." With the notable exceptions of Benedetto Cairoli, Gabriele Rosa, Eugenio Birzio, and Giuseppe Piolti de' Bianchi, who vowed to support him, the followers abandoned their messiah who brooded and agonized across the Swiss border.[100]

February 6, 1853, the date chosen for the Milan uprising, was the last Sunday of the Carnival season, a festive moment when soldiers mixed freely with civilians in the city's streets, parks, and cafés. It would be misleading to suggest that what happened that day was scripted by Mazzini, whose role was probably limited to lending his name to a project run by others, who were in close touch with people and events on the ground. Mazzini, however, was certainly responsible for conveying the impression that he had means at his disposal to make sure that an insurrection in Milan would be answered by insurrections elsewhere. In reality, he was out of touch, isolated, and prey to the extremes of depression and euphoria that he experienced in moments of crisis. The appeal that he issued at the last moment, too late for it to be posted, was a truculent call on "soldiers, women, educated youth, and the people" to wage "war to the knife" against enemy soldiers and public officials. Attacks on army posts, barricades in the streets, and the ringing of church bells completed his scenario of revolution. In Mazzini's imagination, Milan was to repeat the glorious feats of the Five Days of 1848.[101]

What ensued was a lesser drama that brought tragedy to many and liberation to no one. Few of the several thousand conspirators who were expected to gather at points appeared at the appointed time. An attempt by a handful to seize an army post was quickly repulsed and the scattered violence that followed was hard to distinguish from common criminality. Eleven soldiers and four civilians lost their lives in sordid street encounters that had little in common with revolutionary violence. The authorities declared martial law in the city and arrested more than four hundred suspects. Speedy military trials resulted in fifteen executions. Officials levied a special tax to pay for the restoration of law and order and compensate victims or their families.

Mazzini watched and waited in Switzerland, hoping against hope for news that the Milanese were still fighting, but by nightfall he knew the truth, that failure was total and irremediable. He knew that the damage would be great, but he tried to contain it by arguing that he had not initiated the conspiracy, had only responded to pleas for help when no one else would, and had supported it with the limited means at his disposal because he felt that it was the only honorable thing to do. What he said was factually true, but he forgot to mention that his own assurances and encouragement had surely played a role, and he exaggerated by claiming that if others had helped instead of obstructing and if the revolt could have been prolonged for just another twenty-four hours, then all of Italy would have responded. Even in failure the revolt had not been wasted, he insisted, because acting was better than doing nothing, people learned by fighting, and people who knew how to fight could hope better of the future. [102]

This was Mazzini's way of claiming moral victory in the face of defeat, but his defense did not save his reputation or the fortunes of the republican movement from lasting damage. In the eyes of many middle-class Italians he was now seen as an irresponsible agitator who played on class hatreds. Wealthy Milanese shut their minds and purses to his appeals, forcing him to rely almost entirely on what he could raise abroad. He had to ask Herzen for money to return to England, where he also faced problems. In London, the executive committee of the National Association resolved not to support popular agitation in the future; Mattia Montecchi broke publicly with Mazzini.[103] Kossuth accused him of making unauthorized use of his name among Hungarian troops in Italy and criticized him for continuing to rely on conspiracies and local insurrections when it took massive military power to obtain results. In Paris, Montanelli called Mazzini an inept agitator who engaged in *congiure parlanti* (talking conspiracies) and charged that his tactics harmed the very cause of revolution. Cattaneo was so outraged that he informed on Mazzini's fellow conspirators in Switzerland. Medici sought to exclude Mazzini from the leadership of the republican movement, demanding that "no headquarters from abroad should impose ideas or determine the time and manner of insurrection."[104]

Cavour and Garibaldi were the indirect beneficiaries of the Milan debacle. Garibaldi was in America, but his stock among republicans rose as Mazzini's fell; he emerged as the most prestigious figure among democrats, a republican who did not allow his personal convictions to stand in the way of collaboration with the monarchy for the good of Italy. Bertani, Mario, Medici, and Mordini were prominent republicans who began to gravitate toward him after 1853. From then on they would regard Mazzini as someone worth listening to, but not necessarily worth following. Cavour was the rising star among moderates and liberals; though independent and willful, he was a servant of the Savoy dynasty.

Mazzini did not refuse to collaborate with either Cavour or Garibaldi, but his principled, stubborn republicanism relegated him to the margins. Monarchists suspected him of harboring subversive designs; intransigent republicans found him too accommodating. Few republicans attacked him openly, but the very respect expressed for him was a sign of his political marginalization.

NOTES

Works frequently cited in the notes have been identified by the following abbreviations:

BDM　　　　　　*Bollettino della Domus Mazziniana*

EN　　　　　　　*Edizione Nazionale, Scritti editi ed inediti di Giuseppe Mazzini* (1906–90), 106 vols.

PGI　　　　　　*Protocollo della Giovine Italia. Appendice agli scritti editi ed inediti* (1916–22), 6 vols.

RSR　　　　　　*Rassegna Storica del Risorgimento*

SEI　　　　　　*Scritti editi ed inediti di Giuseppe Mazzini* (1861–91), 18 vols.

1. PGI, VI, 297.
2. PGI, VI, 324.
3. PGI, VI, 328.
4. EN, XXXIX, 4–5.
5. PGI, VI, 28.
6. According to Jessie White Mario, *The Birth of Modern Italy* (New York: Scribner's Sons, 1909), 137–38, the Milanese boycott was inspired by Carlo Botta's description of the Boston Tea Party in his *Storia della guerra dell'indipendenza degli Stati Uniti d'America*, first published in 1809.
7. From Dennis Mack Smith, ed., *The Making of Italy, 1796–1870* (New York: Harper and Row, 1968), 148.
8. Quoted in Mario, *The Birth of Modern Italy*, 145–46.
9. PGI, VI, 347.
10. EN, XXXV, 111–14.
11. From Ferrari's subsequent account of the meeting in Antonio Monti, *Un dramma fra gli esuli* (Milan: Risorgimento, 1921), 12–16, 77–85.
12. EN, XXXVIII, 22–24. See also the autobiography of Gabriele Rosa, in Gabriele Rosa and Silvio Pellico, *Due patrioti allo Spielberg* (Milan: Palazzi Editore, 1971), 109.
13. EN, XXXV, 207–9. Also, Luigi Fagan, ed., *Lettere ad Antonio Panizzi di uomini illustri e di amici italiani (1823–1870)* (Florence: Barbera, 1880), 168; Giorgio Pallavicino, *Memorie* (Turin: Ermanno Loescher, 1882–95), II, 26.
14. EN, XXXV, 268–70.
15. EN, XXXV, 270–71.
16. EN, XXXV, 272.
17. Giuseppe Garibaldi, *Memorie autobiografiche* (Florence: Giunti Marzocco, 1982), 194–95.
18. EN, LXVIII, 160.
19. EN, XXXV, 20, 266.
20. Giuseppe Gabussi, *Memorie per servire alla storia della rivoluzione negli Stati Romani dall'elevazione di Pio IX al pontificato sino alla caduta della repubblica* (Genoa: Tip. de' Sordomuti, 1851–52), II, 272–73.

21. Domenico Demarco, *Una rivoluzione sociale, la repubblica romana del 1849 (16 novembre 1848–3 luglio 1849)* (Naples: M. Fiorentino, 1944), 50–57.

22. EN, XXXVII, 220. Also, R. Corrado, "Filippo De Boni, i circoli popolari e la legazione di lui a Berna," in *Studi e documenti su Goffredo Mameli e la Repubblica Romana* (Imola: Galeati, 1927), 63–64.

23. EN, XXXVII, 207–8, 212–13, 220, 238.

24. Livio Pivano, *Mazzini e Giuditta Sidoli* (Modena: Guanda, 1936), 260–61.

25. Ferdinando Martini, *Il quarantotto in Toscana* (Florence: Bemporad, 1918), 267–71. See also Giuseppe Montanelli's somewhat different account of the events in *Appunti storici sulla rivoluzione d'Italia* (Turin: Chiantore, 1945), 49, 279–80n, and in *Memorie sull'Italia e specialmente sulla Toscana dal 1814 al 1859* (Turin: Società Editrice Italiana, 1853), II, 445–47, where he ascribes opposition to union with Rome to the Tuscan Giuseppe Mazzoni, the third member, along with Guerrazzi and Montanelli, of the Tuscan triumvirate.

26. EN, LXXVII, 341.

27. Alberto Caracciolo, *Roma capitale dal Risorgimento alla crisi dello Stato liberale* (Rome: Edizioni Rinascita, 1956), 5–10. On the economy of the Papal States before 1848, see John Bowring, *Report on the Statistics of Tuscany, Lucca, the Pontifical, and the Lombardo-Venetian States* (London: Clowes and Sons, 1837), 70–92.

28. *Le assemblee del Risorgimento* (Rome: Tipografia della Camera dei Deputati, 1911), *Roma*, III, 573.

29. Ibid., 590.

30. Gabussi, *Memorie per servire alla storia della rivoluzione degli Stati Romani*, III, 200.

31. EN, XLI, 77–78, 86–88, 119–21

32. George M. Trevelyan, *Garibaldi's Defense of the Roman Republic, 1848–49* (London: Longman, Green and Company, 1914), 114–34.

33. EN, XL, 73.

34. EN, XL, 123–24.

35. Franco Rizzi, *La coccarda e le campane. Comunità rurali e Repubblica Romana nel Lazio, 1848–49* (Milan: Franco Angeli, 1988), 17–22, 39–55, 61–63, 85–113.

36. *Le assemblee del Risorgimento*, *Roma*, IV, 653–54.

37. EN, XXXIX, 26.

38. EN, XLI, 206–7. Republican decrees from May 16 to July 5, 1949, including special measures and proclamations, appear in EN, XLIII, 3–182.

39. Mario, *The Birth of Modern Italy*, 199.

40. Trevelyan, *Garibaldi's Defense of the Roman Republic*, 227.

41. EN, XLIII, 168.

42. EN, XL, 107, 113.

43. *Appendice epistolario*, EN, IV, 183.

44. EN, XLIII, 174–82.

45. Mario, *Della vita di Giuseppe Mazzini* (Milan: Sonzogno, n.d.), 343.

46. Federico Comandini, *Cospirazioni di Romagna e Bologna nelle memorie di Federico Comandini e di altri patriotti del tempo, 1831–1857* (Bolo-

gna: Zanichelli, 1889), 218. Also, Filippo Spatafora, *Il Comitato d'Azione di Roma dal 1862 al 1867. Memorie* (Pisa: Nistri-Lischi, 1982), I, 56–63.

47. *Carteggio politico di Michelangelo Castelli* (Rome/Turin: L. Roux, 1890–91), I, 52.

48. EN, XL, 222.

49. EN, XL, 237, 307, 310, 374–75.

50. EN, XL, 263.

51. EN, XXXIX, 103–4; XL, 249.

52. Daniele Manin, *Lettere a Giorgio Pallavicino, con note e documenti sulla quistione italiana* (Turin: Unione Tipografico-Editrice, 1859), 117.

53. EN, XLII, 46.

54. EN, XLII, 42, 46–47.

55. EN, XL, 345, 351–52; *Appendice epistolario*, EN, VI, 577–78.

56. EN, XLII, 69–75, 79–81, 100–103, 106–08, 115, 180, 223–24, 260.

57. EN, XLII, 15–16, 135.

58. EN, XXXIX, 203–21.

59. EN, XLII, 108, 120; XLVI, 18–19, 253; XLVII, 83–84, 107–9, 254.

60. EN, XLII, 114.

61. Massimo d'Azeglio, *I miei ricordi* (Turin: Einaudi, 1949), 480.

62. Felice Orsini, *Lettere edite e inedite di F. Orsini, G. Mazzini, G. Garibaldi, F. D. Guerrazzi intorno alle cose d'Italia* (Milano: F. Sanvito, 1862), 294.

63. EN, XL, 140–42; XLII, 99.

64. EN. XLII, 110–11; LII, 239.

65. Mario, *Della vita di Giuseppe Mazzini*, 347–48.

66. EN, XLII, 160–61, 198, 203, 220, 230. Also, Mario, *The Birth of Modern Italy*, 219–20.

67. EN, XLII, 309–10.

68. EN, XLII, 228.

69. EN, XLII, 204; XLIV, 7.

70. EN, XLII, 85–91, 152–56, 169–73; XLIII, 199–203, 207–16; XLVI, 35–37. See also Arthur Lehning, *From Buonarroti to Bakunin. Studies in International Socialism* (Leiden: Brill, 1970), 169–70.

71. EN, XLII, 98, 162.

72. Domenico Giuriati, *Memorie d'emigrazione* (Milan: Treves, 1897), 237, 240–43.

73. See also the slanderous pamphlet by Giuseppe Lucarelli, *Le spie: Rimembranze storico-politiche del secolo XIX* (Genoa: Tip. Como, 1853).

74. Albert B. Cler, *Mazzini jugé par lui-même et par les sieus* (Paris: Plon Frères, 1853), 6.

75. See Terenzio Grandi, "Lettere inedite di Mazzini a Depretis," BDM, XIV, 1 (1968), 185–95.

76. EN, XLIV, 99–118; XLVI, 78; XLVII, 25–26, 39–40, 94, 111–12. See also Carlo Agrati, *Giuseppe Sirtori, il primo dei Mille* (Bari: Laterza, 1940), 120–22, and Carlo Cattaneo, *Epistolario*, (Florence: Barbera, 1949–56), II, 44–48.

77. Aurelio Saffi, *Ricordi e scritti* (Florence: Barbera, 1892–1905), IV, 89. See also Gian Biagio Furiozzi, *L'emigrazione politica in Piemonte nel decennio preunitario* (Florence: Olschki, 1979), 114–15, Piero Cironi, *Giuseppe Mazzini*

(Florence: Lumachi, 1901), 70–71, and Giovanni Visconti-Venosta, *Ricordi di gioventù* (Milan: Cogliati, 1904), 208, 217–21.

78. EN, XLII, 309; XLIII, 319.

79. EN, XLIV, 25.

80. EN, XLVII, 128; XLVIII, 142–45, 149–50.

81. Alexander Herzen, *My Past and Thoughts* (New York: Knopf, 1924–28), IV, 167.

82. *The Reminiscences of Carl Schurz* (New York: McClure, 1907–8), I, 371. See also pages 380–82, where Schurz describes Mazzini's appearance, manners, and lodgings.

83. EN, XLVI, 179.

84. EN, XLVII, 83–84, 107–9.

85. EN, XLVI, 208–9.

86. EN, XLV, 246.

87. EN, XLII, 307–8; XLVII, 255; XLVIII, 209–12; XLIX, 134.

88. EN, XLVIII, 125.

89. Tullio Urangia Tazzoli, "Giuseppe Mazzini e don Enrico Tazzoli," RSR, XXXVII (1950), 488–99.

90. Quoted in Emilia Morelli, *Giuseppe Mazzini; saggi e ricerche* (Rome: Edizioni dell'Ateneo, 1950), 83–85.

91. Cironi, *Giuseppe Mazzini*, 136–40.

92. EN, XLVII, 366.

93. *Mazzini's Letters to an English Family, 1855–60* (London: John Lane, 1922), II, 13–14n.

94. EN, XLIX, 286, 292, 299–301. Also, Visconti-Venosta, *Ricordi di gioventù, 1847–1860*, 229–34.

95. The tangled relationship between Kossuth and Mazzini is discussed in Jeno Koltay-Kastner, *Mazzini e Kossuth. Lettere e documenti inediti* (Florence: Le Monnier, 1929), 3–29.

96. EN, XLIX, 279–80, 306, 310, 316–17, 340, 349.

97. EN, XLVIII, 43.

98. See the account in Franco Catalano, *I Barabba. La rivolta del 6 febbraio 1853 a Milano* (Milan: Mastelloni, 1953), 29.

99. EN, XLVIII, 130, 215.

100. Raffaello Barbiera, *Il salotto della contessa Maffei* (Milan: Istituto Editoriale Italiano, n.d.), II, 116–26, 138–49.

101. EN, LI, 7–10; XLVIII, 186–87, 194–97. Also, SEI, IX, xlvi–xlvii.

102. EN, XLVIII, 245, 255–58, 262–64, 342–44, 366–67.

103. EN, XLVIII, 280–93, 303–5; Nicomede Bianchi, *Vicende del mazzinianesimo politico e religioso dal 1832 al 1854* (Savona: Sambolino, 1854), 230–31, 242–45; Giovanni Cadolini, *Memorie del Risorgimento* (Milan: Cogliati, 1911), 242–45.

104. Koltay-Kastner, *Mazzini e Kossuth*, 82–83, which shows that before leaving for America Kossuth had indeed agreed to work with Mazzini, and Montanelli, *Memorie sull'Italia e specialmente sulla Toscana*, 253–55, 266–67.

CHAPTER 7

After the Triumphant Fact (1853–1860)

"The *fact*, the triumphant fact only is worshipped. Let us try quietly to grow into a triumphant fact."[1] Mazzini's confession that he yearned for vindication was for Emilie, who was always there to console him. The "triumphant fact" that he sought was the victory that would redeem him and the republican cause; he would search for it tirelessly, sometimes frantically, in the course of the next seven years. Those years would decide the outcome of the national movement. *L'Italia chi la fa se la prenda!* (Let those who make Italy take it!), said Agostino Bertani of the contestants.[2] Mazzini, one of many players, did what he knew best: "Conspire to achieve" was the watchword of the Party of Action that he launched in the spring of 1853.

Like the first Young Italy, the Party of Action combined conspiracy with propaganda. Mazzini described it as the "militant church of the national movement," and used it to address the "unknown youths of Italy" who were ready to "disseminate forbidden literature or mount the barricades."[3] Book and rifle symbolized the party's split personality, which was democratic politically, but not organizationally. Disregarding objections from Italians that no one living abroad should presume to direct operations in Italy, Mazzini sought to control activities from London. The party was never the centralized operation that he wished it to be, because of distance, problems of communication, and faulty organizational design. Even with more effective means of control he would have found it difficult to control the network of local cells, which consisted in theory of groups of ten, one hundred, and four hundred organized like units of the army of ancient Rome. Local authority was divided between military commanders and political secretaries, whose orders came from London. Friction developed almost immediately. Within months of its founding, a schism weakened the party in Rome, where a group of "fusionists" led by Cesare Mazzoni demanded freedom to work with constitutional monarchists.[4]

The party's commitment to action appealed to Felice Orsini, who found Mazzini the conspirator more to his liking than Mazzini the diplomat he had known in Rome. Coming together in London in the spring of 1853, the two plotted tirelessly to stir up insurrection. The site they chose was the mountainous area called the Lunigiana, which stretches across the regions of Liguria and Tuscany in central Italy. The Lunigiana touched on the Kingdom of Sardinia and the duchies of Parma, Modena, and Tuscany, and overlooked the Po Valley. From that mountain redoubt, insurgents could strike out against five states and the Austrian army deployed in the Po Valley. They tried a landing in September of 1853, failed, and they tried again the following May, with the same result. The incidents were trivial in and of themselves, but they throw light on Mazzini's state of mind, the kind of collaborators he attracted, and the extremes to which he would resort in pursuit of the "triumphant fact." Perhaps he also wanted to test the temper of the rural populations, after the failure of urban conspiracies in 1853. If that was indeed his intention, the lack of response should have made it clear that peasants were no more revolutionary in 1854 than in 1848.[5]

The attention that governments lavished on these conspiracies magnified Mazzini's reputation. A popular ditty from these years described him as an ubiquitous presence: *Mazzini è in ogni loco ove si spera / Versare il sangue per l'Italia intera*" (Mazzini is wherever people are willing to shed blood for Italy).[6] The Austrians, distrustful of both Mazzini and Louis Napoleon, suspected them of plotting revolution together. Mazzini repaid the attentions of governments by following their policies and trying to divine their motives. For instance, when the British showed signs of strengthening their presence in the Mediterranean, he worried that such designs would encourage autonomist sentiment in Sicily. To deal with that possibility he invited the Sicilian republican Francesco Crispi to such London. Crispi had incited Sicilians to take to the streets in 1848 and was not a separatist; his quick temperament and disposition to act made him an ideal Action Party figure. Mazzini sent him to Sicily to "Italianize" the island and organize it for the party. He also advised Garibaldi in America to prepare for the time when he might have to lead an expedition to Sicily. He was planting seeds that would bear fruit in the future.[7]

MAZZINI'S INTERNATIONAL DIPLOMACY

The search for the "triumphant fact" took him in other directions. The war between Turkey and Russia in October of 1853 opened a new chapter in European international relations. The Crimean War was ostensibly about access to religious shrines in the Holy Land, but the real issue was control of the eastern Mediterranean. Great Britain looked to contain Russian expansion toward the Middle East and to protect the lifeline of its empire, which passed through the Mediterranean. France sought an alliance with great Britain to end its isolation, and its emperor, Napoleon III, was eager to assert leadership in foreign affairs. The British design to form a European coalition against Russia required that Austria join the other powers in an alliance. Austria's reluctance to be drawn into war with Russia increased British interest in bringing Piedmont into the coalition, as a guarantee that Austria would not have to face war in its Italian provinces if it fought against Russia in the east. But Austria hesitated, and was still hesitating when France and Great Britain declared war on Russia in March of 1854.

Mazzini welcomed revolutionary wars, but not this conflict. A British-French-Austrian-Piedmontese alliance was a political nightmare, for it seemed to Mazzini that it aimed at propping up the existing system. In April of 1853, when the war was still in the future, he expressed doubt that a conflict in the east could be to Italy's advantage. Such a war might be useful if Austria became embroiled in it and the Italians were prepared to take advantage of the opportunity; but if the Italians remained passive, the great powers would find a way to settle their differences at Italy's expense.[8] An alliance that brought together Piedmont and Austria could not possibly be in Italy's interest. He feared also that friendship between France and Great Britain would encourage Muratists in Naples and separatists in Sicily, creating a "mess worse than that of 1848."[9] As the prospect of war increased and the British continued to press for an alliance, Mazzini concluded that such a monarchist coalition spelled trouble for republicans everywhere.

The imminence of war compelled Mazzini to act, which meant pushing the Party of Action to seize the initiative. Pulling out all the stops, he mobilized his contacts in the Tyrol, Lombardy, the Central Duchies, Rome, and Sicily, and among Hungarian troops. Orsini's conspiracies in the Lunigiana were part of this larger strategy of revolution. He urged the Lombards to form death squads and the Romans to exert themselves for the "total and unprecedented destruction of domestic and foreign enemies in a manner splendid and decisive."[10]

It was a critical moment. Piedmont was negotiating to join the alliance, and the chief negotiator was Camillo Benso, Count of Cavour, prime minister since November of 1852. Cavour, as he is generally known, was the new man on the political scene, and his diplomacy at the time of the Crimean War caught Mazzini's attention. He had first taken notice of Cavour in 1847, when he had dismissed him too summarily as a mere servant of the Savoy dynasty. Cavour may have been a servant of the monarchy, but he also had strong ideas about what royalty should do, which was to reign and leave the business of government to elected parliaments and those who knew how to work with them. Cavour did not expect the Crimean War to solve the Italian problem, but he did think it could improve Piedmont's international standing and its ability to influence Italian affairs. Relations with Austria were tense when negotiations began, Cavour having antagonized Piedmont's powerful neighbor by granting asylum to Lombard refugees after the Milanese uprising of February 1853, and then having made matters worse by championing their demands for restitution of confiscated assets. As a sop to the Austrian government, he had agreed to expel some refugees, who turned out to be mostly republicans for whom Mazzini had to provide in London. There was no love lost between Cavour and Mazzini, who regarded one another more as enemies than as opponents.

Mazzini misread the intentions of British policy-makers in thinking that he could win their support if he showed them that the Party of Action was capable of making trouble for Austria.[11] That was the intent of Mazzini's conspiracies, but the more he exerted himself, the more the British wanted an alliance with Piedmont to reassure Austria that it had nothing to fear from that quarter. It was in fact the sentiment of all powers that the time had come to crack down hard on agitators. The ensuing repression confirmed Mazzini's fears that monarchist governments were orchestrating a campaign against all republicans.

In April of 1854 Mazzini paid a secret visit to Switzerland. It had an inauspicious start when his ship collided with another vessel and he distracted himself during the rough crossing by downing a bottle of brandy. In Lugano everybody seemed to know about his supposedly secret presence. The press accused him of sending out incendiaries to burn down the forests and blamed him for the assassination of Duke Charles III of Parma, who had been stabbed by an unknown assailant. These fears were exaggerated, for the only thing that disturbed the peace was Orsini's raid the following month, and Orsini soon landed in an Austrian jail. If Italy was ever unified, Mazzini commented, Italians would deserve no credit: "We may be free and united as a nation one day because it is written, because the European movement will carry us along, because a better people will find the right man, and it will be our fault if he is against us."[12]

The news in January of 1855 that the alliance with Piedmont was signed and that Piedmontese troops would go to Crimea deepened Mazzini's frustration to the point that he started to drink absinthe, the powerful concoction of Bohemians seeking oblivion: "I never did foresee that I would despise my own country," he wrote.[13] Back in England, he was persona non grata with the government. David Urquhart, a sensationalist reporter, accused Mazzini of being a Russian spy; Austrian agents may have believed him, because they offered Mazzini money to change sides. Mazzini called Urquhart an ass and a scoundrel, but also declared that he felt free to join anyone "to destroy a common enemy." When he accused the British ruling class of ignoring the people and questioned the authority of the government, he came perilously close to equating Great Britain with the powers that he despised. The conservative press mounted a campaign against him and forced the temporary shutdown the Friends of Italy Society. Even friends like James Stansfeld had to distance themselves for a while.[14]

The uproar grew when an associate of Mazzini tried to assassinate Napoleon III. He was one Giovanni Pianori, a shoemaker from Faenza who had a reputation for violence. After being released from jail for a previous offense, Pianori had killed a man whom he suspected of being his wife's lover. He arrived in London in December of 1854, Mazzini received him, and they practiced target shooting together at a range in Wimbledon. Pianori was supposed to be a crack shot, but on April 28, 1855, he missed two shots at the emperor who was riding in his carriage in the Bois de Boulogne. Pianori was guillotined. Mazzini denied charges of complicity, but defended the killing of tyrants. Perhaps he was trying to make amends later on, when he censured anarchists who defended their right to assassinate heads of state, not excluding Queen Victoria herself. But the anarchists that he criticized were French and what they advocated was indiscriminate violence; Mazzini preferred his violence more precise.[15]

THE NATIONAL MOVEMENT AFTER THE CRIMEAN WAR

Garibaldi arrived from America in March of 1854, brought back to Europe by the news that war was imminent. Mazzini welcomed him in London with open arms, but noted his trust in King Victor Emmanuel and his lack of faith in republican initiatives. He was trying to fashion a surrogate Garibaldi in the person of one Silvino Olivieri, a dashing Neapolitan who had fought in Rome in 1849 and had gone on to make a name for himself as a guerrilla fighter in Argentina. Mazzini was confident that with the right publicity he could create in Olivieri a charismatic figure to rival Garibaldi's; that project was interrupted by Olivieri's death at the hands of disgruntled followers in 1856.[16] The danger with Garibaldi was that he would fight anybody's wars, even Cavour's. Cavour was no firebrand patriot, but his policy of engagement played to the sense of national pride that ran strong in Garibaldi and many other republicans.

Garibaldi did not fight in the Crimean War, and Piedmont received nothing more tangible for its participation than an invitation to the Paris Peace Congress that ended the war. Cavour was in Paris from February to April of 1854, keeping a low profile at sessions of the congress but making himself known in the social and political circles of the capital. He did not neglect Italian exiles, whom he would have had no opportunity to meet elsewhere. One of those he sought out was Daniele Manin, the former head of the Venetian republic in 1849, and a highly respected republican who was critical of Mazzini.[17] The monarchist Cavour and the republican Manin hit it off well. They were both practical men, who could set aside differences of principle for the sake of political cooperation. In the course of several conversations, they laid the groundwork for cooperation between republicans and monarchists for the sake of Italian independence. Manin's chief collaborator, the Lombard nobleman Giorgio Pallavicino, called on Italians to rally behind the goal of "national unification." National unification, according to Pallavicino, was something quite different from Mazzini's program of "national unity," for "unification" implied a gradual process, whereas "unity" set a fixed goal. Mazzini tried to avoid an open break by arguing that the differences were only semantic, but unification as an ongoing and presumably open-ended process accorded more with the pragmatic politics of Cavour than with Mazzini's republican goals. It was also important that "unification" appealed to the "gentlemen of revolution," as Pallavicino called them, who wanted no Mazzinian surprises.[18]

The dispute reached the larger public on May 25, 1856, when the London *Times* published a letter by Manin that condemned the tactics and goals of the Party of Action, describing it as a party of murderers: "The great enemy of Italy is *the doctrine of political assassination* or, in other words, *the theory of the dagger*."[19] Mazzini was never mentioned by name, but it was obvious that he was the target of the attack. Any lingering doubts were dispelled by the reference to conspiracies that were based on nothing more than a few sacks of coins and a few hundred rifles. Pallavicino observed that Piedmont, by contrast, had an army of 100,000, which Victor Emmanuel was not likely to commit if he thought that republicans would rob him of the fruits of victory. It would be better, therefore, to take one's chances with the monarchy than to face defeat with Mazzini.[20]

Mazzini stressed the harm of Manin's letter to the national movement, and argued that the call to rally behind the king smacked of unprincipled opportunism and that it would lead to a repetition of the errors of 1848. His own counterproposal stressed unity under a "neutral banner," which would not exclude a monarchical solution. The "neutral banner" position was preferable to "unification" because it did not confuse expediency and principle. Patriots of all political persuasions could come together under his "neutral banner" without fear of acting against their consciences. As for the theory of the dagger, Mazzini denied that he had ever formulated it; he had condoned violence against tyrants as a last recourse and only in the absence of freedom, but never had he justified violence on theoretical grounds. Manin's accusations, he charged, defamed the entire Italian people.[21]

Manin's letter to the *Times* provided publicity for the Italian National Society that was formed in the summer of 1856. Its slogan of "Italy and Victor Emmanuel" was incompatible with Mazzini's religious republicanism and even with his "neutral banner" stance. Pallavicino spoke for the National Society, but it was Manin's name that gave it cachet. Cavour supported it silently, to avoid offending Austria and the other powers. The National Society acknowledged Victor Emmanuel's claim to the throne of Italy, but also sought to give the monarchy a popular basis. The popular element needed a leader who was not suspected of hiding subversive designs under conciliatory slogans. That ruled out Mazzini and opened the door to Garibaldi, who hastened to offer his services. The intention was to isolate Mazzini, but also to pressure Cavour into pursuing a course more national and less dynastic than the traditional Piedmontese policy of piecemeal territorial expansion. There was never perfect understanding between the National Society and the Piedmontese government, but together they set the course of the unification movement after 1856. Its day-to-day operations were taken over by its secretary, Giuseppe La Farina, a resourceful Sicilian who became the intermediary between Cavour and the National Society. La Farina had been Mazzini's man in Paris in the early 1850s, but by 1856 he had come to the conclusion that "in practical politics, the impossible is immoral."[22]

Manin did not live to see the results of his labors. He suffered a mental breakdown, which his friends said was brought on by the polemic with Mazzini, and died suddenly in September of 1857. His final thoughts were for Mazzini: "Mazzini does not doubt, Mazzini does not hesitate; in that lies the secret of his strength."[23] But Mazzini also suffered. In those years he began to call England his real home; that showed affection for the country that sheltered him, and disillusionment with his own. Perhaps more than anything else, the polemic with the National Society made him aware of his growing isolation among Italians. The death and misfortune of close friends also saddened him. Scipione Pistrucci, "the last friend of the old nucleus" and "the man who loved me the most," died in 1854; Nicolao Ferrari, a young man on whom he relied in Genoa, died in 1855. The bankruptcy that year of the Zurich banker Filippo Caronti, on whom he also relied heavily, hampered his operations on the continent. Republicans in Italy denied him access to their funds and Italians in London increasingly looked to the moderates among them for leadership. Antonio Panizzi, never a friend of Mazzini, held the purse strings in London; it was he who organized the rescue of Luigi Settembrini and other southern patriots from Neapolitan jails. Mazzini felt abandoned, avoided contact with strangers, and received only those whom he trusted.

The sense of being abandoned by Italians from the middle classes played a role in Mazzini's decision to organize workers politically, and that decision in turn drew fire from Mauro Macchi, a democratic deputy in the Piedmontese parliament who was often on Mazzini's side against Cavour. Macchi credited Mazzini with a sincere desire to improve the lot of workers, but faulted him for his visceral opposition to French socialism, which, Macchi claimed, kept Italian workers isolated and weak. Macchi charged that Mazzini's tactics of encouraging collaboration across class lines deprived workers of the opportunity to act on their own. Politics distracted workers from pursuing economic goals that were of more pressing concern. Mazzini's tactics, Macchi concluded, kept workers "in the fetal stage of mere theory, even though he believes that the social question is the only one that matters."[24]

French socialists, as far as Mazzini was concerned, were more interested in securing dominance of the worker's movement than in international cooperation. In 1856, when Macchi published his pamphlet, Mazzini was attempting to establish an international workers' front as part of a broader popular alliance against monarchy. His immediate objective, however, was to protest against Napoleon III's visit to England. He distanced himself from the project when it was taken over by followers of Proudhon, who angered Mazzini by questioning his political motives and opposing Italian unification. National unity for all oppressed nationalities was an unquestionable axiom for Mazzini, who insisted that there could be no genuine cooperation among workers unless all nationalities were free and on an equal footing.[25]

MAZZINI VERSUS CAVOUR

Mazzini left for Italy in June of 1856. He explained that he went there to quench his thirst for action: "I hate idle talk, beginning with my own; my only thought is for action, and [I] am feverish to carry it out."[26] He urged his Genoese collaborators to organize workers. National unification would solve their economic problems, provided they had the political power to take full advantage of the economic opportunities offered by a national market of twenty-four million people. To have that power in the unified state they had to be active in the national movement. Once masters in their own house, the Italian people would show what could be achieved without resorting to socialism:

Without any socialistic squabble, our National Insurrection would achieve wonders for the "people" with only three measures. First, the reform of Taxation, starting with the principle that life cannot be taxed, that taxation must begin from the surplus, leaving the average of necessities for human life untouched, and the surplus being taxed in proportion of the amount. Secondly, the opening of works in all branches, roads, railways, arsenals, maritime establishments, docks, bridges, Pantheon, House of National Assembly, fortresses, drainage of marshes, etc., which would afford employment to millions of men. Thirdly, the formation of a gigantic National Fund, the elements of which would be the ecclesiastical property . . . , the property (national) of Kings, Princes, etc., the Austrian property . . . , the property of a few aristocratic families who would fight or plot in the ranks of the enemy, etc., etc.[27]

To achieve this vision Mazzini was willing to work with everyone, even King Victor Emmanuel, who figured in Mazzini's plans as a possible ally because he knew that the king resented the political ascendancy of Cavour, yearned for military glory, and wanted to be king of Italy. If the king was looking for a pretext to intervene militarily, Mazzini would provide it with uprisings in Genoa, the Lunigiana, and the towns of Massa and Carrara. What happened after that would depend on Austria's reaction; if Austria chose war, a national war would give the republican movement a new lease on life, and an armed citizenry would have a say in the final disposition of the country's affairs. Mazzini claimed that agents of the king expressed an interest in the plan. Making contact with the king was perhaps one reason for Mazzini's visit to Giuditta, who lived in Turin. There was no direct contact, but the overture set a precedent for other intrigues between Mazzini and Victor Emmanuel behind the back of government ministers. In Genoa, Bertani and Medici agreed to work with him to raise money to arm the people (the Ten Thousand Rifles Fund), but rejected his other proposals for immediate action.[28]

The overture was a poorly kept secret. Pallavicino suspected early on that the real purpose of Mazzini's visit was to entrap the king. That suspicion may explain the timing of the revelation that in 1833 Mazzini had plotted the assassination of Charles Albert. Someone was trying to embarrass Victor Emmanuel by making public Mazzini's role in the attempt on his father's life. Curiously, that someone was none other than Antonio Gallenga, who made the revelation in his two-volume history of Piedmont published in 1856, without mentioning his own role in the plot. Gallenga was now a member of parliament and an ally of Cavour, who could not have been pleased that the king was conducting his own foreign policy behind his back with Mazzini's help. Mazzini retaliated by revealing that Gallenga was the one who had volunteered to assas-

sinate Charles Albert, and for good measure threw in the information
that Luigi Melegari was also an accomplice. Melegari was also a member
of parliament, and a supporter of Cavour, and was on the public payroll
as professor of constitutional law at the University of Turin. The ensuing
scandal forced Gallenga out of public life. Melegari chose to challenge
the paper that had made the revelations in court, and won the case when
the paper could not produce evidence to back up its allegations. Only
Mazzini could have provided proof, and he probably yielded to Giuditta's
pleadings on behalf of Melegari, who was still her friend.[29]

Having failed to win the king's support for war in the north, Mazzini
turned his attention to the south. There, Cavourians were a growing but
still exiguous minority, whose rise was contested by autonomists and
republicans of various descriptions. Autonomists were more interested
in liberalizing the government than in national unity, which they envisaged as a loose federation of states in which the Kingdom of the Two
Sicilies would retain a large measure of self-government. Some looked
to the candidacy of Lucien Murat, cousin of Napoleon III, to gain French
support for their cause. Their goal of independence without unity under
French patronage worried Mazzini more than was warranted by the
strength of the Muratist movement. The most prominent Muratist was
Aurelio Saliceti, formerly a Mazzinian republican, who was attached to
the Murat family in Paris as tutor to their children. Mazzini worried
that the presence of a Muratist party would give Napoleon III political
leverage in the south, but because his own influence in the south was
limited he also hoped to take advantage of agitation promoted by the
Muratists.[30]

Except in Naples, where there was a Mazzinian organization headed
by Giuseppe Fanelli, a veteran of the Roman campaign of 1849, southern
republicans looked to Nicolà Fabrizi. The Sicilian baron Francesco
Bentivegna, who led a revolt on the island in November of 1856, worked
with Fabrizi. Mazzinians in the south often acted in isolation, like the
soldier Agesilao Milano, who tried to bayonet King Ferdinand during a
military parade. It is doubtful that Mazzini had anything to do with
either Bentivegna or Milano, but he may have had a role in Naples,
where a navy ship loaded with ammunition blew up under mysterious
circumstances in January of 1857. It was suspected that the explosion
was to be the signal for an uprising that never materialized.[31]

A proposal by Carlo Pisacane made shortly after Mazzini's return to
London in December of 1856 rekindled Mazzini's hope for an initiative
in the south. Pisacane envisaged an armed expedition to galvanize
popular discontent against the Bourbon regime in Naples. They agreed
that Garibaldi should head the raid; when Garibaldi refused, Pisacane
offered himself. Saffi went on a lecture tour to raise money. Help came
from James Stansfeld, Peter Taylor, Ledru-Rollin, and a new English

friend, Jessie Meriton White (Bianca to Mazzini), who was soon to be the wife of fellow republican Alberto Mario. By April of 1857 they had a war chest of 25,000 francs, and Pisacane went off to Genoa to collect volunteers, purchase weapons, and arrange transportation. The expedition would first land on the prison island of Ponza to liberate political prisoners, press on to the coast, then march toward the capital and seize it with the help of peasants gathered along the way and insurgents within the city. Mazzini promised to orchestrate uprisings with workers in Genoa and Livorno to give the insurrection a national character.[32]

In May of 1857 Mazzini went to Genoa to do his part. Hiding in the house of Ernesto Pareto, he complained about many "little inharmonious things" that bothered him about the city (the sound of church bells, the windy streets) and the habits of Italians (they spit in public and lacked civility).[33] He is said to have hid in a mattress and disguised himself as a butler while the police repeatedly searched the house, but perhaps they were not looking too hard. Cavour had a general idea of what Mazzini was plotting and may not have minded making a little trouble for the Bourbons in the South.[34] Cavour's tolerance ended quickly, however, when he realized that Mazzini was planning an insurrection in Genoa and the press alleged that he was also involved with one Paolo Tibaldi, who was arrested in Paris for plotting to assassinate the French emperor.[35]

Mazzini and Pisacane had overestimated popular support for insurrection. Setbacks in Naples delayed Pisacane's departure until late June. In Genoa support was strong only among workers who resented Cavour's plan to relocate the city's naval base to La Spezia. Mazzini intended to unleash workers against the military forts around the city to distract the troops while Pisacane embarked men and supplies. He called off the attacks when he learned that the authorities knew of his plans, but one group of conspirators who did not receive the counterorder went ahead according to plan. In the ensuing clash an army sergeant was killed. Pisacane's volunteers sailed on a steamer that they commandeered on the high seas, only to meet a tragic end after landing near the town of Sapri, in upper Calabria. Hunted down by soldiers and peasants, most were killed or taken prisoner. Pisacane took his own life. Jessie White, Alberto Mario, Rosalino Pilo, and others were jailed in Genoa, but most of the other leaders escaped abroad. Six, including Mazzini, were later condemned to death in absentia.[36]

Charges of cowardice and reckless disregard for the lives of others, as well as defections engulfed Mazzini once again. Cavour called him "the chief of a band of ferocious and fanatical assassins" and threatened that he would be hanged in the central square of the Acquasola in Genoa.[37] Mazzini responded to the death sentence like Socrates accused, claiming credit for the very crimes imputed to him: "To me, to us, slanders and accusations make no difference. We recognize no judges except God, our conscience, and the Italy that will exist in the future."[38] That prediction came true. A later generation of grateful patriots erected a monument to Mazzini on the very spot where Cavour threatened to hang him.

Mazzini justified himself in public by reminding his critics that he had only responded to Pisacane's request for help; his sorrow for what had happened and for the death of Pisacane, to whom he was genuinely attached, he kept to himself. He spent most of August and September in seclusion at the Stansfelds' summer home at Hastings, and then returned to London to pick up the pieces. Nervous and gloomy, he looked for a "hole" in which to hide. He turned his attention to unfinished business, calling for a new republican organization to combat the French-dominated international association. He busied himself with the school, planned the publication of his collected writings, started the journal *Pensiero e Azione* to stimulate theoretical debate, and encouraged everyone to keep the faith. The "triumphant fact" had eluded him once again, but the contest was far from over.[39]

On the evening of January 14, 1858, Felice Orsini and two accomplices threw three homemade grenades at the carriage bearing Napoleon III and Empress Eugenie to a performance of the Paris Opera. Eight people died and almost 150 were wounded, but, miraculously, the imperial couple emerged from the wreckage with only minor injuries and went on to attend a performance of Wagner's appropriately heroic opera *Tannhäuser*. The bombs had been manufactured by a London engineer named Thomas Allsop, who was a member of Mazzini's Friends of Italy Society. That was enough to link Mazzini's name to Orsini's, but, in fact, they had not been on good terms for a while. After his escape from jail in the fortress of Mantua, where the Austrians had relegated him, Orsini had lost interest in Mazzini and had begun to gravitate toward Cavour, like many other republicans. Mazzini, he claimed, had not exerted himself enough to help his escape and surrounded himself with gossipy women in London, whom he suspected of spreading unflattering rumors about himself. While in London, Orsini obviously used some of Mazzini's friends, but he did not trust Mazzini enough to let him in on his plans.[40]

It was not Mazzini but Cavour who benefited from Orsini's attempt on the emperor's life. While waiting in jail for the death sentence to be carried out, Orsini expressed public remorse for his actions, but defended his political motives. Respectfully, he warned Napoleon III that he would not be safe as long as Italians were oppressed by foreign rule: "May Your Majesty not reject the words of a patriot on the steps of the scaffold! Set my country free, and the blessings of twenty-five million people will follow you everywhere and forever."[41] Then he went to the guillotine. The publicity given to Orsini's plea could not have occurred without the emperor's permission. This was followed by close contacts with Cavour, who reciprocated by passing on to the French police information about Mazzinian plots. Diplomatic exchanges occurred outside normal channels, culminating in the famous meeting of Plombières on July 20, 1858. In the pleasant surroundings of that fashionable spa, Cavour and Napoleon III agreed to wage "nonrevolutionary war" against Austria if a plausible pretext could be found. According to their agreements, the Kingdom of Sardinia enlarged with the acquisition of Austria's Italian provinces and the papal Romagna, would form a kingdom in upper Italy, ruled by the House of Savoy. Tuscany augmented by papal territory would constitute a separate kingdom in central Italy, while the pope would retain sovereignty over the city of Rome and its environs. The Kingdom of Naples would remain untouched, but would possibly be ruled by the Murat dynasty. The four independent states would form a loose confederation under the presidency of the pope, who would thus be consoled for the loss of territory. In compensation, France would receive the region of Savoy and possibly the district of Nice. The alliance was to be sealed by the marriage of Victor Emmanuel's daughter to the emperor's cousin. The agreement of Plombières was a personal understanding, but it was soon ratified by a secret treaty of alliance that endorsed most of its provisions, and specified further that the Kingdom of Sardinia would pay for the war.

The agreement met opposition in many quarters. Against it were the Empress Eugenie, Foreign Minister Alexandre Waleski, and Catholics who did not want to offend the pope. Republicans opposed it as well, none more vehemently than Mazzini. He found out about it in November from an unknown source, who provided a fairly accurate account of its provisions.[42] They were hardly a secret anyway, because Cavour also leaked information to impress influential people. Mazzini was alarmed. Even worse than the surrender of Nice and Savoy was the prospect that the war would be "nonrevolutionary" and that Italy would become a satellite of France. That would be the ultimate victory for the man who had suppressed the Roman Republic of 1849. A dark hint that there was "only one remedy to all of this" was followed by the arrest of a certain Donati, who, according to the French police, confessed that he and Mazzini had hatched a plot in James Stansfeld's London brewery to assassinate Napoleon III. Letters made public corroborated the confession, but Mazzini charged that they were forgeries, and the affair ended with Donati's mysterious death in prison.[43]

January of 1859 marked a turning point. A diplomatic bombshell fell on New Year's Eve, when Napoleon III expressed his regrets to the Austrian ambassador that relations between their countries were not what he wished them to be. That was news to the ambassador, as well as to the papal legate, who fainted on hearing the emperor's words. Mazzini's reaction when he read about the incident in the *Times* revealed his fears: "The die is cast; we're done for!" According to Saffi, who was present, Mazzini feared that the coming war would end "the heroic phase of the Italian *Risorgimento*" and surrender "the nation to the discretion of the foreigner."[44] His pessimism was not widely shared, and the republican movement suffered another split. Republicans like Agostino Bertani, Nino Bixio, and Giacomo Medici rejected Mazzini's appeal to oppose the war and warned that they would break with him openly if he spoke out against it. The faithful ones included Federico Campanella, Maurizio Quadrio, Saffi, Filippo De Boni, Francesco Crispi, Alberto Mario, Mattia Montecchi, and Antonio Mosto. They were the true believers, but they were a minority.[45]

Mazzini himself wavered at the approach of war. It excited him to think that the name of Italy would "be heard with an accompaniment of bombs and cannon-firing such as to make the earth shake from the surface to the center."[46] He even bought Piedmontese war bonds, which he cashed in later to buy weapons for republican volunteers.[47] His quarrel was not with war in general, but with what he called the "Bonapartist-Italian War." If the war could not be stopped, however, it could be given a popular character and made revolutionary against the intentions of its promoters. The north might be in Cavour's grasp, but something could perhaps be done in the south with the help of republicans. Fabrizi had funds, operated out of Malta with English connivance, and headed a network on the mainland. Crispi, Giovanni Corrao, and Rosalino Pilo were Sicilians with contacts on the island. Mazzini was impressed by Corrao and Pilo, whom he had met recently in London. He sent them to Sicily to "nationalize" an insurrection that was said to be in progress.[48]

That was the call that Mazzini issued on April 1 from the columns of *Pensiero e Azione*: the war was to become national, so that the people could take charge of their own destiny. For that to happen republicans had to act quickly to separate Piedmont from France and Cavour from Victor Emmanuel. He granted that the king was a patriot and blamed Cavour for refusing to involve the people. That negative assessment was not shared by those who knew how hard Cavour was working to bring on the war in spite of British efforts to keep the peace and the emperor's vacillating resolve. He succeeded by provoking Austria into declaring war on Piedmont on April 29, 1859.

Mazzini hoped that republicans might regain the initiative if Austria surrendered after a short fight and the volunteer forces that were being trained by the government chose to carry on the struggle as a popular war.[49] His hopes were revived when the French emperor acceded to an Austrian request for an armistice on July 11, without consulting his

Piedmontese partners. The armistice of Villafranca followed concentrations of Prussian troops along France's Rhine border, mounting domestic opposition to the war, and evidence that Italians were acting independently. Uprisings in the Central Duchies and the papal Romagna during the ten weeks of fighting had installed provisional governments that demanded union with Piedmont. By the terms of the armistice, Piedmont was to receive Lombardy and the rulers of the Central Duchies were to be restored to their dominions. Cavour took umbrage because the armistice was a repudiation of his policy and provided a political windfall for the opposition. He resigned after a stormy interview with Victor Emmanuel, who wisely resisted his prime minister's demand that Piedmont continue the war alone.

The political prospects that Cavour feared and Mazzini welcomed were not imaginary. There were thousands of volunteers in arms, many of whom had served in the war under Garibaldi's command. Their military contribution had been minor, but they had distinguished themselves in difficult mountain operations and the republican press saw to it no exploit by volunteer troops went unnoticed. Garibaldi emerged from the war with the rank of major-general and with an even greater reputation for leadership. Volunteers were receptive to the message of the political opposition that the armistice of Villafranca betrayed the national cause.

MAZZINI TRIES TO STEAL THE REVOLUTION

Mazzini left London at the end of July with a program for action already formulated. With Cavour hoisted by his own petard, the republicans could pick up where the monarchists left off: *Al centro, al centro, mirando al sud!* (To the center, to the center, on the way south) was his rallying cry.[50] He was disappointed to discover that Victor Emmanuel and Napoleon III were popular with Milanese patriots, who did not seem to mind the armistice, which did provide for the union of their region with Piedmont. Milan was only a stop on the way to Florence. In the Tuscan capital, which he reached on August 8, he found more to work with. Tuscany was one of the duchies that had revolted during the war and installed a provisional government. The strongman of Tuscany was Baron Bettino Ricasoli, who held the title of dictator. When Ricasoli heard that Mazzini might be hiding in the city he forced the *capopopolo* Giuseppe Dolfi to confirm the agitator's presence. Far from evicting him, the Iron Baron, as Ricasoli was called, was delighted to have in his grasp the man who was "the terror of Europe."[51]

Mazzini wrote to Ricasoli "patriot to patriot," expressing the hope that they could work together. Respectfully, he explained that he was working to bring war to the south through Tuscany and hoped that he could count on Ricasoli's support to unify Italy. Ricasoli did believe in national unity, but not by republicans. He nevertheless made sure that Mazzini was not disturbed by the police. Mazzini cooperated by living under an assumed name, staying out of sight during the day, and taking solitary walks at night to admire the moonlit city. If the plan for union with Piedmont misfired, or if anyone tried to restore the deposed dynasty, Ricasoli was prepared to let Mazzini do in Florence what he had done in Rome in 1849. The aristocrat who wanted an orderly transition toward a new monarchy and the republican agitator who dreamed of revolution formed an alliance, agreeing on nothing except that Italy should be united.[52]

While in Florence, Mazzini wrote an open letter to Victor Emmanuel, whose prestige had been increased by the war and the support of France. The letter urged the king to resume the war without the help of France and with only the Italian people on his side. If he did that, he could be king of Italy or president of an Italian republic, according to the choice of the people. If he refused, he would miss an historic opportunity to be the father of his country. It was the same tone and technique that Mazzini had used in his earlier letters to Charles Albert and Pius IX. Victor Emmanuel's reaction was said to be one of interest and curiosity, perhaps because republicans and monarchists were already coming together to unite the former Central Duchies and the Papal Romagna with Piedmont.[53] Mazzini was not content with that partial solution. It was the duty of republicans to push relentlessly toward unification: "Left alone, the people will go along with anything. If you arouse them, they will follow the better course." What they needed was "a splendid, daring deed" to make them go "where they did not dream of going the day before."[54]

Who else but Garibaldi could perform the "splendid, daring deed?" But Mazzini complained that Garibaldi was like a peasant in awe of royalty and that he would not associate openly with him. Therefore, only if he remained invisible behind the scenes would he be able to influence Garibaldi's actions and the course of events. Sicily featured prominently in Mazzini's plans, as it had since 1853, but not in the same way. What he envisaged in 1859 was not a landing in Sicily, but a land operation from Tuscany to link up with insurgents moving up from Sicily. The problem was that neither he nor his collaborators had the resources for such an operation. Crispi, who was in Sicily, turned to Fabrizi, who appealed to Luigi Carlo Farini, head of the provisional government in Fabrizi's native Modena. Farini initially promised funds, but changed his mind after consulting with Ricasoli, who did not want Tuscany to become a base for Mazzini's operations. Garibaldi, who had also shown interest, yielded to Victor Emmanuel's promise of a "Million Rifles Fund" to be used for future ventures with the king's approval.[55]

Ricasoli lost interest in sheltering Mazzini when it became clear that there were no obstacles to the union of Tuscany and Piedmont. Mazzini was proving to be a troublesome guest who incited subversion and boasted that he could make enough bombs like Orsini's to equip an army of his own. He did not have the money to equip an army, but even on a lesser scale bombs could wreak havoc, as Ricasoli discovered personally when two exploded in the courtyard of his palace.[56] Mazzini left Florence quietly on a a rainy day in the second part of September of 1859, after Ricasoli had let him know that his presence in Florence "was more troublesome to the population than to [Ricasoli] himself."[57]

Mazzini repaired to Lugano, close enough to return quickly if his presence was needed. From Lugano he continued to press for a military invasion of the Papal States captained by Garibaldi, but Garibaldi went back to his farm on the island of Caprera in November, cherishing the gift of a splendid hunting rifle from Victor Emmanuel. Caprera, off the larger island of Sardinia, was a convenient refuge in moments of uncertainty from which he could easily return to the fray at the right moment. Mazzini was left to wonder what had gone wrong. He claimed to have on his side "the vague instinct of the popular classes and the majority of the military elements, volunteers, noncommissioned officers, and some of the officers," and against him the arts of deception and intrigue of his enemies. But he would "try to get Garibaldi doing the thing and realizing my scheme, promising that I shall make him *the* hero of the national movement and abdicate my own individuality, which is the easiest part."[58] "Preaching so as to conquer," he invoked filial piety toward the suffering mother that was Italy: "And he who will refuse help to a dying mother while there is still a chance of restoring her to life, let him cast the first stone."[59]

By New Year's Eve Mazzini was back in London to usher in the new year with his friends. The visit, which should have lasted only a month, stretched into spring. January of 1860 brought news that Cavour had returned as prime minister, which meant resumption of the diplomacy that Mazzini dreaded. Cavour's top priority was a new deal with France: In return for the region of Savoy and the district of Nice, the French government would recognize a Kingdom of Italy consisting of the Kingdom of Sardinia minus the ceded provinces, Lombardy, the former Central Duchies, and the papal Romagna. Parliament dismissed a Mazzinian protest that had gathered some 8,500 signatures. Garibaldi took the loss of his native Nice as a personal affront and had an acrimonious verbal confrontation with Cavour in parliament. Cavour survived undiminished; his critics discovered once again how hard it was to argue with him successfully.

Mazzini's tactic was to outbid Cavour by insisting on complete unification, which meant annexing Rome, still under the pope, and the entire

Kingdom of the Two Sicilies. But while Mazzini pondered how to do it, Cavour sought to convince the young King Francis II, who had come to the Neapolitan throne in May of 1859 at the death of his father, to grant a constitution and accept a partnership with Piedmont. Piedmont would be the dominant partner and the peninsula would be governed by two friendly monarchies. Mazzini opposed the agreement for the obvious reasons and decided on his own course of action. In December of 1859 Crispi and Pilo had made plans for an expedition to Sicily. Mazzini promised them funds, but his most important contribution was to insist that Garibaldi be offered command, not because he trusted him politically, but because he had developed an almost irrational faith in his military abilities and in his good star. He called on his own lucky star to protect him after making the case for Garibaldi. "Storm is my pilot," he wrote, as he prepared for the adventure.[60]

Garibaldi agreed to lead the expedition on condition that a revolt be in progress before he sailed with his own men. Mazzini's appeal of March of 1860 to the Sicilian people to rise against their government was part of the republican campaign to convince Garibaldi that Sicilians were ready to fight for national unity. A revolt did break out in Palermo on April 4; suppressed in the city, it lingered in the countryside long enough to convince Garibaldi to go. That it was sustained by peasant grievances and resentment of the government in Naples rather than by sentiment for national unity was something that no patriot could admit. Pilo and Corrao left for Sicily after consulting with Mazzini to steer the insurrection toward a national goal. Their promise of outside help materialized when Garibaldi landed in the port of Marsala on May 11, 1860, with his volunteers.[61]

Garibaldi's *I Mille* (The Thousand) became legendary. Their unexpected victories against seemingly overwhelming odds, the seizure of the capital city of Palermo, the liberation of the island, and their victorious march on Naples seemed like the heroic feats of ancient times. The original nucleus of volunteers eventually swelled to more than forty thousand, and Garibaldi, already a hero, became a power. Mazzini played a role in the background to save himself, he told Fabrizi, "for a time in the future when he could take charge of [the movement]."[62] Was this not the "triumphant fact" that he had anticipated before anyone else? It was his hour, too, and he would not be denied.

If Mazzini could not change Garibaldi's program of "Italy and Victor Emmanuel," he could at least subvert it with the familiar arts of conspiracy and infiltration. He could do so because republicans like Bertani and Crispi, who were closer to Garibaldi, also wanted to radicalize the movement and because Garibaldi could not do without them in spite of his loyalty to Victor Emmanuel. It was a peculiarity of many republicans that they supported Garibaldi's program of cooperation with the monarchy without ceasing to think like republicans. That was true even of Garibaldi himself. They therefore felt bound to Mazzini even if they had to keep him at arm's length for political reasons. For that reason Mazzini could count on being listened to, but not necessarily on being heeded. The source of his influence was his prestige, and he hoped to leverage it into real power.[63]

Mazzini left London for Lugano on May 3, just before Garibaldi sailed for Sicily. He started for Genoa on May 8, two days after the expedition had sailed. He was ill, but even if he had been well sailing with the expedition would have been out of the question. Mazzinian volunteers who did sail from Genoa left the main body of the expedition en route, when they learned that Garibaldi intended to fight for Victor Emmanuel. By staying behind, Mazzini saved Garibaldi the embarrassment of his presence and gave himself time to work out his own strategy. As he told Adriano Lemmi, now a businessman in Constantinople who helped him fund his ventures, he had plans "that in their daring and importance will restore honor to the party."[64]

His party was the republican, but on this occasion Mazzini presented himself with the seemingly neutral slogan of "Italy One and Free," which did not mention the king. Freedom was a loaded word in the vocabulary of revolution. For Mazzini it meant giving the people a voice, but moderates were free to interpret it narrowly as freedom from arbitrary government and as representation for organized groups. They could not fault Mazzini for upholding freedom, but they did not have to take him at his word either. In the ears of moderates, the word freedom when used by Mazzini smacked of barricades and tumbrels. They felt safer with Cavour, who practiced the arts of diplomacy. That is precisely what Cavour was doing with Francis II by offering him the friendship of Piedmont in return for political reforms and a pact of federation.

To ward off that prospect Mazzini planned his own move on Naples with the help of Bertani, Crispi and, he hoped, Garibaldi, counting on a brigade of two thousand assembled in Tuscany with Ricasoli's connivance; an additional nine thousand volunteers were waiting in Genoa, uncertain whether they would reinforce Garibaldi in Sicily or be sent on some other venture. Mazzini had his own plan of action: Instead of heading for Sicily, the volunteers were to converge on Rome by land and sea. Once in possession of Rome, they would continue south to link up with Garibaldi's forces moving up from Sicily. Rome would be liberated and national unification achieved before others could react. The volunteers would have the initiative and be in a position to influence, if not to dictate, the final settlement of the Italian question. Cavour would have no choice but to come to terms with Mazzini.

The plan was imaginative, but difficult to implement. When Cavour made it clear to Ricasoli that France and Piedmont would not countenance any infringement of papal territory, Ricasoli ordered that the volunteers in Tuscany be shipped to Sicily. Giovanni Nicotera who was in command was arrested when he tried to countermand the order.[65] The same thing happened to the volunteers in Genoa, except that there it was Cavour who gave the orders, shipping the volunteers first to Sardinian waters, and then to Sicily. For him, the advantage of having them in Sicily was obvious: From Sicily they could not be deployed against Rome, saving him the embarrassment of having to intervene militarily to stop them or acquiesce in another French mission to save the pope. Mazzini, too, may have been relieved. "Gentlemen," he told his collaborators, "we do not want to slaughter one another just now. . . . There will always be time for that."[66]

Garibaldi swept up the peninsula from Sicily and made a triumphal entry in Naples on September 7, 1860. While the crowds welcomed Garibaldi well ahead of his troops, Neapolitan soldiers still in arms looked on in disbelief. Garibaldi's rapid progress was made possible by the military incompetence of the other side, by political intrigue in the capital that sapped the government's will to resist, and by the defection of local notables who were more interested in maintaining law and order than in saving the Bourbon dynasty. Once the dynasty proved unable to protect them, local potentates were quick to change sides. Mazzini himself hardly played a role in these events, but it is possible that networks of Mazzinian clubs like the one headed by Nicola Mignogna in the Basilicata region hastened by the collapse of royal authority at the local level; perhaps that was just enough to justify Mazzini's later claim that he had played the role of "the spur" in the events of 1860.[67]

Mazzini's arrival in Naples was not triumphal. He arrived on September 17 with Carlo Venturi, Emilie's second husband, as his sole companion. They made the rounds of six hotels before finding one that had one small room, which they shared. The city was jam-packed with journalists on the prowl, businessmen hungry for deals, and thousands of tourists and curiosity seekers. Fighting was still going on, but the city put on a friendly face. The antechambers of government were filled with petitioners. Garibaldi, who hated administration, entrusted the administration to Giorgio Pallavicino. He preferred to be with the troops than to have to deal with political matters in the capital. Mazzini had a hard time getting an audience. While waiting to be received by Garibaldi, he took in the sights and marveled at the exuberance of life in the streets.[68] When they finally met, the conversation was cordial but inconclusive. "I have seen the Hero," he wrote sarcastically, "He was very friendly! But I could only have ten minutes with him."[69]

Mazzini's arrival alarmed the moderates, who began to orchestrate a campaign against him in the streets and in the press. "The week has been stormy," Mazzini wrote one month after his arrival, "demonstrations have been taking place against me; groups with flags and torches have amused themselves with shouting Morte! [Death] under my windows."[70] What hurt him more was that he was excluded from the inner circles of power, unlike Cattaneo, who was just as republican as he was, but who was consulted and heeded. The issues on the table were indeed urgent ones. Was the south to become part of the Italian state by negotiation or by outright annexation? If it was to be annexed, how was the transition to a new system of government to be arranged? How long would Garibaldi's provisional government retain power in the south? Would he agree to a quick and peaceful transfer of power or hold out to campaign against Rome? Moderates feared that the longer Garibaldi retained power, the easier it would be for Mazzini and Mazzinians to entrench themselves in government.

Garibaldi was in the field most of the time, occupied by fifty thousand Bourbon troops that resisted stubbornly north of Naples and threatened to retake the city. With an army of forty thousand, he was hard pressed to contain them. That was reason enough for him to welcome the military assistance of the Piedmontese army. Mazzini did not welcome it, preferring instead to delay a Piedmontese presence in Naples to gain time for political reasons. He made no mystery that his objectives were the liberation of Rome and Venice, the convening of a national assembly, and the creation of a republican power base in the south. Garibaldi's accommodating disposition confirmed Mazzini's poor opinion of his political capacities. He was, Mazzini wrote to Fabrizi, "a reed that bends to every wind, a nullity off the field, who lacks even the capacity to choose someone who can do everything for him in his name."[71]

Cavour's bid to regain control of the unification process took the form of a military invasion of the Papal States, accomplished with French approval after he assured Napoleon III that the Piedmontese would leave Rome to the pope. But he made no promises about the large swath of papal territory that the Piedmontese army would have to cross in order to reach the south. Mazzini's presence in Naples worried him less than it worried Pallavicino, who feared the influence of radical elements. It was Pallavicino who employed against Mazzini the device of the open letter. Like similar letters that Mazzini himself had written, Pallavicino's was respectful in tone and hostile in intent. Mazzini, said the letter, should sacrifice himself for the good of the country; the best service that he could render Italy at that moment was to remove himself voluntarily from the city, where his presence caused dissension and rifts among patriots.[72]

Mazzini replied that as a citizen he had the right and the duty to speak his mind on public matters, and went about his business. His major goal was to make a republican stronghold of Naples, which was surely a delusion, but one that was perhaps justified by the heavy concentration of republicans in Naples at that moment.[73] He did what he could to place trustworthy lieutenants in positions of responsibility, like strongly recommending Adriano Lemmi to Crispi and Sirtori for government contracts to build railroad lines in Sicily. A good republican like Lemmi, he assured them, would contribute part of his profits to the party coffers.[74] He founded the paper *Il Popolo d'Italia* and the *Associazione Unitaria Italiana* (Italian Unity Association) to influence public opinion. Given time, he did not despair of building in Naples the kind of political machine that he had built in Rome in 1849.

That was all very alarming to moderates, who were more likely to overestimate Mazzini's influence than to underestimate it. Their fears were mirrored in a play that was all the rage in Paris that fall. *The Donkey and the Three Thieves* showed Cavour and Garibaldi quarreling over a stolen donkey (Naples), while Mazzini made off with the prize: "I am the one you cannot stop, I am the one you cannot kill, I am the Revolution."[75] In the real world, to stop the revolution in its tracks Pallavicino engineered the plebiscite of October 21, which, as expected, produced an overwhelming vote for immediate union with the rest of Italy and for the Savoy dynasty.

Mazzini and Garibaldi had their most productive meeting on November 5, after the Piedmontese had taken over and Garibaldi was again a private citizen. They agreed to work "for Venice and Rome without and against Louis Napoleon, and try to overthrow Cavour during the winter, then try if we can raise a movement in the spring, when, if we succeed as we did in Sicily, Garibaldi will come out with some Marsala-like expedition and join us."[76] There was perhaps some sarcasm in the reference to another "Marsala-like expedition," for Marsala is also the name of a powerful Sicilian dessert wine, but the understanding meant a great deal to Mazzini. His task would be to prepare public opinion and gather funds, Garibaldi's to take command of field operations. Garibaldi's sole condition was that he must be free to work with the king, while Mazzini promised that he would not raise the "Institutional Question" until Rome and Venice were liberated.

Garibaldi sailed from Naples three days later, to be remembered as a modern Cincinnatus who gave up power for the good of the country. He also had a good nose for the popular gesture: Onlookers reported that he carried on his shoulders a sack of seeds for spring planting. What they could not see was his burden of resentments. He was resentful toward Cavour for the loss of Nice, toward the regular army for its shabby treatment of his volunteers, toward politicians in general for making his life miserable in Naples, and toward priests for corrupting the people and sapping their will to fight. Those resentments were a major reason for his alliance with Mazzini at that moment. Mazzini left Naples on November 24. He traveled by land to see for himself how the people reacted to the new order; not surprisingly, he found them not joyous that they were one, but "dazed and nullified."[77] The people's distress would justify the campaigns that he was already planning.

NOTES

Works frequently cited in the notes have been identified by the following abbreviations:

BDM	*Bollettino della Domus Mazziniana*
EN	*Edizione Nazionale. Scritti editi ed inediti di Giuseppe Mazzini* (1906–90), 106 vols.
RSR	*Rassegna Storica del Risorgimento*
SEI	*Scritti editi ed inediti di Giuseppe Mazzini* (1861–91), 18 vols.

1. EN, XLIX, 143, 38–51; LI, 87–94.

2. Jessie White Mario, *Agostino Bertani e i suoi tempi* (Florence: Barbera, 1888), 228.

3. EN, LI, 107–10.

4. On the organization of the Party of Action, see Andrea Giannelli, *Aneddoti ignorati ed importanti, brevi ricordi mazziniani dal 1848 al 1872* (Florence: Nerbini, 1905), 14–16. On the schism in Rome, see EN, XLIX, 134, 328–31, and Filippo Spatafora, *Il Comitato d'azione di Roma dal 1862 al 1867: memorie* (Pisa: Nistri-Lischi, 1982–84), II, 91–92, 842.

5. EN, XLIX, 110–11, 177, 185, 192, 210, 214, 284, 354–55, 364–72; L, 40, 138–40; LI, 25. Also, Felice Orsini, *Memorie politiche* (Turin: De Giorgis, 1858), 90–109, and Elena Sanesi, "Inediti mazziniani," RSR, LIX (April 1972), 235–41.

6. Quoted in Jessie White Mario, *The Birth of Modern Italy* (New York; Scribner's Sons, 1909), 274. Also, Giorgio Asproni, *Diario politico, 1855–1876* (Milan: Giuffrè, 1980–91), I, 643.

7. EN, XLII, 159–60, 168, 252–57; XLIV, 148–50; XLV, 101–2; XLVII, 87–88.

8. EN, XLIX, 79.

9. EN, L, 203.

10. EN, L, 50; also 31–32, 36–38, 138–40. See also *Lettere edite e inedite di F. Orsini a G. Mazzini, G. Garibaldi e F. D. Guerrazzi intorno alle cose d'Italia* (Milan: F. Sanvito, 1862), 311–15, and Silvia Pelosi, *Della vita di Maurizio Quadrio* (Sondrio: Arti Grafiche Valtelli, 1921–22), II, 29–33.

11. EN, L, 226–28, 261–64, 268–69, 270–77. Also, Terenzio Grandi, "Lettere inedite di Mazzini a Depretis," BDM, XIV, 1 (1968), 199.

12. EN, LI, 249–54; LII, 60.

13. EN, LIII, 353; LIV, 104.

14. EN, LIII, 299. Also, EN, XLV, 321; LII, 125–27; LIV, 312–18, 371–94; LV, 23–38, and *Appendice epistolario*, EN, V, 87.

15. EN, LIV, 91, 349, 352–53, 360. Federico Comandini's *Cospirazioni di Romagna e Bologna, nelle memorie di Federico Comandini e di altri patriotti del tempo, 1831–1857* (Bologna: Zanichelli, 1889), 323–33, exonerates Mazzini, but Piero Zama's *Giovanni Pianori contro Napoleone III* (Modena: Società Tipografica Modenese, 1933), 92–101, does not.

16. On Olivieri, see EN, XLIX, 223–24; L, 180; LI, 175–85; LII, 154–55; LIV, 227, 296–98; LVI, 19–21, 97–98, 118–19, 165–66; *Appendice epistolario*, EN, V, 106. Also, SEI, IX, lxxviii–lxxix, and Gaetano Bernardi, *La vita del colonnello Silvino Olivieri* (Naples: Stampe e Cartiere del Fibreno, 1861).

17. Asproni, *Diario politico*, I, 254–55.

18. Baccio Emanuele Maineri, ed., *Daniele Manin e Giorgio Pallavicino. Epistolario politico* (Milan: Bortolotti, 1878), 501–6. Also, Giorgio Pallavicino, *Memorie* (Turin: Ermanno Loescher, 1882–95), III, 250.

19. Daniele Manin, *Lettere a Giorgio Pallavicino, con note e documenti sulla quistione italiana* (Turin: Unione Tipografico-Editrice, 1859), 134–35. Also, Giorgio Pallavicino, *Memorie*, III, 225–27, 231–32.

20. EN, LVI, 336–37. Also, Manin, *Lettere a Giorgio Pallavicino*, 50, 71, 172.

21. EN, LV, 147–60.

22. Quoted in Raymond Grew, *A Sterner Plan for Italian Unity. The Italian National Society in the Risorgimento* (Princeton, N.J.: Princeton University Press, 1963), 142.

23. Pallavicino, *Memorie*, III, 274.

24. Mauro Macchi, *La conciliazione dei partiti. Risposta a Giuseppe Mazzini* (Genoa: Moretti, 1856), 35.

25. Julius Braunthal, *History of the International, 1864–1914* (London: Nelson, 1966), I, 77–78, 81–82.

26. Quoted in Marc Vuilleumier, "Les papiers d'Angelo Umiltà: Quatre lettres inédites de Mazzini à Attilio Runcaldier," RSR, LVII (April–June 1970), 239–40.

27. EN, LVIII, 31–33; LIX, 165–69.

28. EN, LVI, 284–87; LIX, 237. Also, Mario, *Agostino Bertani e i suoi tempi*, 172.

29. Domenico Giuriati, *Memorie d'emigrazione* (Milan: Treves, 1897), 250, and Pallavicino, *Memorie*, III, 280–81, 284–90, 309–12.

30. EN, LIV, 282–83. Also, Fiorella Bartoccini, *Il murattismo. Speranze, timori e contrasti nella lotta per l'unità italiana* (Milan: Giuffrè, 1959), 83–92.

31. See Giuseppe Berti, *I democratici e l'iniziativa meridionale nel Risorgimento* (Milan: Feltrinelli, 1962), 646–48, and the brief study by Giovanni Greco, *La cospirazione mazziniana nel Mezzogiorno, 1853–1857* (Salerno: Palladio, 1979).

32. EN, LVIII, 24–25, 61–65, 68–70, 91–95, 138–42; LIX, 197–223. Also, Ersilio Michel, *L'ultimo moto mazziniano (1857). Episodio di storia toscana* (Livorno: Belforte, 1903), 27–39.

33. *Mazzini's Letters to an English Family, 1855–1860* (London: John Lane, 1922), II, 77.

34. Camillo Cavour, *Epistolario* (Florence: Olschki, 1962 to date), XII, 402; XIII, 62, 461, 513, 521.

35. EN, LXXVIII, 78–87. Also, Paolo Tibaldi, *Da Roma a Cajenna, lotte, esigli, deportazione* (Rome: Società Cooperativa fra Tipografi, 1888), 41–46, 110–11.

36. Bianca Montale, "Giustizia e magistratura nel Piemonte cavouriano. Il processo politico genovese del 1858," in *Saggi mazziniani dedicati a Emilia Morelli* (Genoa: La Quercia, 1990), 105–24.

37. Cavour, *Epistolario*, XIV, 296–97.

38. EN, LIX, 69.

39. EN, LXI, 54–59, 363, 372. Also, *Mazzini's Letters to an English Family*, II, 89–91.

40. Orsini, *Memorie politiche*, 325–30, 338–39, 350–53.

41. Quoted in Michael St. John Packe, *The Bombs of Orsini* (London: Secker and Warburg, 1957), 273.

42. EN, LXVII, 254–55; LXXXIV, 134.

43. EN, LXII, 11; LXXVIII, 81–82n. Also, Luigi Ambrosoli, *Giuseppe Mazzini.Una vita per l'unità d'Italia* (Manduria: Lacaita, 1993), 220–21.

44. SEI, X, lvi.

45. EN, LXII, 21–22, 33–34, 53, 109–10, 115, 127, 137, 184, 186–87, 217, 249–62.

46. *Mazzini's Letters to an English Family*, II, 126.

47. EN, LXIII, 224, 238–39.

48. *Appendice epistolario*, EN, V, 285, 291–92, 330; VI, 3–4, 6. Also, SEI, XI, xxxii–xxxiv.

49. EN, LXIII, 221, 263–64; LXIV, 9–21.

50. EN, LXIV, 57–66.

51. *Lettere e documenti del Barone Bettino Ricasoli* (Florence: Le Monnier, 1887–94), III, 247. Also, Mario Puccioni, *L'Unità d'Italia nel pensiero e nell'azione del Barone Bettino Ricasoli* (Florence: Vallecchi, 1932), 132–35.

52. EN, LXIV, 76. Also, Marco Tabarrini, *Diario 1859–1860* (Florence: Le Monnier, 1959), 82–83, 88.

53. EN, LXIV, 137–52. Also, Mario, *Agostino Bertani e i suoi tempi*, 293.

54. EN, LXV, 44, 47.

55. EN, LXV, 50, 75, 83, 98–102, 137, 222.

56. EN, LXV, 61. On the attempt on Ricasoli's life, see Tabarrini, *Diario*, pp. 117–18.

57. Quoted in W. K. Hancock, *Ricasoli and the Risorgimento in Tuscany* (London: Faber and Faber, 1926).

58. *Appendice epistolario*, EN, VI, 69–70, 71.

59. EN, LXVI, 230–31.

60. EN, LXVII, 112. Also, Gaetano Falzone, *Ricerche mazziniane* (Palermo: Flaccovio, 1976), 107–20.

61. Francesco Crispi, *I mille (da documenti dell'archivio Crispi)* (Milan: Fratelli Treves, 1911), 103–9.

62. EN, LXVII, 62.

63. On Garibaldi's willingness to work with Mazzini, see Giuseppe Nuvolari, *Come la penso: aneddoti sconosciuti di storia contemporanea* (Milan: Ambrosoli, 1881), 120–22, and Giovanni Pittaluga, *La diversione. Note garibaldine sulla campagna del 1860* (Rome: Casa Editrice Italiana, 1904), 5–6, 21–24.

64. EN, LXVIII, 74, 82–86.

65. *Lettere di Giuseppe Mazzini ad Andrea Giannelli: con prefazione riguardante il lavoro della democrazia toscana specialmente dal 1849 al 1859* (Prato: Lici, 1888–92), 147–61.

66. EN, LXVIII, 257–58. Also, Luigi Pianciani, *Dell'andamento delle cose in Italia* (Milan: Editori del Politecnico, 1860), 69, and Pittaluga, *La diversione*, 124–28, 132–56.

67. EN, LXX, 261. Also, Giuseppe Pupino-Carbonelli, *Nicola Mignogna nella storia dell'unità italiana* (Naples: Morano, 1889), 65, 202–18.

68. EN, LXX, 78–79.

69. EN, LXX, 99.

70. EN, LXX, 155.

71. EN, LXX, 113.

72. Pallavicino, *Memorie*, III, 611.

73. EN, LXVI, 254–56. Also, Pallavicino, *Memorie*, III, 611.

74. EN, LXX, 3–4.

75. Quoted in Jasper Ridley, *Garibaldi* (London: Constable, 1974), 488–89. Also, Federico Sclopis, *Diario segreto, 1859–1878* (Turin: Deputazione Subalpina di Storia Patria, 1959), 287, 289, 294.

76. EN, LXX, 184.

77. EN, LXX, 202.

CHAPTER 8

The Monarchy's Outlaw (1860–1872)

After 1860 Mazzini was in the anomalous position of being regarded both as a founder of the nation and as an enemy of the state. As a founder of the nation he was entitled to reverence, as an enemy of the state he was the target of censure. A conciliatory gesture would have cleared him, but he refused to make it. When Victor Emmanuel offered him a pardon, his reply was worthy of Socrates: Mazzini, he said, deserved the nation's gratitude, not the king's mercy. Personal pride and political calculation mixed in that retort. The politician in him urged his followers to insist on a pardon, which he would always refuse. Pardons and refusals would work to his advantage. They would show that while others rushed home to feed at the public trough, he lived poor but principled. He called himself, proudly, *il proscritto della monarchia* (the monarchy's outlaw).[1]

In 1860, at the age of fifty-five, Mazzini was on the threshold of old age by the standards of his time, and old age brought the prospect of deprivation. His inheritance was almost spent and the annuities produced a modest income that barely covered the cost of living. He suffered from recurring back pains, fatigue, dizziness, fainting spells, and nausea. Depression and irritability indicated a precarious mental state. Recurring nightmares throubled his sleep; the worst nightmare of all was one that he did not understand. In it three veiled, gigantic female figures advanced on him without ever speaking. He could not explain why that vision filled him with fear, but he often woke up from it screaming in terror. Because of these nightly ordeals he refused offers

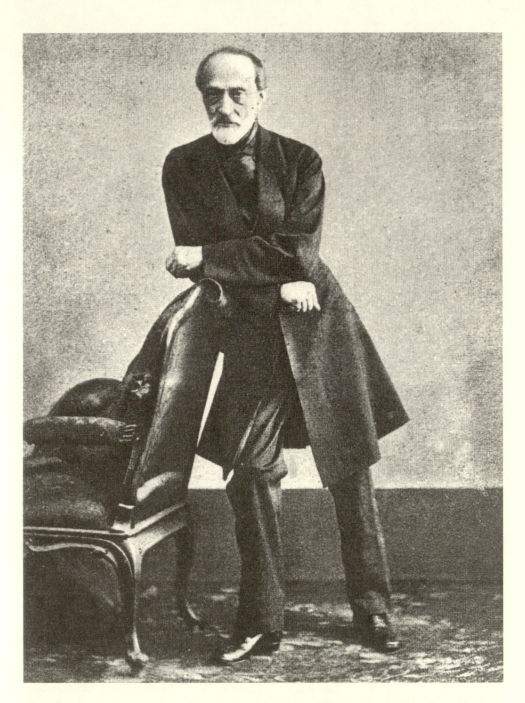

Photograph of Mazzini, ca. 1865. From *Edizione Nazionale*, vol. XL (Cooperativa Tipografico-Editrice Paolo Galeati of Imola, 1912–1924).

of hospitality; he preferred to stay in hotels, and he would not share his quarters. He was, he claimed, a "living ruin."[2]

After returning to London in December of 1860 he lived modestly in two rooms on the ground floor of a three-story house on a quiet stretch of Fulham Road, a front sitting room where he worked and received visitors and a back room where he slept; the landlady cooked his meals, his sole companions were canaries and finches, books and papers covered every surface, and the pungent smell of cigar permeated the premises. The location had the advantage of being on the omnibus route to Stansfeld's brewery, where he sometimes received visitors and mail. The pseudonyms of Signor Ernesti and Signor Fiore (Mr. Flower) protected him from the curious.

London was less welcoming after 1860. The British saw no need to prolong the revolution in Italy once constitutional monarchy was secure there. Italians in London were relieved and grateful that the country was unified and looked to others for leadership; they found moderates more to their liking. Mazzini severed his connection with the school for workers totally in 1861. While Italians turned toward moderate leaders, expatriates of other nationalities were becoming more radical. Mazzini's views, considered daring twenty years before, now seemed tame. He warned against the dangers to society from the growing power of "the financial-industrial element" in England and other industrial nations, but the remedies he proposed seemed to lack bite.[3]

To refurbish his image and earn money, Mazzini took up an offer inspired by Cattaneo to prepare a comprehensive edition of his political and literary writings. The contract with the Turin publisher Gino Daelli was signed on March 17, 1861, the same day that the Kingdom of Italy was made official.[4] It was perhaps for that reason that he described the project as a *cattedra di repubblica* (a podium for republicanism). Independently of that project, he had already collected a volume of his writings on the Social Question, which he prided himself on having been among the first to raise thirty years before. The book, based on pieces published since the early 1840s, was entitled *Doveri dell'uomo* (The Duties of Man); by the end of 1860 two editions had already appeared, one published in Lugano and the other in Naples. With an estimated one million copies published in the century after its publication, this became Mazzini's most widely disseminated work.[5]

Nothing in *Doveri dell'uomo* was new, but, brought together in one volume, his writings showed the organic unity of his social thought. Dedicated to Italian workers, the book started by reminding them of their duties: "I want to speak to you of your duties . . . , listen to me with love, as I speak to you with love."[6] That set the tone, which was meant to be loving but which strikes modern ears as condescending and paternalistic. The preachy tone suggests perhaps a desire to speak a language different from that of socialism. He did not deny that workers had rights, but he stressed that, like all members of society, they also had obligations (duties) toward others; workers were entitled to material benefits, but their spiritual and intellectual needs were just as if not more important than their material satisfactions. *Doveri dell'uomo* encouraged workers to unite, but, even more, it aimed at forging bonds of solidarity across class lines. Capitalism and socialism were equally wrong in their stress on rights, the economic rights of the individual in the case of capitalism, and the economic rights of the working class in the case of socialism. Socialism and capitalism defined happiness similarly in material terms, and each pursued no more than a partial good. The solution was to sever all ties with materialistic philosophy and affirm the spiritual aspects of life. Workers had a special obligation in that regard, because they were the ones that gave shape, beauty, and meaning to lifeless matter: "Just as the individual is called to transform, improve, and master the moral and intellectual faculties, he is also called on to transform, improve, and master the physical world through *labor*."[7] *Doveri dell'uomo* was dedicated to workers, but its message was that it was wrong to set them apart as workers, because their human needs took precedence over their class interests. All the rest followed: no separation of rights from duties, of individuals or classes from society, of liberty from authority. The exclusive concern with rights and liberties was what Mazzini criticized in the writings of his friend John Stuart Mill, whose 1859 essay *On Liberty* he described as *arriérée* (behind the times).[8]

Doveri dell'uomo stressed the role of education as an instrument of liberation. Education to Mazzini meant not instruction but moral training, and he regarded it as essential to democratic society, where individuals were free "to choose the means of doing good freely and according to talent."[9] That narrow definition of liberty (was he denying individuals the right to define the nature of the good?) stressed that democracy entailed responsibilities, including the responsibility to cultivate the intellect. Only educated workers could overthrow the worst form of oppression, which was the tyranny of the educated over the uneducated. Oppression, he pointed out, rests ultimately on claims of cultural superiority: "Does the history of oppression not teach you that the oppressor always makes his case on some imagined fact?"[10]

In fact, *Doveri dell'uomo* reminded workers that they were not alone in the fight against oppression. Their natural allies were women ("from whom we expect inspiration and solace and the education of our children"), slaves, serfs, and oppressed nationalities.[11] Workers could not remain indifferent to their plight without doing injury to their own cause. Unfortunately, the oppressed were just as likely to fight against one another as against the oppressors, because their material interests did not necessarily coincide and often clashed. Social movements that spoke only the language of material interest were therefore bound to fracture and die. Solidarity required a principle of unity that transcended temporal realities, and that principle was the idea of God. Mazzini introduced the idea of God early on in *Doveri dell'uomo* and returned to it in the end; his definition of labor as the activity that puts God's imprint on the material world buttressed the notion that labor had a God-given mission to fulfill.[12]

Unlike Karl Marx, who addressed workers in the language of social science, Mazzini relied on religious invocation and paternalism (the "language of love") to convince workers of their special mission. The consequences of that choice for the labor movement that he inspired are not clear. Socialists used religious symbolism to good effect in their efforts to organize workers. In Italy in particular, where religious symbolism and paternalism were part of the culture, and where small workshops were far more common than large, impersonal factories, Mazzini's tone and language were not liabilities. Mazzini counted on the prevalence of small-scale production to get his message across. His proposal for "the union of capital and labor in the same hands"[13] found special resonance among artisans in the Romagna, the Marches, and Tuscany, where small establishments were especially numerous and Mazzinian organizers were first on the scene after national unification. In these regions the Mazzinian labor movement held its own against socialists and Catholics well into the first decades of the twentieth century.

A charter for the *fratellanze* (brotherhoods) of workers that Mazzini had prepared in Naples was adopted as a national charter at the ninth congress of workers, which met in Florence in September of 1861 (Italian worker congresses were numbered consecutively after the first in 1853). Mazzini prepared it and followed its deliberations from London without appearing in person; his name was mentioned only once as that of the author of *Doveri dell'uomo*, which workers were urged to read. Mazzinian delegates packed the congress, but not all participants were workers. The principle that all men are "called by God to help one another" in a spirit of brotherly love meant that nonworkers were welcome and could hold office in the brotherhoods.[14] Mazzini defended the practice as the logical corollary of the principle of collaboration across class lines.

More controversial than the charter was the Mazzinian contention that worker societies must commit themselves to political causes, particularly to the liberation of Rome and Venice, universal suffrage, and women's rights. On that last issue, Mazzini reiterated his belief that women should be organized separately on the basis of their gender and that they could help out politically as fund-raisers.[15] Representatives of organizations that stressed economic assistance weighed in against worker involvement in politics; they were particularly strong in the regions of Piedmont, Lombardy, and Liguria, which had a longer history of labor organization. That suggests that the Mazzinian message of political involvement was received most readily by first-generation workers and by workers without previous experience of collective action. The Mazzinian position was endorsed by a majority, while the dissenting minority decided to meet separately. The political commitment gave the Mazzinian organizations a subversive image that made them more suspect than unions that concerned themselves with economic matters, including for a time many socialist unions. The subversive image was reinforced by Mazzini's condemnation of labor strikes for being economically motivated. Clearly, moderate politicians preferred strikes against owners to strikes that called government on the carpet.[16]

VENICE AND ROME: REVOLUTION BY POLITICAL MEANS

The political support of workers mattered greatly to Mazzini at a time when the republican movement appealed less to the middle classes. Lack of interest in prolonging the national revolution explains the difficulties that Mazzini and Garibaldi encountered. Nothing was ready in the spring of 1861, when, according to their earlier agreement, they should have been acting in unison. They blamed each other, Mazzini complaining that while he moved heaven and earth to get things going Garibaldi planted cabbages on his farm. They agreed to work on organization first, encouraging sharpshooter societies to teach Italians how to use firearms and gymnastic societies to keep them physically fit. They agreed to arm the nation, but disagreed on how to do it. Mazzini set up the Unitary Italian Association, while Garibaldi worked with local committees (*comitati di provvedimento*) staffed by independent democrats. These activities alarmed moderates and conservatives, whose fears increased when Cavour came to a natural but untimely end in June of 1861. Mazzini was rather looking forward to a series of weak governments now that Cavour was out of the picture. That sentiment was not shared by responsible people like Massimo d'Azeglio, who predicted that without a strong hand at the helm the law of the mob would soon prevail.[17]

Cavour's immediate successor was Baron Bettino Ricasoli, who resigned after less than eight months in office, apparently because he felt undermined by the king's tendency to conduct his diplomacy. Mazzini was not enthusiastic about Ricasoli, but he positively detested his successor Urbano Rattazzi, whom he called unprincipled and, even worse, pro-French. The parliamentary maneuvering surrounding these changes of government struck him as unworthy of the nation; there were always the same discredited politicians (*il cerchio fatale della consorteria*), playing musical chairs, and spreading corruption that originated higher up.[18] Higher up meant the king, with whom he was nevertheless trying to negotiate secret deals. He advised fellow republicans in parliament to take the oath of office if they felt inclined to do so, which meant swearing loyalty to the king. He did not consider taking the oath to be morally correct, and refused to do so in 1865, when he was elected in absentia. Still, he did not object to other republicans doing what he himself would not do; how else could he make his voice heard in the halls of power?[19]

The liberation of Rome and Venice was at the top of the republican agenda. That was the objective of the Emancipation Society that Mazzini and Garibaldi sponsored jointly in the spring of 1862. It billed itself as a counterparliament and called for national unity and popular war. There was little unity in the Emancipation Society itself, however, as Mazzini and Garibaldi fell out again on issues of tactics and priorities. The question was which should come first, the liberation of Venice or of Rome? Mazzini argued for Venice on the ground that Austria's defeat would bring down the entire European system and that Rome would then fall by itself like a fruit deprived of sustenance. Attacking Rome would antagonize Austria and France simultaneously, expose Italy to war on two fronts, and make a martyr of the pope. Mazzini's insistence on Venetia however, was also motivated by the consideration that the national movement in Rome was controlled by moderates, and that republicans were stronger in the regions of Venetia, Istria, and the Trentino, which were still under Austrian rule.[20]

Except perhaps for the king, who fancied himself a war leader, there was little official enthusiasm for war. Democrats themselves were seriously split on the issue, with Agostino Bertani, Francesco Crispi, Alberto Mario, and others warning Mazzini and Garibaldi to tread cautiously. The prevailing view was that national unity was too recent and fragile to be risked by going to war. Mazzini ignored such warnings. His decision to send Carlo Venturi to do some military scouting in Venetia caused a rare ripple of discord in his relationship with Emilie, who feared for the safety of her husband, who had defected from the Austrian army and risked his life by going back to Austrian territory. While Mazzini pursued the Venetian plan, Garibaldi acted on his own for Rome. Throughout the summer of 1862 he gathered volunteers in Sicily, while the government tried not to see what was happening. Mazzini, Fabrizi, Medici, Mordini, and other prominent figures of the opposition did not approve, but Mazzini stopped objecting when he realized that Garibaldi would go ahead with or without him. He came on board, promising Garibaldi that he would foment mutiny in the regular army if the government gave it orders to stop him.[21]

On August 29, 1862, the army fired on and dispersed a force of two thousand volunteers that Garibaldi was leading toward Rome. The clash that occurred in the Aspromonte mountains of Calabria reverberated throughout Italy. Mazzini heard about it in Lugano, where he had arrived that very day to be closer to the scene, and he marked the day on the calendar as one of national mourning. Jessie White Mario, who brought the news, reported that "such a cry burst from Mazzini's lips as 'erst from David of his son bereaved.'" The grief was greater for knowing that Garibaldi had been wounded in the encounter, but she noted that "the first paroxysm of their grief over, Mazzini did not doubt for a moment that the Italians would rise as one man to avenge their outraged chief."[22] The failure of Italians to rise as one stunned Mazzini. The blood of Garibaldi, he told Alberto Mario, was on the head of others: "The ghosts of the martyrs appeared, accusing him of having killed them to revive the *land of the dead*."[23] He turned down an Englishwoman's offer to "blow up Rattazzi, the King, and Parliament," but vowed that Aspromonte would initiate "the period of extralegal action."[24]

Falange Sacra (The Sacred Phalanx) was to be Mazzini's instrument for extralegal action. Little need be said about this association founded in May 1862, which, like other Mazzinian societies, existed mostly on paper. Its interest lies in its involvement with the peasantry.[25] It found little support among democrats, but Mazzini pinned his hopes on it for a while; he returned to London at the end of September confident that *Falange Sacra* could play an important role in revolution. Italians might be lethargic, but the Danes were up in arms over Schleswig and Holstein; Greece, Poland, Hungary, and Serbia were on the verge of revolution, and the recently freed serfs of Russia demanded land and justice. Perhaps he had been wrong to think that Italians would take the initiative; perhaps that distinction of leading the revolution belonged instead to the Slavic nationalities of Eastern Europe.[26]

With what amounted to civil war raging in many provinces of the south and discontent with taxes, conscription, and bureaucracy rife everywhere, few Italians were eager for adventures abroad. It was all that the government could do to hold the country together. Peasant unrest in the south was particularly dangerous, because it provided endless opportunities for mischief to the many enemies of the state. The fear was that supporters of the deposed Bourbons and of the pope, as well as agents of foreign powers would direct peasant discontent toward political goals. The government called the popular resistance to the state brigandage, which did not make it less legitimate in the eyes of peasants long accustomed to regarding brigands as popular heroes.

Falange Sacra's interest in the peasantry was not unrelated to the turmoil in the south. It had been Mazzini's and Bianco's dream to wage guerrilla warfare with peasant support. It could still happen, Mazzini thought, if someone summoned peasants "with promises of love and help."[27] Given that peasant unrest was real, why should it be allowed to serve reactionary ends? Why could it not be harnessed for progressive purposes? In the end, however, he did not play the peasant card. Although some who called themselves Mazzinians may have done so without his knowledge, making common cause with peasants, *papalini,* and brigands, Mazzini was not prepared to jeopardize political unity by catering to regional and class interests.[28]

Mazzini chose instead to advance the national revolution by pursuing the Venetian project. That was in accordance with his conviction that the people attain power by being politically active, but in pursuing his design he did not neglect to work with the other end of society, namely, with the king. Hence a new round of intrigue centered on a shady figure from the days of the Roman republic. Demetrio Diamilla-Muller had served time in a papal jail for stealing and selling art objects in 1849; released, he had insinuated himself in the court circle in Turin. His republican past and new connections made him the ideal link between Mazzini and Victor Emmanuel. The king talked to Mazzini through intermediaries, ostensibly to liberate Venice, but perhaps also hoping to control Garibaldi, who was thought to be working hand in hand with Mazzini. Garibaldi, however, was the rock on which their cooperation foundered; initially Mazzini seems to have supported the king's design to send Garibaldi to Poland, where an insurrection had broken, but later changed his mind to keep Garibaldi in Italy, where he hoped to make use of him for a move on Venice. It was probably no coincidence that the king's plan for Garibaldi was made public by a newspaper owned by Mazzini's friend Adriano Lemmi.[29]

The Venetian project brought Mazzini back to Lugano from May to August of 1863. Bands of insurgents made sporadic appearances in the Austrian provinces of northern Italy; they were not all connected with Mazzini, although he is said to have provided considerable sums of money to support their activities. Back in London, he found himself implicated in another plot to assassinate Napoleon III, although this time he was as much victim as instigator. It is quite likely that he was set up by Italian and French police agents bent on discrediting him and putting an end to his intrigue with Victor Emmanuel. The man who allegedly volunteered to carry out the attempt was one Pasquale Greco, who may have been working simultaneously with Mazzini and the police. At the time of his arrest in December of 1863 Greco also implicated James Stansfeld, who had to resign from a cabinet post in Palmerston's government.[30]

While the British parliament debated the Greco-Mazzini-Stansfeld affair, Mazzini prepared to receive Garibaldi in London for what he hoped would be a fund-raising tour. "His making money is the only thing

I care about," he wrote to Peter Taylor, who was organizing the tour, but he also hoped that the visit would strengthen republican sentiment among English workers, whom Garibaldi was expected to address in the provinces.[31] He was disappointed on both counts. From the minute Garibaldi stepped ashore on April 3, 1864, until his departure on April 28, Garibaldi was kept busy with dinners, balls, and formal receptions arranged by conservative admirers, who made sure he had no time left for anything else. A record crowd of several hundred thousand did greet him in London, but the tour of industrial cities never materialized. Mazzini and Garibaldi managed to meet a few times. At a banquet offered by Alexander Herzen, Mazzini toasted "to the freedom of the Peoples; to the union of the Peoples; to the man who in our day stands as the living incarnation of these great ideas; to Giuseppe Garibaldi." In reply, Garibaldi referred to Mazzini as the counselor of his youth: "He alone was awake when all around were slumbering, he became my friend and has remained my friend for ever; in him the holy fire of love for fatherland and freedom has never dimmed; that man is Giuseppe Mazzini: I drink to him, to my friend, to my teacher."[32] That moving moment, often cited as evidence of deep rapport between the two, was short-lived. The day after the banquet Mazzini was asked whether he did not agree that Garibaldi's face resembled that of a lion. "Have you noticed the face of a lion?" he asked in reply, "Do you not think it is a very foolish face? Well, that is Garibaldi's."[33] Later, he complained that the visit cost him 40,000 pounds in lost contributions.

Relations were hardly better with other democrats. In September of 1864 the Italian government signed an agreement with France (the September Convention) that pledged respect for the pope's sovereignty over Rome in return for the removal of French troops still there from 1849. Francesco Crispi rose in parliament to protest the agreement, which appeared to acknowledge the legitimacy of the pope's claim to the city. The protest sat well with Mazzini, but not the statement that Crispi made in his speech that he still supported the monarchy because "the monarchy unites us, the republic would divide us."[34] That speech elevated Crispi to the role of chief of the loyal opposition and brought down on him Mazzini's ire. He would forgive Crispi, he wrote years later, only if he died on the barricades. When riots broke out in Turin to protest the transfer of the capital from Turin to Florence, which was also a consequence of the September Convention, Mazzini welcomed the disturbances as retribution against the government for an agreement that he thought shamed the nation.[35]

With republicans defecting to the monarchy and the Polish revolt sputtering away, Mazzini feared for the future of democracy. The impression that there was a resurgence of conservative sentiment was reinforced by Pius IX's encyclical *Quanta cura*, issued in December of

1864. Appended to the encyclical was the notorious Syllabus of Errors, which was the pope's list of the transgressions of modern society. Mazzini was not in complete disagreement with the list of errors, which included communism, socialism, and secularism. It was the pope's attack on modern civilization as a whole that offended him, especially the inclusion of the idea of progress among the errors to be combated. It was time for another open letter to the pope, this time to argue that by condemning progress he had transgressed against the law of God.[36]

The emergence of materialistic movements was equally unsettling. Most worrisome to Mazzini was that of the *libero pensiero*, or free thought movement. Freethinkers gravitated toward the materialistic philosophy of positivism and were fanatically anticlerical; their simple message that the evils of society stemmed from the obscurantism of religion was not without popular appeal. The government supported the free thought movement because it deflected resentments toward local targets and because it also provided justification for the expropriation of ecclesiastical properties that was national policy. Freemasons helped propagate its ideas, and distinguished academics endorsed it in the name of science and freedom of thought. Every village seemed to have its small cadre of freethinkers, who focused popular resentments on the local priest. Local societies of freethinkers sprung up by the hundreds with the enthusiastic endorsement of Garibaldi, who did not share Mazzini's qualms about making scapegoats out of priests. On the issues of free thought and anticlericalism Mazzini broke with Luigi Stefanoni, a former Mazzinian who was an effective popularizer of Positivist Culture.

Anticlericalism was particularly reprehensible in Mazzini's eyes. He was a critic of the papacy and the Roman Catholic Church, but not of the clergy, which he would have liked to win over to the side of revolution. The philosophical implications of free thought also disturbed him, for it seemed to him that free thought implied lack of commitment. He did not shy away from asserting that dogma was beneficial, although he qualified that claim by explaining that dogma did not mean unassailable truth: "The Greek word *dogma* corresponds to the Latin *placitum*, which only means an accepted truth, a principle of faith. I do not understand the anathema, which is itself more than dogmatic, hurled against it by free thinkers. The movement of the earth is today a scientific dogma."[37] The real threat came not from having too much faith, but too little. Therefore "truth and justice are ignored; ignored also is the obligation to act on them. Italy is neither monarchist nor republican, nor anything else; it is *opportunistic*."[38]

The dysfunction of free thought was not confined to Italy, according to Mazzini. Never did he sound more Victorian than when he deplored the "selfishism" and "forgetfulness of high duties" that he saw everywhere.[39] Liberalism and socialism were different manifestations of "selfishism," liberalism expressing the "selfishism" of individuals, socialism that of a class.[40] Mazzini's critics on the left found it easy to depict him as an enemy of socialism, but that was not his view of himself. He claimed that he was not out to combat socialism, but to help define it. The debate on the nature of socialism reached a turning point in London in the 1860s, kicked off by an initiative that on the surface had little to do with the rarefied theoretical debates of intellectuals and political exiles. What developed into an international movement for revolution began as a modest effort to regulate the labor market by representatives of British workers, who feared the competition from immigrant laborers and women. What they wanted was self-regulation of the labor market to protect wages, and to start that they proposed that workers be organized along ethnic lines. Mazzini did his part in the early stages of the campaign by organizing Italian workers in a Society for Mutual Progress. It was small, but its few hundred members gave him a foothold in labor politics.[41]

When labor representatives met in London's St. Martin's Hall on September 28, 1864, to set up the International Working Men's Association, better known as the First International, Mazzini was represented by a German acolyte named Adolphe Wolff, to whom he often entrusted confidential missions. Wolff proposed a charter, which a spectator named Karl Marx, who represented no workers at all, immediately volunteered to revise.[42] The original proposal has never been found in the archives of the International, but we have Marx's word for it that it was Mazzinian through and through. Not surprisingly, the revised version that he produced was not Mazzinian at all. He left in "zwei *duty* und *right* Phrasen" (two phrases about duty and right) as a sop, he explained, but reassured his partner Friedrich Engels that they were too innocuous to do harm.[43]

Marx and Mazzini differed, but they were not instant enemies. Marx was often sarcastic at Mazzini's expense and intrigued against him, but he was also careful not to offend him in public. Mazzini simply ignored Marx, until their differences over the Paris Commune of 1871 made their breach irreparable. From Mazzini's silence one would never guess that they lived in the same city for many years. Their paths seem not to have crossed, although they moved in some of the same circles. Socialism was diverse enough in the 1860s to accommodate two figures such as Mazzini and Marx, who disagreed on philosophy and religion but were both democrats, republicans, and critics of capitalism and the bourgeoisie.[44]

The political itinerary of the Russian anarchist Mikhail Bakunin crossed both Mazzini's and Marx's. Mazzini and Bakunin first met in London in 1861 through Alexander Herzen, and Mazzini introduced

Bakunin to his contacts in Genoa and Florence on the occasion of his visit to Italy in January of 1864. The purpose of the visit was to raise money and public support for the languishing Polish insurrection, a mission that Mazzini endorsed enthusiastically. What Bakunin accomplished is not clear, but in Florence, where he stayed, he met a great many democrats. He approached Marx after returning to London in October of that same year, and returned to Italy the following month as an internationalist and as a critic of Mazzini. Perhaps he realized that Mazzini's name was not universally popular in Italian democratic circles and that the depth of popular discontent in Italy called for a different and more decisive approach to revolution. In his next phase Bakunin was in effect an agent for Marx, but still outwardly respectful and deferential toward Mazzini. In the end, Bakunin played his own game in Italy. He is remembered as the most prominent anarchist of his generation, but in the context of the 1860s he was another radical democrat ranged against the state, much like Mazzini and Marx.[45]

With Bakunin presumably "laying mines" against Mazzini in Italy, Marx managed to expel Mazzinian delegates from the policy-making general council of the International in April of 1865.[46] The sense of having been duped by a cabal of English, French, German, and Russian socialists is one reason for Mazzini's increasingly nationalistic appeals to Italian workers, whom he warned to resist foreign influences and pursue the Italian road to social justice. At the same time, however, he also urged them to remain active in the International to counteract "tendencies that want to intensify the antagonism between the working classes and the middle classes."[47] Perhaps he was trying to deal with Marx as he had dealt with Buonarroti thirty years before, infiltrating the other man's organization and attempting to subvert it from within.

Mazzini also fought the International from the outside. Marx rightly suspected that Mazzini's real motive in launching the Universal Republican Alliance in September of 1866 was to set up a rival organization.[48] Mazzini had great hopes for this organization, which found followers in Europe and America. The defeat of the conservative slave-holding South in the American Civil War and the enfranchisement of Blacks gave him confidence that the American government was ready to exert itself on behalf of republican movements in Europe. He counted on public and private help from America to support international progress toward a "Universal Republic." He admired President Lincoln, revered John Brown, and regarded abolitionists as his natural allies; William Lloyd Garrison and Sarah Parker Remond were personal friends. "Those are to be pitied who die doubting," he commented when he learned of Lincoln's assassination; at least he had died knowing that he had won. Mazzini cultivated prominent American republicans, particularly the New York philanthropist Gerrit Smith, from whom he optimistically expected shiploads of dollars. The Universal Republican Alliance turned out to be another small sect of idealists (a "militant church" he called it in 1868), with its own secret rituals and petty squabbles.⁴⁹

More effective than the Universal Alliance was its Italian affiliate, the Italian Republican Alliance, which developed in the climate of war and gave Mazzini an organizational footing in national politics. The Seven Weeks' War of 1866, known in Italy as the Third War of Independence, was fought to acquire Venice from Austria. Italy's ally was Prussia, which would do to Austria in Germany what Piedmont and France had done to it in Italy: curb its power to make way for a new national state. Italy could perhaps have gained Venice and the region of Venetia without fighting, because Austria agreed to turn it over in return for Italian neutrality. That seemingly good offer had an insidious aspect. Accepting Venice would have put the government in the politically embarrassing position of accepting as a gift from the traditional national enemy what it was entitled to have but could not win by force of arms. The democratic opposition, which wanted a war of liberation, stood ready to accuse the governing coalition of being timid, weak, and unpatriotic. Mazzini was on the side of those who wanted war. "Oh! for six months of power in Italy, just as I had in Rome. How I would manage these rotten cowardly immoral Powers. I dream of going first to Vienna, then to Pesh, then to Berlin, finally to Paris, with 300,000 Italians."⁵⁰ That was the democratic passion for revolutionary war and citizens' armies toppling reactionary regimes and liberating the oppressed. The role of the Republican Alliance was to orchestrate popular support, recruit volunteers, and regain the revolutionary initiative.⁵¹

There were republicans who thought that this was wishful thinking. They pointed out that if Italy won, the monarchy would take credit and become stronger, and if it lost, it could lose everything, particularly its still fragile political unity. Mazzini himself had second thoughts after the first enthusiasm, but what worried him was that the government would find ways to prevent a people's war as it had done in 1859. Believing that popular war was the key to victory, he feared that the government would choose to fight conventionally, courting military defeat to deny political victory to the opposition. Victory for Mazzini meant full mobilization, support for guerrilla operations, arming the nation, and stirring up the oppressed nationalities of the Austrian Empire. Otherwise Austria would win, with its better-trained soldiers and impregnable bases. Should Italy not fight if the government refused to wage a popular war? Mazzini's answer was that "a defeat might prove useful in its ultimate result; still, although I would try to make the best of it for our own good, I cannot afford to calculate now on it."⁵²

As the hour approached, Mazzini agonized over whether he should leave London or stay: "The thought appears, reappears, torments. Still, unless the army is beaten, what could I do in Italy now?"[53] He did not have to wait for long to decide: the government went to war on June 20, 1866, and the army was defeated in battle four days later. The battle of Custozza may not have been the military disaster that critics made it out to be, but it was certainly felt as a national humiliation. The silver lining was that the Italian army's retreat to safe positions may have frustrated Austrian hopes that a defeat would bring down the state, and democrats found something to cheer once again in Garibaldi's well-publicized exploits. The memory of Custozza, however, poisoned the political atmosphere for years to come.

Although Mazzini predicted the defeat, he felt confounded and humiliated by it. Ill and hesitant because he thought that the French police would try to arrest him, he left around the middle of July to be Sara Nathan's guest at her recently bought villa La Tanzina, in Lugano, which became Mazzini's favorite place of refuge and his political headquarters. The acquisition of Venetia gave Mazzini little comfort. The transaction through the good offices of France was particularly galling for him, because it confirmed Italy's status as a client state. With Venice part of Italy, Mazzini's strategy shifted toward Rome and the frontier of the Alps: "The Alps must be ours, and Rome; that is our watchword; republicanism is the means."[54] He urged Garibaldi not to disband his volunteers, as the government ordered, but to lead them instead against the pope in Rome; Garibaldi refused.[55] As long as there were territories that could be claimed in the name of nationality, Mazzini could insist that *patria* and *libertà* went together: "Prepare, preach, and work for both simultaneously; seize the one that comes first, in the knowledge that one will hasten the advent of the other."[56]

From London, where Mazzini returned at the end of October, he followed events in Rome and in the south. Giacomo Medici had repressed a large-scale uprising in Palermo in September, in which separatists and republicans had mixed freely. Rome was quiet for the time being and the Italian government did not want to offend France by claiming it, but Garibaldi demanded it as the national capital. Mazzini urged his Roman contacts to take measures against public officials, build tension, and create the impression of widespread disaffection with papal rule. Garibaldi did not believe that Romans were ready to revolt, and had even less faith in Mazzini's emissaries. He preferred to attack from the outside, with the help of volunteers whom he knew would answer his call. The stage was thus set for a repetition of the disaster in Aspromonte five years before. As in 1862, Rattazzi was prime minister. Mazzini suspected that Rattazzi and the king were setting up Garibaldi for a tragic fall in the likely event that the "march on Rome" failed. Together with Agostino Bertani, Francesco Crispi, and the Marios he warned Garibaldi that he took a great risk if he went ahead with his plan. But

Mazzini soon succumbed to the lure of action and to his faith in Garibaldi's star. Was defeat worse than inaction? And was it not Rome's fate to be "either an immense, prophetic ruin, or the temple of the Italian Nation"?[57]

Mounting physical disabilities did not keep Mazzini in London this time; joking that the stomach cramps that plagued him came from the landlady's cooking, he was in Lugano again in August of 1867. Two international congresses took place nearby, but he attended neither. He was not invited to the second congress of the First International, and he declined an invitation to the first meeting of the League for Peace and Liberty: Peace would be desirable if liberty and justice were secure, but until that happened war was as holy as peace. Garibaldi attended both gatherings, assuring the Internationalists that he was with them and the pacifists that he valued peace above all else. Then he excused himself in a hurry; he had to leave to "deliver the final blows to the monster" of papal power.[58]

Thus began the debacle of Mentana. The volunteers who crossed into papal territory in October of 1867 were a disorganized force that never came together, Garibaldi was not at his best, and the Roman insurrection that Mazzini had hoped to deliver did not come off. The Italian army did not intervene, as it had done in Apromonte; this time it was a force sent by the French government that routed the would-be liberators near the town of Mentana on November 3, 1867. The defeat left another legacy of discord. Garibaldi directed his ire at Mazzini, whom he accused of sabotaging the campaign, sowing dissension, and turning family members against him.[59] Herzen saw in Mentana the end of democratic revolution: "Count Bismarck, it is your task now. And you, Mazzini, Garibaldi, last of the Mohicans, fold your hands and take your rest. You are not needed now. You have done your part. Make room now for madness, for the frenzy of blood in which either Europe will slay herself or the reaction will."[60]

As if acting on cue, barely two weeks after Mentana, Mazzini turned to Prussia's Chancellor Otto von Bismarck: If Prussia provided him with one million francs and two thousand rifles, he would prevent an Italian alliance with France in case France and Prussia went to war. It was widely expected after Prussia defeated Austria in 1866 that there would be a Franco-Prussian confrontation in the near future. There was no doubt that Mazzini would support the Germans, but until then he had supported German patriots who were politically liberal. Mentana and his hatred of France threw him into Bismarck's arms instead. The reversal was surprising, but perhaps no more so than Bismarck's interest in Mazzini's overture. Far from dismissing it, he instructed Prussian diplomats to stay in touch with the agitator, until the Italian government got wind of what was going on and forced the recall of the intermediary.[61]

A photograph of Mazzini from around the time of Mentana shows an old man troubled in body and spirit. Just about then his physical health worsened appreciably and his mind plunged deeper into religious mysticism. There were rumors that he dabbled in spiritualism; they may have been false or exaggerated, but he did think more about the afterlife. Many of his oldest and dearest friends were dead or dying. Giuseppe Giglioli and Lorenzo Pareto died in 1865, Giuditta's brother Carlo Bellerio, Jane Carlyle, and Carlo Venturi in 1866, Giovanni Grilenzoni in 1868, and Filippo Bettini in 1869. That people who loved one another were reunited after death was a belief that Mazzini expressed in many consolatory letters to bereaved friends, acquaintances, and even complete strangers. The souls of departed ones gathered, he believed, in distant regions of the universe, where they lived on in perfect harmony. The living had an obligation to remember the dead in rituals and ceremonies. Monuments were sacred altars that consecrated the tie between the living and the dead and gave a religious dimension to the concept of *patria*.[62]

Something resembling a personal cult developed around him. Its chief priestess was Emilie Venturi. "When I am asked what is my religion, I answer that I am a Mazzinian," she would say.[63] As she summed it up, Mazzinianism rejected the doctrine of original sin and viewed man as a perfectible creature; it proclaimed the law of progress and believed that history was controlled by the will of God and by human volition working in unison.[64] A Danish enthusiast named Rosalia Nielsen also claimed to have been sent to establish the religion of Mazzini. Mazzini denied sending her, but called her *chère soeur* and recommended her to his friends in Italy.[65]

Mazzini's summary of his religious views appeared in an essay of March 1870, in which he addressed the cardinals who were gathered in Rome for the First Vatican Council, which produced the doctrine of papal infallibility. It was a rambling essay that repeated much of what Emilie had written in her pamphlet on religious republicanism. Mazzini's essay was perhaps more emphatic in calling for a Third Way between materialism and traditional religion. The Third Way was to affirm "the continuity of creation, God as the inexhaustible source of energy that transforms the universe, thought made action, concepts that become substance in separate worlds."[66]

Carlo Venturi's death from a heart attack in 1866 left his wife Emilie precariously dependent on Mazzini for emotional support and may have accentuated her possessiveness and jealousy. She quarreled with Jessie White Mario over the right to translate Mazzini's writings. Something less obvious was going on between Emilie and Sara Nathan. Perhaps it was gossip that one of Sara's twelve children, Ernesto Nathan, was Mazzini's son, or it may have been Mazzini's undeniable predilection for

Sara's company that made her jealous. For whatever reasons, Emilie sensed a mysterious intimacy between them and looked upon Sara as a rival. Jealous rage drove her to attack a portrait of Sara that she herself had painted and cut it into shreds with a knife. That incident occurred at La Tanzina and was first blamed on the servants. When Mazzini found out what happened, he made excuses for Emilie; she had a complex character, he wrote to Sara, and she wanted to believe that no other woman understood him.[67]

Mazzini was back at La Tanzina in August of 1868 to keep an eye on unrest in Italy and make sure that Bakunin did not exploit it for his own purposes. The unrest was nothing new. What was new was the presence of Bakunin's Alliance for Socialist Democracy, which did its best to foment and take advantage of popular discontent. Mazzini had little organization of his own with which to oppose the Alliance. His records consisted of a little book of names and addresses that he kept on his person. After he lost the notebook on the way to Lugano he had to rely on his memory. To add insult to injury, a Genoese banker who had extended credit in the past refused to honor his promissory notes.[68]

Disturbances broke out in January of 1869 in protest against a grist tax that went into effect on the first day of the year. They caught Mazzini by surprise, because he was busy planning demonstrations for later in the spring. Far from abetting the protests, Mazzinian agents actually tried to calm the peasants who were sacking mills and municipal offices. The Mazzinian demonstrations of March and April were to protest the suspension of civil liberties brought on by the January disturbances.[69] In June Mazzini was expelled from Switzerland at the request of the Italian government. He was accused (correctly) of promoting the disturbances, and suspected, perhaps wrongly, of plotting the assassination of Victor Emmanuel. He left Switzerland, but returned surreptitiously in August. For the next sixteen months he moved continually to keep a step ahead of the police. It is impossible to document his actions precisely in the months when he was on the run, but the police in Italy quashed mutinies in the army that were attributed to him. One mutiny resulted in the execution of Pietro Barsanti, an army sergeant whose name topped off the long list of Mazzinian martyrs. Armed bands appeared sporadically in Lombardy, Romagna, Tuscany, and Calabria; those in Lombardy were subsidized and led by Sara Nathan's son Joseph Nathan; those in Calabria by members of Garibaldi's family.[70]

Prime Minister Giovanni Lanza jibed that these bands were a new form of national entertainment, but the government was concerned. There were too many of them, parts of the south were still under martial law, and the army maintained order with a heavy hand. Medici kept the lid on in Sicily, with a strictness that belied his origins in the democratic movement. He retained a personal affection for Mazzini, but was ready to do anything necessary to stop him. Stop him is what he did when Mazzini was drawn into a Sicilian conspiracy in which republicans and separatists mixed uneasily. Wary of Sicilian separatists, Mazzini was determined not to leave Sicilians to their own devices; if they must rebel, better that they do so with his guidance.[71] To warnings that he stay out of Sicilian affairs he replied that a regional insurrection could become national in the right hands. A Sicilian uprising, he thought, could give the republicans one last chance to liberate Rome; if Sicilians were willing to take the risk, he would be with them "flag in hand," come what may.[72]

Rumors of imminent war between France and Prussia encouraged Mazzini to play the Sicilian card. If the French withdrew their garrison from Rome, republicans stood a chance to regain the initiative; hence his renewed promises to Bismarck that he would make trouble for the Italian government if it decided to support the French.[73] Traveling under a false name with a British passport, he reached Palermo by steamer on the morning of August 14, 1870. He was expected by the police; in the harbor crowded with warships, before he could step ashore, he was placed under arrest by a polite but firm official, removed to a navy vessel, and carted off to the prison.

THE FINAL PROTESTS

During the two months that Mazzini spent in jail in the then isolated town of Gaeta, the French lost the war, Napoleon III was deposed, and Rome became the capital of Italy. Government troops broke into the city on September 20, 1870, after overcoming the token resistance of the papal army. As Mazzini had foreseen, the French had withdrawn their troops to France to fight the Prussians, but it was the monarchy, not the republicans, that took advantage of the situation. For that reason, he reacted with mixed feelings to the liberation of the city. Rome under the pope was a powerful reminder of the monarchy's lack of national spirit and of its political impotence. A monarchist Rome did not fit the scenario of revolution that he had envisaged since his youth. How could he continue the struggle without Rome's magic name?[74]

While Mazzini pondered that question, naval vessels patrolled the waters beneath the fortress where he was held captive, confined in the same place where Pius IX had found refuge in 1849. The quarters assigned to him were spacious and comfortable; a local innkeeper sent up excellent meals, but he ate little and saved the choicest morsels for the guards, who were in awe of their illustrious prisoner. Officers kept him company when he promenaded on the ramparts, and the commander dropped in for tea.[75] He read Shakespeare again, marveling at the complexity of Hamlet's character, whom he saw as torn between

clarity of vision and inability to act.[76] Emilie came from England to be
his daily companion. Foreign Minister Emilio Visconti-Venosta, another
former Mazzinian, gave her special permission to enter the country and
stay with Mazzini. He was supposed to be isolated from the outside
world, but he received and sent messages through Emilie or some other
channels. Thus, he learned of the impending army attack on Rome two
days before it happened. When he found out that Giuseppe Petroni was
free after twenty years in a papal prison, he invited him to help start a
newspaper. He already had a title for it, *La Roma del Popolo* (The Rome
of the People). With or without a king, Rome was a sacred city with a
special mission.

When he heard that the French emperor had been deposed and that
France had become a republic, he lamented at the double blow that
deprived him of Rome and gave France the initiative: "The double dream
of my life has vanished, the republican initiative has come not from Italy,
but from France, where it is bound to remain precarious and sterile."[77]
He feared that the main beneficiaries of the republican initiative would
be the socialists, whose gain would be another defeat for democracy. For
a moment he allowed himself to hope that Garibaldi would come to the
rescue. He was fighting for the French republic and holding his own
against the Prussian Army, to the honor of those Italians who fought
with him. Perhaps they would restore the fortunes of the republican
movement in Italy. "If I am still alive at that time," Mazzini speculated,
"he will have to get together with me."[78]

Released from Gaeta on October 13 by a general amnesty, Mazzini
protested. He did not wish to benefit from royal clemency, and he would
leave the country immediately. No train reached Gaeta in those days,
so he traveled by coach to the nearest railroad station, surprised to see
that people greeted him along the way as if he were a victorious general.
His response to a toast raised in his honor was "To the future!" The train
took him to Rome, where he had to stop overnight, but he refused to visit
the city. He would rather remember it as the glorious republican ruin of
1849 than as the desecrated capital of the Kingdom of Italy. From Rome
he went on to Livorno and Genoa, where he stopped just long enough to
visit his mother's grave; then he proceeded for Lugano, and from Lugano
he went to London. His companion on the last leg of the journey was
Joseph Nathan, who was going to England to study engineering and
stay out of trouble.

Health problems and a fall from a carriage kept Mazzini in London
until the beginning of February, when he said farewell to his friends in
the British capital for the last time and started for Lugano. It was a hard
journey in the middle of winter. At one point during the crossing of the
Alps, a sled that belonged to the party plunged down an embankment,
fortunately with no loss of life. Mazzini's spirits lifted as he proceeded

south. At a hotel in Basel he met a young German academic who was traveling to Italy for health reasons. Friedrich Nietzsche was not in a talkative mood, but there was no escaping the garrulous old man who sat in the coach wrapped in a blanket and quoted from Goethe: "Get rid of compromise and live resolutely in that which is whole, full, and beautiful." According to Elizabeth Nietzsche, who was present, the words that Mazzini drummed into their heads set the course for the rest of her brother's life.[79]

Mazzini found little rest during the next thirteen months, when he visited Lugano, Milan, Genoa, Florence, Livorno, and, finally, Pisa. He traveled under the name of George Brown, also spelling it Braun or Brünn, posing variously as a retired British gentleman, a German tourist, or a Jewish merchant. It is assumed that he used those identities to deceive the police, who were not at all deceived. It is more likely that he disguised himself for the sake of his pride and to make a political statement: As long as he did not acknowledge his true identity Giuseppe Mazzini would still be *il proscritto della monarchia*. The reason he gave, however, was different: A false name saved him from being importuned by members of his own party.[80]

Giuditta's death in March of 1871 broke another link with the past. "I have never stopped thinking of you, cherishing and loving you as one of the best beings (*una delle migliori anime*) that I have ever encountered in my life," he wrote to her when they both knew she was dying.[81] There was still time left to exchange anathemas with Garibaldi. "Mazzini and I are old men," Garibaldi wrote to Petroni, who tried to make peace between them, "Let us not even talk of reconciliation between us: Infallibilities like him die but do not bend."[82] Mazzini kept busy writing articles and letters. In the more than fifty articles that he wrote for *La Roma del Popolo* he lashed out at government and at socialism. He called the members of the governing coalition Germanic worshippers of power. That was a reference to the Hegelian philosophy espoused by prominent members of the governing right. The socialists he accused of being slavish followers of the French. Neither, he charged, understood Italian traditions and ideals. He made sure that the newspaper welcomed young radical writers who were not socialists; one of its contributors was Anna Maria Mozzoni, a founder of the Italian feminist movement.[83]

The rise of the Paris Commune in the spring of 1871 gave Mazzini's anti-socialist polemic a concrete target. His first reactions were by no means unsympathetic, but he turned against the Commune when he concluded that it had been taken over by socialists. "People who hate and cannot love" was how Mazzini described the socialist Communards, urging republicans to stay away and reminding everyone that "capital represents the fruits of labor, that property is the sign of the mission given to man to transform the material world, that the bourgeoisie descends from the artisans of our republican communes, that it liberated Italy from its feudal lords, and enriched the country and itself with its own labor."[84] In the heat of the debate Mazzini described Marx as "a man of sharp but corrosive intelligence like Proudhon, of dominating temperament, jealous of the influence of others, devoid of strong philosophical or religious convictions . . . with more anger than love in his heart."[85]

Opposition to the Commune cost Mazzini dearly. Andrea Costa, the founder of Italian socialism, believed that Mazzini "alienated the most enthusiastic and generous elements among the young who were shaped by the new science with his unremitting attacks on the fallen Commune, and by attributing the defeat of France to the influence of materialist doctrines."[86] Mazzini answered his critics in increasingly strident nationalist tones, calling Bakunin a Cossack and urging Italian workers to reject foreign leadership. He declared before a gathering of pacifists that a general European war might be needed to satisfy national aspirations, establish representative government, meet the needs of workers, and protect human rights.[87]

After the defeat of the Commune, Marx and Engels decided to fight Mazzini on his home ground in Italy. The opening shot was fired by Carlo Cafiero in an article that appeared on August 31, 1871, in the anti-clerical paper *Il Libero Pensiero*. Mazzini interpreted the move as an admission of defeat for the tactic of revolution and as a shift to the tactic of seeking change through the organization of labor.[88] Hence the importance that he attached to the labor congress that met in Rome in the first week of November of 1871. Mazzinians controlled most of the 135 worker societies that were represented, and they generally followed the instructions that Mazzini sent from London. A young republican named Giuseppe Marcora, who had been handpicked by Mazzini, saw to it that the congress voted for mutual aid, cooperativism, and progressive taxation, and against strikes as a means of economic negotiation. It was a Pyrrhic victory. A minority made up of internationalists and free thinkers left the hall rather than accept the resolutions. The congress divided the labor movement and reinforced its image as a politically subversive force.[89]

While the labor congress met in Rome, Mazzini was in Lugano, recovering from what seemed to be a severe case of bronchitis. News of the death of his brother-in-law Francesco Massuccone reached him while he was convalescing. He offered to visit his widowed sister Antonietta, but she urged him not to come "on account of her principles" and in conformity with her dead husband's wishes. "It is the old excommunication," Mazzini commented, "and from her it came rather bitter to me."[90] By the first week of February of 1872 he was feeling better and decided to go to Pisa, where the climate was milder and Sara's daughter Janet Nathan Rosselli offered him hospitality. In Pisa he had little to do but write, walk, and smoke. He wrote to his old friend Enrico Mayer to repay a debt of 3,000 lire contracted thirty-five years before. He thanked him, apologized, and explained the delay: In all those years he had never had that much money to call his own.[91]

The Rossellis called in their family physician, Giovanni Rossini, who described his patient as a man of at least seventy (Mazzini was not quite sixty-seven), gaunt, ashen, suffering from severe digestive and respiratory problems, and unable to swallow. The doctor suspected an abscess or tumor, but did not feel that there was any imminent danger. The patient had the mannerisms of an English gentleman. He lost his composure only once, when the doctor complimented him on his excellent Italian; then the normally polite gentleman became quite agitated. He was not a foreigner, he replied, but an Italian who loved his country deeply and tried to serve it well.[92]

The doctor was summoned again on March 7 and found that the patient had a fever and a high pulse; he complained of chest pains and breathing difficulties. Lung cancer was not ruled out, but Rossini and a consultant agreed on a diagnosis of bronchial pneumonia. Little could be done, said the doctor, except make the patient comfortable and prepare for the worst. Only then did Janet realize what was happening and hurry to inform Mazzini's friends. Sara Nathan, Felice Dagnino, and Adriano Lemmi arrived while he was still conscious. Death came so quietly that several minutes elapsed before anyone realized that he was gone. It was 1:30 P.M., March 12, 1872.

THE FINAL RITES

The quiet of the final moments was broken by the scramble to claim Mazzini's political legacy. Lemmi had the advantage of having been at his bedside; he claimed that with his last words Mazzini exhorted Garibaldi to continue the revolution. That put Mazzini firmly on the side of Lemmi's freethinkers, anti-clericals, and Masons. A popular lithograph showed Mazzini on his deathbed surrounded by Lemmi, Agostino Bertani, Federico Campanella, Dagnino, Alberto Mario, Maurizio Quadrio, and Aurelio Saffi, who might be called the general staff of the Masonic order in Italy. They kept away the archbishop, who offered to come and pray, and made sure no other clergyman approached the corpse. Catholics said that the presence of so many anti-clericals showed that there was a plot to prevent Mazzini from seeking a reconciliation with the Church.[93]

The image of the master surrounded by anti-clericals and atheists did not sit well with many of Mazzini's English friends either. They saw their spiritual, gentle, and prophetic Mazzini purloined and transfigured by crafty Italians. Emilie complained that they had been deliberately kept in the dark about the seriousness of his illness. Harriet Eleanor King, a religious zealot who later converted to Catholicism, went into deep mourning for a year. She was not at his bedside when he died, but her account of his last moments made up in drama what it lacked in authenticity. "On the last day," she wrote, "he suddenly appeared to enter into some tremendous conflict with an invisible enemy. There seemed a terrible struggle against a mortal foe, with incoherent and broken words of agony. All at once, he sat up strongly in bed, and in a loud voice cried out, *'Si! Si! Credo in Dio!'* (Yes! Yes! I do believe in God!)."[94] That account was published in 1912, when all the eyewitnesses had joined Mazzini in the grave.

Georgio Asproni, a former priest who looked upon Mazzini as a secular Christ, observed other struggles going on around Mazzini's body. Some complained that the women monopolized the funeral rites, and that they were Jewish. One mourner said that the corpse had been seized by the tribe of Manasse; that was a play on the double meaning of greedy and Jewish that the word *manasse* had in the dialect of Lombardy.[95] The body was actually seized by Paolo Gorini, a geologist who claimed to have discovered an embalming process that made cadavers as hard as rocks. He showed human remains that did indeed roll as if made of marble. Gorini promised that Mazzini's petrified body would defy the ages. But something went wrong when he set to work, however, and the body started to decompose at an alarming pace. It was patched up and sent off to Genoa, where Gorini managed to stabilize it long enough for it to be shown to the public in a cavernous space inside the railroad station.

Several thousand mourners accompanied the body to the cemetery at Staglieno on Sunday, March 17. The banners of over 150 associations lined the route—red ones for the revolutionists, tricolored ones for the patriots, black ones for the anticlericals and freethinkers. The most prominent banner was the tricolor of The Thousand, ordered there by Garibaldi, who did not attend. Campanella eulogized Mazzini speaking for the men. Sara Nathan was to speak for the women, but she was overcome by emotion; she stood under a drizzling rain weeping helplessly, the silence broken only by the sobbing of mourners, until they dispersed along the paths of the cemetery and went back to the city.[96]

Giosuè Carducci, then the country's most eminent poet, proposed an epitaph to "The man who sacrificed everything, loved much, pitied much, and did not hate." That set the tone for what was to come. The Mazzini who hated would always be an uncomfortable figure. For the sake of national concord, he had to be remembered as shown in a popular lithograph, standing at Victor Emmanuel's and Cavour's side, the three welcoming Garibaldi, who was the last to die in 1882, into patriot's heaven. It might have been more fitting to quote the last words attributed to the medieval pope Gregory VII: *Dilexi justitia, odivi iniquitate, ergo in exilio moro* (I loved justice and hated iniquity, hence I die in exile). Mazzini was Gregory's equal in loving justice, hating iniquity, and asserting his own righteousness. But perhaps the best epitaph of all is the one on the marble mausoleum that holds his remains: the name of Giuseppe Mazzini, engraved in the stone. The power was always in the name. Paul of Tarsus had said it: "When I am weak, then I am strong."

NOTES

Works frequently cited in the notes have been identified by the following abbreviations:

BDM	*Bollettino della Domus Mazziniana*
EN	*Edizone Nazionale. Scritti editi ed inediti di Giuseppe Mazzini* (1906–90), 106 vols.
RSR	*Rassegna Storica del Risorgimento*
SEI	*Scritti editi ed inediti di Giuseppe Mazzini* (1861–91), 18 vols.

1. EN, LXXI, 6–27; *Appendice epistolario*, VI, 142.

2. EN, XCI, 165, 183–84, 186, 283, 302–3, 311, 332, 339–40, 344. Also, Harriet Eleanor King, *Letters and Recollections of Mazzini* (London: Longman, Green, 1912), 57.

3. EN, LXXII, 105; LXXIII, 199–202, 325–27; LXXV, 142; LXXVI, 82–84.

4. EN, LXX, 233–35; LXXVII, xvii–xl.

5. See Terenzio Grandi, *Appunti di bibliografia mazziniana* (Turin: AMI, 1961), 21–26. Also, Vittorio Parmentola, "Doveri dell'uomo. La dottrina, la storia, la struttura," in *Mazzini e i repubblicani italiani* (Turin: Istituto per la Storia del Risorgimento Italiano, 1976), 355–420.

6. All references to *Doveri dell'uomo* are from the Naples 1860 edition as reproduced in EN, LXIX, 1–145.

7. EN, LXIX, 121.

8. EN, LXIII, 170. Also, LXXIV, 187–88; LXXXVII, 54.

9. EN, LXIX, 97.

10. EN, LXIX, 73.

11. EN, LXIX, 145.

12. EN, LXIX, 29.

13. EN, LXIX, 127.

14. EN, LXVI, 373–81.

15. EN, LXXI, 269–70, 277.

16. Bianca Montale, *Mazzini e le origini del movimento operaio italiano* (Genoa: Tilgher, 1973), 64–66. Also, Nello Rosselli, *Mazzini e Bakunin. Dodici anni di movimento operaio in Italia, 1860–1872* (Turin: Einaudi, 1967), 108–10.

17. EN, LXXII, 26–28. Also, Romualdo Bonfandini, *Vita di Francesco Arese con documenti inediti* (Turin: Roux, 1894), 297; *Carteggio politico di Michelangelo Castelli* (Rome; Roux, 1890–91), I, 352; Demetrio Diamilla-Muller, *Politica segreta italiana, 1863–1870* (Turin: Roux, 1891), 16–18, 26; *Mazzini's Letters to an English Family*, III (London: John Lane, 1922), 20, 29.

18. EN, LXXII, 250; LXXVII, 72.

19. EN, LXXVII, 72.

20. EN, LXXI, 126, 230–31, 332–34, 339–40, 344–49; LXXII, 35–41; LXXIII, 2; LXIV, 407–15.

21. EN, LXXII, 367–69; LXXIII, 3–4, 9–11, 37–38, 44–45, 47. Also, SEI, XIII, cxxiv–cxxv, and Andrea Giannelli, *Aneddoti ignorati ed importanti, brevi ricordi mazziniani dal 1848 al 1872* (Florence: Nerbini, 1905), 37–38.

22. Jessie White Mario, *The Birth of Modern Italy* (New York: Scribner's Sons, 1909), 325.

23. Ibid., 326, 423, 424.

24. EN, LXXIII, 126, 185, 210. Also, Leo Morabito, "La cospirazione mazziniana dal 1863 al 1865. Lettere inedite di Giuseppe Mazzini ad Antonio Mosto, Giuseppe Guerzoni e Giuseppe Garibaldi," BDM, XXXVII, 2 (1991), 121–65.

25. EN, LXXIII, 126–30, 140–42, 239–40; LXXV, 36–39.

26. EN, LXIX, 274; LXXII, 102, 167–68, 200–201, 367–69; LXXIII, 162; LXXIV, 26–27, 31–32, 44–50. Also, Eugenio Koltay-Kastner, "Lettera inedita di Mazzini nell'Archivio di Stato ungherese," RSR, LVII (January–March 1971), 94–96.

27. EN, LXXIX, 90; LXXXIII, 175. Also, *Mazzini's Letters to an English Family*, III, 7.

28. EN, LXXXI, 307–8. For Mazzini's southern strategy, see Mario Chini, *Lettere di Giuseppe Mazzini a Giuseppe Riccioli Romano. Documenti sulla cospirazione repubblicana in Sicilia tra il 1864 e il 1872* (Palermo: Società Italiana di Storia Patria, 1951), 36–42. Also, EN, LXXIX, 236, 240, 248, 266, 300. For evidence of later contacts between Mazzinians and Bourbon supporters, see SEI, XVI, 161–74, and Aldo Romano, *L'unità italiana e la Prima Internazionale, 1861–1871* (Bari: Laterza, 1966), 402–6.

29. EN, LXXIV, 29–30, 33, 188–91, 217. Also, Francesco Cognasso, *Vittorio Emanuele II* (Turin: Unione tipografico-editrice torinese, 1942), 268–72; Diamilla-Muller, *Politica segreta*, 98, 113–15; *Mazzini's Letters to an English Family*, III, 80–81; Luigi Fallani and Lucia Milana, "Demetrio Diamilla-Muller: una singolare personalità del Risorgimento italiano," RSR, LXXV (October–December 1988), 429–60.

30. EN, LXXIII, 27–28, 71, 105–6, 164, 194, 231, 256; LXXIV, 170–71, 205. Also, Demetrio Diamilla-Muller, *Roma e Venezia* (Rome: Roux e Frassati, 1895), 208–10. On the Stansfelds' involvement, see EN, LXXVIII, 31–32, 42–48, and the reconstruction of the incident in Emilia Morelli, *Mazzini in Inghilterra* (Florence: Le Monnier, 1938), 191–201.

31. EN, LXXVI, 308–10; LXXVIII, 6, 29–31, 69–70, 72.

32. *My Past and Thoughts. The Memoirs of Alexander Herzen* (New York: Knopf, 1924-28), V, 64-65. Also, SEI, XIV, lx–lxii.

33. George M. Trevelyan, *Garibaldi and the Thousand* (London: Longmans Green and Co., 1909), 64n. Giacomo E. Curatolo, in his *Il dissidio tra Mazzini e Garibaldi* (Milan: Mondadori, 1928), 241, translates the incriminating words as *una faccia veramente stupida* (a very stupid face), which is stronger than Mazzini's expression as quoted by Trevelyan.

34. Quoted in W. J. Stillman, *Francesco Crispi* (London: Grant Richards, 1899), 118. Crispi reiterated his views in a public letter of March 18, 1865, which provoked Mazzini's angry reply. See T. Palamenghi-Crispi, ed., *Carteggi politici inediti di Francesco Crispi, 1860–1900* (Rome: L'Universelle, 1912), 214–27.

35. EN, LXXIX, 106, 108; LXXXIII, 3–5, 9–13, 23–41.

36. EN, LXXXIII, 45–63.

37. EN, LXXXIII, 203n.

38. EN, LXXXI, 49–53, 124–25; LXXVIII, 350–55. Also, Guido Verrucci, *L'Italia laica prima e dopo l'unità, 1848–1876* (Bari: Laterza, 1981), 179–266.

39. EN, LXXX, 192.

40. EN, LXXXI, 217–18. On the reasons for Mazzini's rejection of Masonry on philosophical grounds, see Alessandro Luzio, *La Massoneria e il Risorgimento italiano* (Bologna: Zanichelli, 1925), I, 221–55.

41. EN, LXXVIII, 182–83, 217. Also, Francesco Fiumara, *Mazzini e l'Internazionale* (Pisa: Nistri-Lischi, 1968), 32–35.

42. Wolff was suspected of spying on Mazzini for the French, and those suspicions were confirmed in 1870, when Communards seized police files; although Mazzini was warned, he continued to trust Wolff. Perhaps Wolff's role is the basis of the rumor that Napoleon III was behind the First International. See EN, LXV, 285n, 304, 306; LXXVI, 325–26. Also, *Mazzini's Letters to an English Family*, III, 76–78, and Francesco Fiumara, *Mazzini e l'Internazionale* (Pisa: Nistri-Lischi, 1968), 32–35.

43. August Bebel and Eduard Bernstein, eds., *Der Briefwechsel Zwischen Friedrich Engels und Karl Marx, 1844 bis 1883* (Stuttgart: Dietz, 1913), III, 189, 190, 191, 195, 249.

44. Karl Marx and Friedrich Engels, *Sull'Italia: scritti e lettere* (Moscow: Edizioni Progress, 1976), 39, 46–48, 106.

45. See also the discussion in T. R. Ravindranathan, *Bakunin and the Italians* (Kingston: McGill-Queen's University Press, 1988), 38–45.

46. Aldo Romano, *L'unità italiana e la Prima Internazionale, 1861–1871* (Bari: Laterza, 1966), 158.

47. EN, LXXX, 218. Also, Aldo Romano, *Storia del movimento socialista in Italia* (Bari: Laterza, 1966–67), I, 222n.

48. Romano, *L'unità italiana e la Prima Internazionale*, 223.

49. EN, LXXX, 126–27, 139–40, 224, 230; LXXXI, 230, 277; LXXXII, 109–10, 278–79, 288–92; LXXXIII, 163–67, 187–89; LXXXIV, 75–81, 87–90, 99–102, 180–84, 191–95, 224; LXXXVI, 25–46, 182; *Appendice epistolario*, EN, VI, 371–72, 382. Also, W. F. Galpin, "Letters Concerning the Universal Republic," *American Historical Review*, XXXIV (July 1929), 779–86, and Ralph V. Harlow, *Gerritt Smith, Philanthropist and Reformer* (New York: Holt, 1939), 469–70.

50. EN, LXXX, 339.

51. EN, LXXX, 137–38; LXXXI, 206–9, 255, 291, 306, 312; LXXXII, 71–72, 121, 215–20, 287–93; LXXXIII, 241–49, 253–63.

52. EN, LXXXII, 112. The quotation is from *Mazzini's Letters to an English Family*, III, 126.

53. Ibid., III, 126.

54. EN, LXXXIV, 30.

55. EN, LXXXII, 297–300; 303–12; LXXXIV, 3–4.

56. EN, LXXXIII, 222. Also, SEI, XIV, ccxxxvi–ccxliii.

57. EN, LXXXV, 153–55, 160–62, 165.

58. EN, LXXXV, 176–79, 189, 192, 194, 274; LXXXVI, liii–lix. Also, *Mazzini's Letters to an English Family*, III, 187, 190–91, 193; and Anthony P. Campanella, "Garibaldi and the First Peace Congress in Geneva," in Anthony P. Campanella, ed., *Pages from the Garibaldian Epic* (Sarasota: International Institute for Garibaldian Studies, 1984), 226–27.

59. SEI, XV, lxxiv–lxxv, lxix–lxxv. Also, Curatolo, *Il dissidio tra Mazzini e Garibaldi*, 263–64.

60. Herzen, *Memoirs*, V, 274–75.

61. EN, LXXXVII, 105–6; LXXXIX, 164–65. Also, Diamilla-Muller, *Politica segreta Italiana 1863–1870* (Turin–Rome: Roux, 1891), 346–47, and Asproni, *Diario politico*, V (Milan: Giuffrè, 1980–91), 280.

62. For Mazzini's letters on death and the afterlife, see the collection edited by Renato Carmignani, *Lettere consolatorie di Giuseppe Mazzini* (Pisa: Domus Mazziniana, 1965).

63. Quoted in King, *Letters and Recollections of Mazzini*, 113.

64. Emilie Venturi's interpretation of Mazzinianism appeared first as an article in *Contemporary Review* (September 1871), and was later published as a pamphlet entitled *Religious Republicanism. Joseph Mazzini As a Religious Teacher* (Bath: Wilkinson Brothers, 1871).

65. EN, LXXXVII, 48–50, 58–64; LXXXVIII, 182–83n. Also, *Mazzini's Letters to an English Family*, III, 161–64, and King, *Letters and Recollections of Mazzini*, 25.

66. "From the Council to God," in EN, LXXXVI, 261; also LXXXIX, 97–98. The notion of a "Third Way" may be derived from Mazzini's reading of the medieval mystic Joachim Flores. See EN, LXXIX, 90.

67. EN, LXXXVII, 274–75; LXXXVIII, 92–96, 119–21; LXXXIX, 307–8.

68. EN, LXXXI, 326; LXXXIV, 150–51; LXXXVII, 22–23, 118, 122, 154, 165–66, 179, 185, 230–33; LXXXVIII, 22–26. Also, Carlo Gentile, *Giuseppe Mazzini uomo universale* (Rome: Società Editrice Erasmo, 1972), 107–36.

69. EN, LXXXVIII, 190–91n, and the report by Edoardo Pantano on a meeting that Mazzini held with his top supporters in February of 1869, in SEI, XVI, 161–74.

70. EN, LXXXIX, 105n, 167n, 191–92, 197, 213–15, 229, 239–40, 298–99. Also, *Carteggio politico di Michelangelo Castelli*, II, 465.

71. EN, LXXXVIII, 278–79.

72. EN, LXXXIX, 118–23, 219–23, 292–95. Quoted in Giacinto Fassio, *Mazzini a Gaeta, 15 agosto–15 ottobre 1870* (Poggio Mirteto: Sabina, 1912), 23.

73. EN, LXXXIX, 313–16. Also, Asproni, *Diario politico*, V, 565, and Bolton King, *The Life of Mazzini* (London: Dent, 1902), 214–17.

74. EN, LXXXVIII, 45–48.

75. EN, XC, 44–48.

76. Mario Chini, *Lettere di Giuseppe Mazzini a Giuseppe Riccioli Romano* (Palermo: Società Italiana per la Storia Patria, 1951), 205–6. Also, Franco Della Peruta, "Lettere di Giuseppe Mazzini a Giuseppe Petroni, 1870–1872," *Annali dell'Istituto Gian Giacomo Feltrinelli*, V (1962), 403–6.

77. EN, XC, 57.

78. EN, XC, 88; XCI, 17–18, 39, 59, 298. Also, Luigi Musini, *Da Garibaldi al socialismo. Memorie e cronache perglianni dal 1858 al 1890* (Milan: Edizioni Avaviti, 1961), 14.

79. Elizabeth Förster-Nietzsche, *The Life of Nietzsche* (New York: Sturgis and Walton, 1912), I, 243–44, and Sander L. Gilman, ed., *Conversations with Nietzsche* (New York: Oxford University Press, 1987), 88.

80. EN, XCI, 121.

81. EN, XC, 325–26; XCI, 9, 53.

82. EN, XCI, 192, 238, 368.

83. EN, XC, 152, 156, 206, 238–40.

84. EN, XCII, 20. Also, XCI, 5, 65, 293, and Chini, *Lettere di Giuseppe Mazzini a Giuseppe Riccioli Romano*, 217.

85. EN, XCII, 306.

86. Andrea Costa, *Bagliori di socialismo. Cenni storici* (Florence: Nerbini, 1900), 7–8. Also, Alfonso Scirocco, "Gennaro Bovio e la crisi del mazzinianesimo dopo la Comune," RSR, LXIII (January–March 1966), 53–74. Also, EN, XCI, 87–88.

87. EN, XCI, 225, 236, 238, 288–89, 304–6; XCII, 328; XCIII, 99–108, 125–46. Mazzini's writings on the International were published separately as *Mazzini e l'Internazionale* (Rome: Roma del Popolo, 1871).

88. *Appendice epistolario*, EN, VI, 415–18.

89. EN, XCI, 158–59, 227, 248, 255; *Appendice epistolario*, EN, VI, 408–9. Also, Bruno Di Porto, *Storia del Patto di fratellanza. Movimento operaio e democrazia repubblicana, 1860–1893* (Rome: Edizioni della Voce, 1982), 90–105, and Rosselli, *Mazzini e Bakunin*, 313–22.

90. EN, XCI, 324–25.

91. EN, XCI, 335–36.

92. Giovanni Rossini, *Dell'ultima malattia di Giuseppe Mazzini, avvenuta in Pisa nel marzo 1872* (Pisa: Tip. Nistri, 1872), 20–21. An account of Mazzini's illness and death based on contemporary reports also appears in Joseph Lloyd Garrison, *Joseph Mazzini: His Life, Writings, and Political Principles* (New York: Hurd and Houghton, 1972), 349–52.

93. Asproni, *Diario*, VI, 287. Also, Gentile, *Giuseppe Mazzini uomo universale*, 11–12.

94. King, *Letters and Recollections of Mazzini*, 112. Also, *Mazzini's Letters to an English Family*, III, 305–7.

95. Asproni, *Diario*, VI, 289, 291.

96. See Giuseppe Cesare Abba's eyewitness description of Mazzini's funeral in his *Scritti garibaldini* (Brescia: Morcelliana, 1983–86), III, 205–8.

Mazzini on his death bed, March 1872. From Lamberto Vitali, *Il Risorgimento nella fotografica* (Turin: Giulio Einaudi Editore, 1979).

Aftermath

Several of Mazzini's friends met after the funeral to commemorate him privately. Everyone expressed personal feelings, except Agostino Bertani, whose mind was on politics; with Mazzini gone, he asked, who would keep the International at bay, who would prevent it from destroying the republican movement?[1] Bertani took it for granted that Mazzini had protected the republican movement and the country from socialism, but his view of Mazzini's role was not shared by all republicans. As if to confirm Bertani's fears, a few weeks later another republican, the journalist Maurizio Quadrio, who worshipped Mazzini, expressed a very different view of the relationship between republicanism and socialism. There were two dominant currents in contemporary society, Quadrio wrote in his diary, one that concerned itself primarily with securing rights, the other with promoting the collective or social will; the first was individualist, the second socialist: "There is no need to say it: We stand with the second; we are socialists."[2]

There was room for disagreement, because Mazzini's mind had embraced and tried to synthesize dichotomous principles. It was possible to arrive at radically different interpretations of the Mazzinian legacy depending on whether one chose to stress rights or duties, liberty or solidarity, patriotism or cosmopolitanism, principle or politics, all of which were embedded in the message of his life. Mazzini was not aware of the contradictions because he lived his creed from the inside out as an organic whole, but others could only perceive that same creed as a set of distinct propositions that required analysis and explanation. The republicans who survived him saw the signs of his intentions, but not the clear program that they needed to launch and sustain a movement.

Republicans therefore went off in different directions. Aurelio Saffi emerged as the leader of the pure Mazzinians who acted as the moral conscience of the nation, refusing to sit in parliament, holding up ideals of public probity, and chastising the monarchy and parliament for playing low politics.[3] The small group of republicans led by Saffi called itself a republican party, but there was no party in the modern sense of the term until 1895 when, five years after Saffi's death, the Italian Republican Party emerged. In 1900 it elected twenty-eight deputies to parliament, where it fought to lower taxes and to curb bureaucracy. Saffi set a precedent for more intransigent republicans who refused parliament. Italian republicans have always been minorities ready to take unpopular positions in the interest of sound policy and honest government; like all other parties, they have claimed to speak for the people, but they have also prided themselves on being select minorities. In that sense, they could rightly claim to operate in the Mazzinian tradition.[4]

Other republicans plunged into politics with mixed results. Bertani was a principled republican who joined the fray, pushing for government action on welfare and health issues, tax reductions, and universal suffrage with limited success. Former republicans like Francesco Crispi, Depretis, Cairoli, Mordini, and Nicotera accepted the monarchy and became leaders of the so-called Liberal Left, which in March of 1876 took control of parliament from the "heirs of Cavour" on the Historical Right. First Depretis, until his death in 1887, and then Crispi, until he was forced out in 1896, became the political arbiters of the country. Crispi's ouster brought to an end an era of politics whose protagonists had actually lived the passions of the Risorgimento that swirled around Mazzini.

Most republicans (with a small "r") of the next generation remembered Mazzini as an anti-socialist crusader and therefore questioned his credentials as a revolutionist. The most notable of the new republicans was Felice Cavallotti, (1842–1898), a radical who looked to the left. Mazzini had noticed the work of this dynamic young man who spoke out against the monarchy, but the monarchy was not Cavallotti's obsession. Elected to parliament in 1873 at the age of thirty-one, he sat with the members of the extreme faction of the Liberal Left, took the oath of loyalty to the monarchy, and announced that he felt no obligation to honor it. A campaign for universal suffrage in which he played an important role was instrumental in bringing about the electoral reform of 1882. Dissatisfied with the results, Cavallotti helped rally republicans and socialists around a Fascio for Democracy (the word *fascio*, later associated with fascism, was a label for political alliances formed for a specific purpose). He was largely responsible for the republican opening toward socialism that Bertani had feared since the death of Mazzini.[5]

The mass arrest of republicans at Villa Ruffi near Rimini in August of 1874 showed that the authorities did not distinguish republicans from socialists or anarchists and regarded all with equal suspicion. If anything, republicans were feared more, because they had both a popular base and representation in parliament. Governments feared conspiracies, but also legal action in and outside of government, where republicans often found collaborators outside their own ranks.[6] The republican drift toward the left was undoubtedly encouraged by conservative efforts to control labor by appropriating the Mazzinian watchwords of mutual aid, cooperation, and collaboration across class lines. Eventually, the socialist movement absorbed most Mazzinian labor organizations, but a government census of 1894 showed that Mazzinian mutual aid societies still outnumbered socialist ones by almost four to one; Mazzinian labor strongholds resisted among artisans and craftsmen in the central regions of Marches, Tuscany, and parts of the Romagna until after World War I. The number of Mazzinian organizations, however, does not tell the whole story, because the Mazzinian impact also made itself felt as moral teaching, exhortation, and practical guidance in nonpolitical matters such as good practices in domestic management, child rearing, nutrition, drinking, personal hygiene, education, and self-help.[7]

One of Mazzini's arguments against socialism lost some of its relevance as socialists began to distance themselves from the more crude forms of philosophical materialism and historical determinism. The revision of Marxism that was inspired by the reorientation of European culture that began in the 1890s renewed interest in Mazzini's teachings. The anti-positivist reaction that rejected the determinism of social science was the work of intellectuals who stressed the role of volition and initiative in human affairs. One of its leading exponents was Georges Sorel (1847–1922) who set out to revive the revolutionary spirit of socialism by injecting it with the kind of crusading fervor that he saw in Mazzini's teachings. It mattered little to Sorel that Mazzini had fought socialism; what mattered was Mazzini's ability to inspire, which Sorel missed in contemporary socialism.[8] Other socialists were also attracted to Mazzini for different reasons. Bolton King (1860–1937), an English admirer of Mazzini who wrote a well-received biography, found precedents for Fabian socialism in Mazzini's voluntary associationism, reformism, and humanitarianism.[9]

Republicans eager to build bridges toward the left stressed the complementary aspects of Mazzinianism and socialism. Stressing the affinities facilitated the political tactic of forming progressive parliamentary alliances, which was favored in the early years of the century by Giovanni Giolitti, the new dominant figure of Italian politics. Giolitti

refused to treat opponents as enemies of the state unless they resorted
to illegal tactics. That shift in attitude ended a political legacy of the
Risorgimento era. Giolitti would deal with anyone, from clericals on the
right to socialists on the left, who would help him form viable parliamentary alliances and second his politics. Giolittian democracy, as some
have called his method of government, made change possible; many
feared that the country would slip into socialism. In the writings of the
republican Napoleone Colajanni (1847–1921) one senses the desire to
take advantage of the new climate of openness. His censure of socialists
who called Mazzini a moral conservative suggests unrequited love. If
socialists could transcend the diatribes of doctrinaire Marxists, Colajanni argued, they would realize that Mazzini belonged to the socialist
tradition.[10]

It fell to Gaetano Salvemini (1873–1957), a socialist who was also an
historian and a gifted polemicist, to sort out the issues. Salvemini
resembled Mazzini in many ways; like Mazzini, he was at his best when
lashing out against corruption and compromise; like Mazzini, he would
spend much of his life in exile, unwilling to acknowledge the legitimacy
of a government he despised. But that would come later, with the rise
of fascism. In the early years of the century Salvemini was very much
committed to working through the system as a socialist. He began to
study Mazzini in 1903 and published his first results two years later.[11]
Salvemini was a secularist and an atheist all his life, yet he understood
the motivational role that faith had played in Mazzini's politics. He just
did not believe that appealing to faith had served Mazzini's political
cause, and argued that the religious tone had actually worked against
him, to his ultimate isolation.

What Salvemini valued in Mazzini was his patriotism, the spirit of
democracy, and the commitment to social justice that, Salvemini argued,
made Mazzini's ideas compatible with those of socialism before Marx.
Mazzinianism and socialism were not to be confused, however, because
Mazzinianism raised moral issues and spoke the language of cooperation, while socialism dealt with economic questions of production and
distribution, and considered class warfare unavoidable. Like Sorel,
Salvemini valued Mazzinian "illusions" like the notion of Italian primacy for their motivational effect, but did not think that Mazzini
understood economic realities. What Salvemini found most attractive
in Mazzini was the ability to infuse moral fervor in politics; that was
what gave universal validity to Mazzini's work.

The critical appreciation that Salvemini brought to the study of
Mazzini was less evident in other quarters. In fact, the process of
sanctifying Mazzini began in earnest at about the time when Salvemini
began to write about him. By then Mazzini had been dead for more than
thirty years, the monarchy seemed reasonably secure and popular, and

republicanism was no longer a threat. Parliament, not without heated debate, passed a law that made an expurgated version of *Doveri dell'uomo* compulsory reading in public schools. King Victor Emmanuel III, who had come to the throne after his father had been assassinated in 1900, had nothing invested in the political diatribes of the past. He lent his royal patronage to the publication of Mazzini's *opera omnia*, and parliament agreed to fund the enormous project that is still going on more than ninety years after it was started.

By the early years of the century, liberals, anti-liberals, Catholics, socialists, and super-patriots all found reasons to praise Mazzini.[12] Gaetano Mosca (1858–1941) and Vilfredo Pareto (1848–1923) approved of Mazzini's critique that liberal governments manipulated the masses and catered to special interests. A Mazzinian party founded in 1900 denounced parliamentary politics, the Triple Alliance that made Italy a partner of Austria-Hungary and Germany, and international socialism. The main goal of this Mazzinian party was to liberate Italian territories from Austrian rule and strengthen the Italian presence in the Adriatic and Balkans. In death, Mazzini seemed to have recovered the power to fire the imagination of the educated young, who read about him in the writings of the popular polemicist Alfredo Oriani (1852–1909), who sought to remind Italians of their mission in the world.[13] Mazzini's name was never more popular than in 1915, when Italy declared war on Austria-Hungary. At that moment, Mazzini was hailed as the prophet of national greatness by interventionists across the political spectrum, who cited Mazzini's anticipation that a general war would set things right in Europe.[14]

The admiring consensus broke down after the war, when political and social conflicts of unprecedented severity divided Italians into warring factions.[15] Giovanni Gentile (1875–1944), a prominent philosopher soon to be identified with the fascist movement, opened the debate with an attack on those who saw Mazzini as a peaceful social democrat and reformer.[16] The real target of Gentile's polemic was Salvemini's Mazzini, who was too much the humanitarian reformer to answer the needs of the moment as Gentile saw them. Gentile's Mazzini was an idealistic warrior who believed in right and wrong, in struggle and conquest. Gentile asserted that Mazzini's thought was essentially religious in nature, but claimed also that Mazzini had transfused his religious fervor into nationalism, making it into a consuming passion that engulfed individuals; according to Gentile, that, made Mazzini the true prophet of modern nationalism.

Gentile made it easier for fascists to appropriate Mazzini as one of their own. Even before fascism came to power in 1922, fascists proclaimed their intention to give Italy the spiritual unity and resolve that had been Mazzini's ideal. There seemed to be a Mazzini to fit every shade of fascist sentiment. Fascist *squadristi*, who took the struggle to the streets, quoted him on the therapeutic value of action, while left-leaning fascists admired the socially conscious patriot, nationalists the patriotic crusader, and "corporatists" the synthesizer who wanted to bring together capital, labor, and the state. Giuseppe Bottai (1895–1959), a fascist who was both intellectual and a man of action, made a case for Mazzini as a protofascist, denying all the while that it was his intention to do so.[17] Mussolini himself bestowed the ultimate seal of approval by citing Mazzini's illiberalism as a precedent for fascism in the entry on fascism that appeared in the authoritative *Enciclopedia Italiana*. The Duce continued to demonstrate his admiration by placing on his desk the volumes of the national edition of Mazzini's writings as they came off the press.

The opposition to fascism was not silent. Pacifists invoked Mazzini the Europeanist, who believed in international cooperation and would surely have approved of what the League of Nations was trying to do. Catholic social activists and theoreticians like Romolo Murri (1870–1944) and Ernesto Buonaiuti (1881–1946) discovered the appeal of Mazzini's democratic views and his spirituality in the repressive atmosphere of fascism. On the left, where revolutionary intentions prevailed, Antonio Gramsci (1891–1937), the most influential Marxist intellectual of his generation, charged that Mazzini's patriotism had deflected the national movement from more radical goals of social reform.[18] Other Marxist intellectuals, particularly those who rose to prominence immediately after World War II, showed a more subtle understanding of Mazzini. They did not challenge Gramsci's contention that Mazzini had led a bourgeois revolution, but they recognized that his airing of social issues and pioneering efforts to organize workers had helped pave the way for socialism.[19]

Anti-fascists who were also anti-communists showed more enthusiasm for Mazzini. The exile brothers Carlo (1899–1937) and Nello Rosselli (1900–1937), descendants of the Rosellis who had befriended Mazzini, were inspired by Mazzini to launch the resistance movement *Giustizia e Libertà* in the early 1930s. The name of the movement reflected the Rossellis' goal of reconciling the demands of personal liberty with those of social justice.[20] Piero Gobetti (1901–1926) also struggled with the Mazzinian problem of how to reconcile opposites from a liberal perspective. According to Gobetti, both Mazzini and Marx recognized that government must respond to groups formed when individuals come together spontaneously to advance collective interests.[21] Others in the middle of the political spectrum also saw Mazzini as a mediator of differences in modern pluralistic societies.[22] In its brief life, the anti-fascist Party of Action (1942–1946) reflected the Mazzinian ideal of a socially progressive democracy. One of its chief exponents was

Guido Dorso (1892–1947), who found in Mazzini's vision of national solidarity support for a program of reform that would address the needs of the south.[23]

History vindicated Mazzini's republican vision when Italy became officially a republic on June 2, 1946. With the monarchy abolished, universal suffrage introduced, and labor proclaimed to be the foundation of the state by the constitution that was adopted in 1947, Mazzini's prophecy that Italy would be a social republic seemed realized at last. Mazzinian celebrations enlivened the early days of the republic; they were joyous events looking to the future, unlike the macabre ceremony that took place on inauguration day, when a select few gathered to view Mazzini's remains in the sarcophagus that had last been opened in 1873. In 1946 Rome finally erected a monument to its champion, and in the coming years sites associated with Mazzini's life became virtual shrines. A new literature stressed the relevance of Mazzinian ideas to the politics of a democratic society ready to make room for diversity. The Christian democrats who governed the country praised Mazzini's religiosity, while religious minorities remembered the Mazzini who had criticized the Church and consorted with Protestants and Jews.[24]

Public enthusiasm waned as it became clear in time that republican government was not a panacea. The republic was certainly more pacifist and more solicitous toward the masses than the monarchy, but it was also more vulnerable to the pressure of private interests; it catered to material expectations, and was not very good at defining or articulating the national mission. Universal suffrage and all the guarantees of the constitution offered little protection against what Mazzini had once called "selfishism." The republican system that lasted from the end of World War II to the mid-1990s adopted many of the political mechanics of republicanism, but was not animated by Mazzini's austere spirit of abnegation and his ideals of citizenship. Admonition was in the air in 1972, when the country observed the centenary of Mazzini's death. Ugo La Malfa, then head of the Republican Party, warned that if civic responsibility was at the heart of Mazzini's message, then his influence on posterity was not much in evidence.[25]

Versions of Mazzini appropriate to the current New Age will be fashioned. Mazzini the critic of corrupt government is a timely topic, especially in Italy where corruption is a political issue. The current discredit of communism resurrects memories of Mazzini as the antagonist of Marx and international communism. Religious fundamentalists can invoke Mazzini's spirituality, Europeanists his Europeanism, feminists his defense of women's rights, holists his view of reality as a unified and interrelated whole. All these Mazzinis are plausible to some degree, although it remains to be seen what resonance they will have, if any.

A few observations can be offered while the story of Mazzini and his legacy continues to unfold. For all the lack of realism that has been imputed to him, Mazzini was on the mark when he sensed the dawning of the era of mass politics. The fact that his main quarrel was with the institution of monarchy may give his pronouncements a quaint flavor in today's world, but that does not detract from the historical significance of his politics, which bridged the gap between royal absolutism and government by popular consent. It is perhaps ironic that one who believed in the unity of thought and action and prided himself on the constancy of his beliefs should have left behind so many mixed messages. But, as he said, weakness can also be strength, and that seems to be true in his case. The message is mixed because Mazzini struggled with recurring issues that have no easy solution, and because he made a valiant effort to resolve contradictions that bedevil the human condition, seeking to relate rights and duties, sentiment and reason, principle and expediency. Mazzini's effort to reconcile such opposites, and his insistence that the resulting tensions must not be allowed to erode faith in ultimate truths is a constant source of fascination. Mazzini appeals because he struggled to avoid both the abyss of uncertainty and the prison of static belief. From the effort to obtain the double benefits of security and freedom comes the protean legacy that makes Mazzini a man for all times. In the spirit of creative tension that characterizes his legacy, this study ends not as a conclusion, but as an aftermath.

NOTES

1. Giuseppe Cesare Abba, *Scritti garibaldini* (Brescia: Morcelliana, 1983–86), III, 209. Sentiments similar to Bertani's were expressed by another Mazzinian, Giorgio Asproni, in his *Diario politico, 1855–1876* (Milan: Giuffrè, 1980–1991), VI, 207.

2. Quoted in Giuseppe Tramarollo, *Risorgimento mazziniano* (Florence: Le Monnier, 1985), 45.

3. See the pamphlet by Francesco Mormina Penna, *La questione morale secondo Giuseppe Mazzini* (Livorno: Tipografia economica A. Debatte, 1896).

4. For an overview of republicanism since Mazzini, see Giovanni Spadolini, *I repubblicani dopo l'unità, 1871–1980* (Florence: Le Monnier, 1980).

5. See Giovanni Quagliotti, *Aurelio Saffi, contributo alla storia del mazzinianesimo, con documenti inediti* (Rome: Edizioni Italiane, 1944), 194–202.

6. For the collaboration between republican and socialist labor leaders, see Gastone Manacorda, *Il movimento operaio italiano attraverso i suoi congressi* (Rome: Editori Riuniti, 1963), 169–92. For an example of local cooperation, see Renato Mori's comments on labor in the marble town of Carrara, in *La lotta sociale in Lunigiana, 1859–1904* (Florence: Le Monnier, 1958), 73–74, 82–83.

7. Maurizio Ridolfi, *Il circolo virtuoso* (Florence: Centro Editoriale Toscano, 1980), 64, and Alfonso Scirocco, "L'associazionismo mazziniano da Porta Pia alla fondazione del Partito socialista," in Istituto per la Storia del Risorgimento, *L'associazionismo mazziniano. Atti dell'incontro di studio, Ostia, 13–15 novembre 1976* (Rome: Edizioni dell'Ateneo, 1982), 3–21. For an interesting case study, see Angelo Varni, *Associazionismo mazziniano e questione operaia: Il caso della Società democratica operaia di Chiavenna, 1862–1876* (Pisa: Nistri Lischi, 1978). Also, Bruno Ficcadenti, *Il Partito Mazziniano Italiano nelle Marche* (Ascoli Piceno: Arti Grafichie Stibu, 1994).

8. Georges Sorel, *Reflections on Violence* (London: Collier Books, 1961. First published in 1908), 41–42.

9. From Bolton King's introduction to Thomas Okey, ed., *Essays by Giuseppe Mazzini* (London: J. M. Dent, 1894), xx–xxxi. Also, Giuseppe Renzi, "Mazzini e il socialismo," in *Mazzini. Conferenze tenute in Genova, maggiogiugno 1905* (Genoa: Libreria Federico Chiesa, 1906), 31–54.

10. See Napoleone Colajanni's pamphlet *Preti e socialisti contro Mazzini* (Rome: Libreria Politica Moderna, 1921), first published in 1903. Another republican who stressed the radical implications of Mazzinianism was Giovanni Bovio (1837–1903), who pointed out that Mazzini saw the social question as a *questione umana* because of the human need to satisfy both material and spiritual wants. See Bovio's posthumous *Mazzini* (Milan: Sonzogno, 1905).

11. Gaetano Salvemini, *Mazzini* (London: L. Cape, 1956), first published in 1905. See Michele Cantarella's *Bibliografia salveminiana* (Rome: Bonacci Editore, 1986), 37.

12. For religious perspectives on Mazzini see the following pamphlets: Tommaso Gallarati Scotti, *Giuseppe Mazzini e il suo idealismo politico e religioso* (Milan: L. F. Cogliati, 1904), Angelo Crespi, *Giuseppe Mazzini e la futura sintesi religiosa* (Florence: Associazione Italiana di Liberi Credenti, 1912), and Ugo Della Seta, *Il pensiero religioso di Giuseppe Mazzini* (Florence: Associazione Italiana di Liberi Credenti, 1912).

13. Alfredo Oriani, *La lotta politica in Italia* (Turin: Roux e Frassati, 1892).

14. For Mazzini's statement on the European war, see *Edizione Nazionale. Scritti editi ed inediti di Giuseppe Mazzini* (1906–90), XCI, 225. Alessandro Levi's *La filosofia politica di Giuseppe Mazzini* (Bologna: Zanichelli, 1917) and Felice Momigliano's *Giuseppe Mazzini e la guerra europea* (Milan: Società Editoriale Italiana, 1916) reflect the interventionist sentiments of Mazzinians who were by no means fanatical nationalists.

15. Sordello (pseud.), *Giuseppe Mazzini e la lotta politica, 1831–1920* (Rome: Libreria Politica Moderna, 1922).

16. Giovanni Gentile, *I profeti del Risorgimento italiano* (Florence: Vallecchi Editore, 1923), first serialized in 1919 in the journal *Politica* (Rome).

17. Giuseppe Bottai, *Incontri* (Milan: Mondadori, 1938), 47–94.

18. Antonio Gramsci's comments on Mazzini are scattered throughout his writings. In the volume of Gramsci's writings entitled *Il Risorgimento* (Turin: Einaudi, 1966), see pages 66, 73, 103–4, 115–19.

19. For the most influential postwar Marxist interpretations of Mazzini see Aldo Romano, *Storia del movimento socialista in Italia* (Milan: Bocca, 1954–56)

and *L'unità italiana a la Prima Internazionale, 1861–1871* (Bari: Laterza, 1966), Giuseppe Berti, *I democratici e l'iniziativa meridionale nel Risorgimento* (Milan: Feltrinelli, 1962), and Franco Della Peruta, *Mazzini e i rivoluzionari italiani. Il partito d'azione, 1830–1845* (Milan: Feltrinelli, 1974).

20. Nello Rosselli, *Mazzini e Bakounine. 12 anni di movimento operaio in Italia, 1860–1872* (Turin: Bocca, 1927) and *Carlo Pisacane nel Risorgimento italiano* (Turin: Bocca, 1932).

21. Piero Gobetti, *Risorgimento senza eroi* (Turin: Edizioni del Baretti, 1926).

22. Federico Chabod, *L'idea di nazione* (Bari: Laterza, 1961), based on lectures delivered in 1943–44; Adolfo Omodeo, *L'età del Risorgimento italiano* (Naples: Edizioni Scientifiche Italiane, 1946), first published in 1931, and *Il senso della storia* (Turin: Einaudi, 1948); Luigi Salvatorelli, *Pensiero e azione del Risorgimento* (Turin: Einaudi, 1960). These interpretations generally reflect the influence of Benedetto Croce, Italy's most influential liberal intellectual.

23. Guido Dorso's *La rivoluzione meridionale* (Turin: Einaudi, 1955) was first published by Gobetti in 1928.

24. Giorgio Falco, *Giuseppe Mazzini e la Costituente* (Florence: Sansoni, 1946); Giuseppe Ardau, *Giuseppe Mazzini, apostolo d'italianità* (Milan: Ceschina, 1946); Arturo Codignola, *Mazzini* (Turin: UTET, 1946).

25. *Giuseppe Mazzini, raccolta di saggi in occasione del centenario della morte di Giuseppe Mazzini* (Rome: Edizioni della Voce, 1972).

Bibliographical Essay

It is not always easy to distinguish between the works of scholarship discussed in this essay and the politically inspired interpretations discussed in the Aftermath. Indeed, Salvemini's studies of Mazzini show that political commitment and moral fervor are fully compatible with sound scholarship. Little of what was written about Mazzini in his lifetime made claims to scholarly objectivity. Albert B. Cler's *Mazzini jugé par lui-même et par les sieus* (Paris: Plon Frères, 1853) was both an anti-Mazzinian tract and a documented exposition of Mazzini's creed and tactics. Nicomede Bianchi's *Vicende del mazzinianesimo politico e religioso dal 1832 al 1854* (Savona: Sambolino, 1854) struck a more objective stance, yet found Mazzinian politics vitiated by religious zeal.

Mazzini responded to his critics indirectly in the introductions to the first eight volumes of *Scritti editi ed inediti* (Milan: G. Daelli, 1861–1891). Later gathered in one volume as part of the National Edition of his works as *Ricordi autobiografici di Giuseppe Mazzini* (1938), and also published separately (1944, 1972), these introductions constitute his Autobiographical Notes. The eight volumes in question were followed by ten others, prepared by Aurelio Saffi after Mazzini's death, and by two volumes of correspondence. These twenty volumes make up the so-called *daelliana* edition of Mazzini's writings, named after the publisher Gino Daelli. Although superseded by the *Edizione Nazionale* published by the Cooperativa Paolo Galeati in Imola, the *daelliana* is still important for the introductions that Saffi wrote to volumes nine

through eighteen, which provide first-hand information from someone
who was very close to Mazzini after 1848.

The *Edizione Nazionale*, also entitled *Scritti editi ed inediti* aimed for
completeness. Authorized by parliament in 1904 in anticipation of the
first centenary of Mazzini's birth, and endorsed by King Victor Emmanuel III and subsequent heads of state in the spirit of national
reconciliation, the *Edizione Nazionale* is an ongoing project. The first of
its 106 volumes appeared in 1906 and the most recent in 1990; additional volumes will appear as long as unpublished writings by Mazzini
continue to surface, as they still do occasionally. The articles that
Mazzini and others wrote for the journal *Giovine Italia* are published in
the six separate volumes of *La Giovine Italia* (Rome: Società Editrice
Dante Alighieri, 1902–1925), edited by Mario Menghini, who was also
chiefly responsible for the *Edizione Nazionale*. The six volumes of
Protocollo della Giovine Italia (Congrega di Francia), 1840–1848 (Imola:
Cooperative Galeati, 1916–1922) contain summaries of correspondence
between Mazzini and Giuseppe Lamberti. Notes that Mazzini wrote
down sporadically from the mid-1840s to 1871 have also been published
separately under the title of *Zibaldone pisano* (Pisa: Domus Mazziniana, 1955).

Political journalists were the first biographers who made use of
Mazzini's reflections in the Autobiographical Notes. The prolific Enrico
Montazio presented Mazzini as a born conspirator in his *Giuseppe
Mazzini* (Turin: Unione tipografico-Editrice, 1862). Montazio's politics
were ambiguous, but in this biography Mazzini's propensity for conspiracy was seen as evidence of his uncontainable patriotic fervor. Also
laudatory was Luigi Stefanoni's *Giuseppe Mazzini, notizie storiche* (Milan: Barbini, 1863), which hinted at Mazzini's desire for harmony among
patriots. Emilie Ashurst Venturi's *Joseph Mazzini: A Memoir* (London:
King, 1877) set the tone for what some scholars regard as a distinctly
Anglo-Saxon school that depicts Mazzini as a spiritual reformer and
moral guide. The religious interpretation was carried on by Harriet
Eleanor King, a convert to Catholicism, in her *Letters and Recollections
of Mazzini* (London: Longman, Green and Company, 1912).

Jessie White Mario's *Della vita di Giuseppe Mazzini* (Milan: Sonzogno, 1886) presented a revolutionist bent on changing the world. Often
inaccurate on details because she relied heavily on her memory and was
denied access to public archives, this work conveyed the radical spirit
of Mazzini's republican crusade. Its captivating illustrations and plain
language facilitated its diffusion at a time when Mazzini's legacy was
being reevaluated. The revisionists were helped by new information that
expanded factual knowledge of Mazzini's personal and public life.
Domenico Giuriati's *Duecento lettere inedite di Giuseppe Mazzini* (Turin:
Roux, 1887) disclosed Mazzini's love affair with Giuditta Sidoli, but also

suggested that Mazzini approached politics impersonally and sacrificed personal feelings and friendships to what he judged to be politically necessary. The *Lettere di Giuseppe Mazzini ad Andrea Giannelli* (Prato: A. Lici, 1888–92) drew attention to Mazzini's political activities after 1849. Revelations of personal conflicts and political dissent in Mazzini's inner circle appeared in Carlo Cagnacci's *Giuseppe Mazzini e i fratelli Ruffini* (Porto Maurizio: Tip. Berio, 1893), in Dora Melegari's *Lettres intimes de Joseph Mazzini* (Paris: Perrin, 1895) and *La Giovine Italia e la Giovine Europa dal carteggio inedito di Giuseppe Mazzini a Luigi Amedeo Melegari* (Milan: Treves, 1906), and in Luigi Ordono de Rosales, ed., *Lettere inedite di Giuseppe Mazzini ad alcuni de' suoi compagni d'esilio* (Turin: Bocca, 1908). The fourteen volumes of Aurelio Saffi's *Ricordi e scritti* (Florence: Barbera, 1892–1905) were also a treasure trove of information for the period after 1848.

In the midst of these discoveries, Bolton King's *The Life of Mazzini* (London: Dent, 1902) made the bold claim that further research was unlikely to reveal anything new. King looked no further than 1848–49, showed little interest in Mazzini's later years, and discussed Mazzini's ideas on literature, religion, nationality, and labor separately; the separation of the ideas from one another and from the person produced an informative but fragmented account of Mazzini's life, which was nevertheless hailed as a major scholarly achievement. More comprehensive and better integrated was the less acclaimed biography by Federico Donaver, *Vita di Giuseppe Mazzini* (Florence: Le Monnier, 1903), which tried to demystify its subject. The centenary of Mazzini's birth produced a collection of essays presented by Giuseppe Macaggi, *Mazzini, Conferenze Tenute in Genova, Maggio-Giugno 1905* (Genoa: Libreria Federico Chiesa, 1906).

Mazzinian scholarship of the period between the two world wars generally did not reflect the extreme nationalism of Giovanni Gentile's *I profeti del Risorgimento italiano* (Florence: Vallecchi, 1923). The frequent criticisms of Mazzinian tactics and the stress on the correctness of royal justice in Alessandro Luzio's *Giuseppe Mazzini carbonaro* (Turin: Bocca, 1920) and *Carlo Alberto e Mazzini* (Turin: Bocca, 1923) reflected perhaps Luzio's monarchist sentiments; these works are important for their documentation, as is Arturo Codignola's *La giovinezza di Giuseppe Mazzini* (Florence: Vallecchi, 1926). Anna Errera's *Vita di Mazzini* (Milan: Casa Editrice E.S.I., 1932) and Giuseppe Ardau's *Giuseppe Mazzini* (Milan: Ceschina, 1941 and 1946) reflected the nationalism of the time in which they were written. The anti-fascist Nello Rosselli initiated the study of Mazzini's labor policies with his *Mazzini e Bakunin. Dodici anni di movimento operaio in Italia, 1860–1872* (Turin: Fratelli Bocca, 1927). Works written by non-Italians reflected different concerns. The three volumes of Mazzini's *Letters to an English*

Family (London: John Lane, 1920–22) presented material that reinforced the image of Mazzini as moral reformer. Gwilyn O. Griffith's *Mazzini: Prophet of Modern Europe* (London: Hodder and Stoughton, 1932) and Stringfellow Barr's *Mazzini: Portrait of an Exile* (New York: Holt, 1935) focused on Mazzini's cosmopolitanism and his democratic convictions.

The debate on Mazzini opened up in the free atmosphere of the Italian Republic after World War II. Federico Chabod's wartime lectures in Paris, later published as *L'idea di nazione* (Bari: Laterza, 1961), connected Mazzini's patriotism to the pursuit of liberty. Michele Saponaro's *Mazzini* (Milan: Garzanti, 1945) covered Mazzini's life in two well-written volumes meant for the educated public. The emphasis of Arturo Codignola's *Mazzini* (Turin: UTET, 1946) on the religious underpinnings of Mazzini's creed could not have displeased the Christian Democratic leadership of the new republic. Alessandro Levi's *Mazzini* (Florence: Barbera, 1955) was a social democratic interpretation that stressed the Mazzinian commitment to patriotism and social justice. Edward E. Y. Hales's *Mazzini and the Secret Societies: The Making of a Myth* (New York: Kennedy, 1956) presented Mazzinian conspiracies as more nuisance than threat and Mazzini as the prototype of irresponsible radical youth.

Scholars of the postwar period reconsidered Mazzini's relationship to socialism and democracy. Mazzini appears as the founder of the social democratic tradition in Giuseppe Galasso's *Da Mazzini a Salvemini. II pensiero democratico nell'Italia moderna* (Florence: Le Monnier, 1974). Further to the left, Giuseppe Berti, Franco Della Peruta, and Aldo Romano drew attention to Mazzini's role in the struggle for social justice. Della Peruta's *Mazzini e i rivoluzionari italiani. II partito d'azione, 1830–1845* (Milan: Feltrinelli, 1974) argued that Mazzinian republicans, if not Mazzini himself, established the first broadly-based revolutionary movement in Italy. Alfonso Scirocco's *I democratici italiani da Sapri a Porta Pia* (Naples: E.S.I., 1969) and *L'Italia del Risorgimento* (Bologna: II Mulino, 1990) present Mazzini in the context of the ideological diversity and decentralization that characterized the democratic movement.

With the exception of Andreina Biondi's *Mazzini uomo* (Milan: Editrice Tramontana, 1969) there were no full-length biographies of Mazzini from the 1960s to the early 1990s. As Lucy Riall has pointed out in *The Italian Risorgimento: State, Society and National Unification* (London: Routledge, 1994), scholarship in those years preferred groups to individuals and processes over events. In Clara M. Lovett's prosopographic study of the process of democratic socialization, *The Democratic Movement in Italy 1830–1876* (Cambridge: Harvard University Press, 1982), Mazzini appeared as one democrat among many. John Breully's

Nationalism and the State (New York: St. Martin's Press, 1982) saw nationalism as a by-product of the process of state formation rather than as an autonomous phenomenon, and completely ignored Mazzini. Maurizio Ridolfi's *Il circolo virtuoso Sociabilità democratica, associazionismo e rappresentanza politica nell'Ottocento* (Florence: Centro Editoriale Toscano, 1990) manages to discuss the Roman republic of 1849 without ever mentioning Mazzini's name. Literary scholarship perhaps made up for the neglect by historians in those years. Starting with Franco Della Peruta's *Giuseppe Mazzini e i democratici* (Milan: Ricciardi, 1969) in the series *Scrittori politici dell'ottocento*, and continuing with Anna T. Ossani's *Letteratura e politica in Giuseppe Mazzini* (Urbino: Argalia, 1973) and Giovanni Pirodda's *Mazzini e gli scrittori democratici* (Bari: Laterza, 1976), works of literary scholarship drew attention to the political features of Mazzini's literary style.

Devoted Mazzinian scholars refused to be swayed by trends and fashions. Salvo Mastellone published a detailed and perceptive two-volume account of Mazzini's early conspiracies in *Mazzini e la "Giovine Italia," 1831–1834* (Pisa: Domus Mazziniana, 1960). Emilia Morelli built on the work of her youth, *Mazzini in Inghilterra* (Florence: Le Monnier, 1938), with articles and essays that were collected in *Giuseppe Mazzini: saggi e ricerche* (Rome: Edizioni dell'Ateneo, 1950) and in *Mazzini: Quasi una biografia* (Rome: Edizioni dell'Ateneo, 1984), the last in particular being an impassioned defense of Mazzini the patriot. The centenary of Mazzini's death produced significant collections of essays, including the *Atti del convegno sul tema: Mazzini e l'Europa* (Rome: Accademia Nazionale dei Lincei, 1974), *Giuseppe Mazzini, raccolta di saggi comparsi in occasione del centenario della morte di Giuseppe Mazzini* (Rome: Edizioni della Voce, 1972), *Democrazia e mazzinianesimo nel Mezzogiorno d'Italia 1831–1872* (Geneva: Droz, 1975), *Mazzini e i repubblicani italiani* (Turin: Istituto per la Storia del Risorgimento, 1976), and Istituto per la Storia del Risorgimento Italiano, *L'associazionismo mazziniano* (Rome: Edizioni dell'Ateneo, 1976). Later came *Mazzini. Tra insegnamento e ricerca* (Rome: Edizioni dell'Ateneo, 1982), and *Saggi mazziniani dedicati a Emilia Morelli* (Genoa: La Quercia, 1990), the latter edited by Giovanni Spadolini.

By the time the last of these collections appeared, Mazzinian scholarship was already reflecting the political concerns of the 1990s. Silvio Pozzani's *Mazzini e Marx: quale socialismo?* (Cremona: Edizioni Evoluzione Europea, 1979) and Bruno Di Porto's *Storia del Patto di Fratellanza Movimento operaio e democrazia repubblicana, 1860–1893* (Rome: Edizioni della Voce, 1982) proposed Mazzinianism as an alternative to collectivist socialism. Romano Bracalini's *Mazzini. Il sogno dell'Italia onesta* (Milan: Mondadori, 1993) holds up Mazzini as a model of political honesty and as an antidote to corruption. The most recent biography, the first in English in more than sixty years, is Denis Mack Smith's *Mazzini* (New Haven: Yale University Press, 1994), which also presents Mazzini as a model of public and private rectitude. The frequent comparisons between Mazzini and Cattaneo in Luigi Ambrosoli's *Giuseppe Mazzini. Una vita per l'unità d'Italia* (Manduria: Lacaita, 1993) relate to the debate on the relative merits of centralized and decentralized government. Salvo Mastellone's *II progetto politico di Mazzini: Italia-Europa* (Florence: Olschki, 1994) revisits Mazzini's early years in light of the current interest in European integration.

A current project of the Domus Mazziniana in Pisa seeks to document the impact of Mazzinian ideas outside Italy. That topic is broached in Gita Srivastava, *Mazzini and His Impact on the Indian National Movement* (Allahabad: Chugh, 1982); William Roberts, *Prophet in Exile: Joseph Mazzini in England, 1837–1868* (New York: Peter Lang, 1989); and Joseph Rossi, *The Image of America in Mazzini's Writings* (Madison: University of Wisconsin Press, 1954).

Mazzini's writings can be sampled in formats less intimidating than those of the *daelliana* or the *Edizione Nazionale*. In Italian, there is a one-volume collection edited by Carlo Cantimori, *Scritti scelti* (Milan: Vallardi, 1915), which includes Mazzini's major essays on a broad range of literary and political topics. In English, the six volumes of Giuseppe Mazzini, *Life and Writings of Joseph Mazzini* (London: Smith, Elder, 1890–91) are still a useful source, although the translations are not always reliable. Selections also appear in N. Gangulee, ed., *Giuseppe Mazzini, Selected Writings* (London: Drummond, 1945); William Lloyd Garrison, *Joseph Mazzini: His Life, Writings, and Political Principles* (New York: Hurd and Houghton, 1872); Thomas Okey, *Essays by Joseph Mazzini* (London: J. M. Dent, 1894); Ignazio Silone, *The Living Thoughts of Mazzini* (New York: Longman's Green, 1939; and *Mazzini's Letters* (London: J. M. Dent, 1930), with an introduction and comments by Bolton King. Useful bibliographies appear regularly in the *Bollettino della Domus Mazziniana* and *Rassegna Storica del Risorgimento*. The periodicals *Archivo Trimestrale* (1975–86) and *Nuovo Archivio Trimestrale* (1987), and the journal *Il Pensiero Mazziniano*, published since 1945 by the Associazione Mazziniana Italiana, relate the Mazzinian creed to current developments.

Index

About the Author

ROLAND SARTI is Professor of History and former department chair at the University of Massachusetts, Amherst. He is the author of numerous works, including *Fascism and the Industrial Leadership in Italy, 1919–1940*; *The Ax Within: Italian Fascism in Action*; and *Long Live the Strong: A History of Rural Society in the Apennine Mountains*.